The Bright Field

Meditations and Reflections for Ordinary Time

Martyn Percy
with
Jim Cotter
Jenny Gaffin
Malcolm Guite
Helen-Ann Hartley
Geoff Miller
Sam Wells
Rowan Williams

Preface by **John Pritchard**
Foreword by **Paula Gooder**

CANTERBURY
PRESS
Norwich

© Contributors 2014

First published in 2014 by the Canterbury Press Norwich
Editorial office
3rd Floor, Invicta House,
108–114 Golden Lane,
London EC1Y 0TG

Canterbury Press is an imprint of Hymns Ancient & Modern Ltd
(a registered charity)
13A Hellesdon Park Road, Norwich,
Norfolk, NR6 5DR, UK

www.canterburypress.co.uk

British Library Cataloguing in Publication data

A catalogue record for this book is available
from the British Library

978 1-84825-612-5

Typeset by Regent Typesetting
Printed and bound in Great Britain by
CPI Group (UK) Ltd

Contents

Part Two: Readings and Reflections for the Weeks of Trinity Season (Compiled by Geoff Miller)   57

Dedication
For Fellow Pilgrims Near and Far –
And all the Peoples of Palestine and Israel
And for Jim Cotter, 1942–2014
Priest, Writer, Liturgist, Campaigner

Contributors

Jim Cotter was formerly the parish priest of Aberdaron, Wales. He was the author of many books of liturgy and prayers under the successful imprint he created, Cairns Publications. He died in 2014.

Jenny Gaffin is Chaplain to the Bishop of Portsmouth. She was previously a Curate in the Diocese of Salisbury. A priest, theological educator and writer, she trained for ordination at Ripon College, Cuddesdon.

Malcolm Guite is Chaplain of Girton College, Cambridge. A performance poet and singer/songwriter, he lectures widely on poetry and theology in Britain and the US. He is a contributor to *Reflections for Daily Prayer*.

Paula Gooder writes and teaches in Biblical Studies. She is Canon Theologian of Birmingham and Guildford Cathedrals, and a Six Preacher of Canterbury Cathedral. She is a former Lecturer at Ripon College, Cuddesdon.

Helen-Ann Hartley is the Bishop of Waikato Diocese, New Zealand. An English priest, she both trained and taught at Ripon College, Cuddesdon. She is a former Dean of Tikanga Pakeha students at St John's College in Auckland.

Geoff Miller is Archdeacon of Northumberland and a Canon of Newcastle Cathedral. He has served as a Diocesan Urban Officer, and prior to ordination was a teacher. He is a Trustee of the Hospital of God at Greatham.

Martyn Percy was from 2004-14 the Principal of Ripon College, Cuddesdon. He writes and teaches on practical and pastoral theology, and modern ecclesiology. In 2014, he was appointed Dean of Christ Church, Oxford.

John Pritchard was Bishop of Oxford from 2007-14, and Chaired the Church of England's Board of Education. He is a best-selling writer on prayer and spirituality. He was Bishop of Jarrow, and a former Archdeacon of Canterbury.

Sam Wells is Vicar of St Martin in the Fields, London. He is a broadcaster, author and editor of many acclaimed books. He was previously Dean of Chapel and Research Professor of Christian Ethics at Duke University, North Carolina.

Rowan Williams is the Master of Magdalene College, Cambridge. He was Archbishop of Canterbury from 2002-2012. Prior to this, he was Archbishop of Wales, and is a former Lady Margaret Professor of Divinity, Oxford.

Foreword – Paula Gooder

The word 'Ordinary' has travelled a long way. Today it often has mildly negative connotations and refers to something commonplace, without any special or distinctive features. It can sometimes even be used as a derogatory description of something – nothing special, just ordinary. This is not how the word began. The word comes via Old French from the Latin word 'ordo' which means 'order'. Something ordinary, then, is something that is ordered.

'Ordinary time' is more closely connected to the word's origins than to its more popular usage today. Ordinary time translates the Latin 'Tempus Ordinarium' which means ordered or measured time, and refers to the emphasis in Ordinary time of measuring the weeks. This measuring takes place not just by counting the weeks past Epiphany or Pentecost that make up the two period of Ordinary time but by an inner measuring – a noting, savouring, and appreciating the time as it passes by. In this way events do not just flow past us in an unnoticed, unappreciated stream of time but are treasured, relished and placed in the presence of God as each week passes by.

This process of measuring time is one that allows us to become more attuned to the details of life, to notice features that otherwise we would overlook driven as we are by busyness, anxiety or ambition. It is this that R.S. Thomas was so keen to drawn our attention to in his poem 'The Bright Field' after which this book is named (see page xxi below). With his usual insight, R.S. Thomas reminds us how easy it is for us to rush through our lives either looking backwards to something we remember with nostalgia or forwards to something we hope will happen but all the time missing those moments when God's eternity breaks through into our lives often in events which seem, at first, to be commonplace, without any special or distinctive features.

Ordinary Time summons us into the discipline of measuring and savouring time so that when God breaks through into our lives, as the sun breaks through to illumine a small field, we are prepared and ready to take the time to turn aside and to recognise in those small events the eternity of God, if only we could see it.

A book such as this challenges us to embrace the unfashionable and often lamented 'Ordinary time' and as we do, through the savouring and measuring of time, to rediscover the importance of the small things of life. It beckons us into ordinariness in both senses of the word: to a rediscovery of the importance of measured time and through that to savour the in-breaking of God into the commonplace things of life. This book offers us the equivalent of the sun breaking through to illuminate a small field, I hope you will enjoy taking time to turn aside and through it to encounter anew the eternity that awaits you.

Paula Gooder

Preface – John Pritchard

Martyn Percy sets the scene clearly: 'There's nothing ordinary about Ordinary time.' And these reflections, prayers, poems and sermons prove it. Just as in the parallel volume *Darkness Yielding* we are offered here a feast of ideas to stimulate the mind and motivate the heart. In every case these ideas shed light on the central premise that there's nothing ordinary about ordinary.

I became convinced long ago that every life we meet is deep in detail and intrinsically fascinating. Sometimes that detail is tragic, sometimes inspiring, sometimes puzzling, but it's always a privilege to be entrusted with its varied landscape. I've also concluded that every person I meet is probably carrying a heavy burden of some sort and I'm well advised to be sensitive to the emotions not obviously on show.

So the word 'ordinary' is dangerous. Many years ago a quote was in vogue which spoke of 'An Ordinary Life', one in which the subject had only lived to his early thirties, had never written a book or been on television, had never spoken to more than a few hundred people at a time, and had been executed as a dangerous rebel before his movement could really take off. And yet this 'ordinary life' had had more impact on world history than any other life before or since.

Ordinary is a lazy word.

What Martyn Percy has done is to assemble a rich array of material to help us feed on the extraordinariness of the ordinary. He uses the helpful word 'graze' in inviting us to explore this material. There are gems aplenty, whether it be the boxing and coxing of Martyn and Jenny Gaffin disturbing the ordinariness of numbers or carrion or walls or corncrake; or whether it be the evocative poems of Geoff Miller and Malcolm Guite, the searching sermons of Rowan Williams, Sam Wells and Helen-Ann Hartley, or the fresh Compline liturgies of Jim Cotter.

At the heart of this book is encouragement in the elusive art of seeing both clearly and deeply. A culture that lives on the surface fears depth. Deep means the danger of engagement, even the possibility of commitment. Better to skim the surface, to experience much and to absorb little. And so we fail to see the deeper contours that give life its distinctive shape, the geomorphology of reality. So too an evasive culture takes flight from God, unable to face the danger of such accountability and possibility.

C.S. Lewis wrote: 'I believe in God as I believe the sun has risen, not only because I see it, but because, by it, I see everything else'. The task this book has set itself is to enable the reader to do a double-take, to look under the stone, to penetrate the mist, to 'see everything else' as suffused with significance and glowing with the divine. There's nothing sentimental about such recognition. 'Everything else' may sting as well as glow. The point is to see.

This is not a systematic theology of Ordinary time. It's a basketful of gifts from a group of able thinkers who believe there is inestimable value in turning aside to a lit bush or a bright field, for it's there that eternity may lie in wait. In our spiritual pilgrimage, to meander aimlessly over familiar territory is to run the risk of boredom and the slow death of commitment. We want more from the stories and practices of faith. We want more from church when we run into Ordinary time. We don't want to play endlessly in the shallow end of faith.

It's under the surface, at the deep end, that we encounter miracles.

+John Pritchard

Introduction

There is nothing ordinary about Ordinary Time. While it is true that the two segments of the Christian year that constitute Ordinary Time are about the regular Sundays and weeks of the Christian year, it is a common misconception that 'ordinary' should be taken to mean 'plain' or 'unexceptional'. Some of the great high days and holy days of the Christian year fall in Ordinary Time, as do some of the most sublime festivals and commemorations. What is so special about Ordinary Time is its richness and depth. So this book is a simple 'primer' of homilies, meditations, sermons, reflections and readings designed to accompany the pilgrim and reader on what can be a full and fertile and spiritual journey.

Ordinary Time consists of two periods within the Christian year: from the Baptism of Christ up to Ash Wednesday, and then from Pentecost Monday to Advent Sunday. Ordinary Time is therefore the longest season of the liturgical year. Yet the length of season also contains great and rich variety. The anticipation of Lent and Easter leads us in a very particular kind of way; and the long months from Pentecost to Advent, likewise. Both seasons lead to times and places of penance and preparation. Both seasons offer us the opportunity to relax and renew our energies – to refresh our souls and revive our spirits as we make preparation for Lent, Holy Week and Easter, or for Advent and Christmas.

The Bright Field brings together one hundred meditations, reflections and homilies for the many and varied journeys of Ordinary Time. Not all the material included here relates directly to the Common Lectionary. Rather, the selections offered are intended to be used either as a complement to the lectionary, or perhaps as a supplement of readings for personal devotions. The variety of offerings is entirely intentional, and mirrors the richness of the Sundays and feast days that occur in Ordinary Time. As authors, our hope and prayer is that readers – individuals and groups – will use the material in the creative spirit in which it is offered.

In choosing the title of this book, each author has been struck by R. S. Thomas' poem 'The Bright Field' – and in turn, therefore, that extraordinary and sacred anarchy of the Kingdom of God. As John Caputo puts it in *The Weakness of God* (Bloomington, IN, Indiana University Press, 2006, p. 10), the Kingdom of God is a world of 'soaring parables and mind-bending paradoxes'. Jesus does not just tell parables; he is a parable. The dead are raised; the sick healed; the poor made rich; those in mourning comforted; deserts bloom. He walks on water or through walls; he suffers, he bleeds, he weeps, he dies, he is raised, he'll be back, he'll never ever leave us.

The Kingdom of God is the place where God uses weakness to subvert power; foolishness and simplicity shames the wise; the poor are made rich; the humble and lowly are crowned; the strangers and outcasts feast at table, as God's most honoured guests. The Kingdom of God – the Bright Field – is the very contradiction of the 'world'. And moreover, this is heaven-in-ordinary. It is the natural state of the world to come. So it seems highly appropriate that this rich vein of gospel truth is the foundation for the meditations and reflections of Ordinary Time.

As with the previous and complementary *Darkness Yielding* (which covers Advent, Christmas, Lent, Holy Week and Easter), the reader of *The Bright Field* is encouraged to graze freely on the writings, and use them for spiritual nourishment. The first three parts of the book offer meditations, reflections and sermons for the 25 weeks of the year that follow Trinity Sunday. The fourth part covers a number of high days and holy days of Ordinary Time (with another 25 reflections). The sermons and homilies here are interwoven with some of Malcolm Guite's exquisite and daring sonnets.

The fifth part of the book consists of two contemporary Compline liturgies written by Jim Cotter, and with some additional seasonal prayers. In providing the Office of Compline at the back of the book, readers are invited to use the meditations, sermons and reflections in the rest of the volume within the context of a liturgy, or as part of a rhythm of daily prayer – and especially as night falls. Indeed, this book takes us from the great season of light (Easter) to the edge of darkness that must always yield to the light (Advent), knowing that the Lord is with us always; for the night and the day and the light and the dark are as one to him.

The Bright Field also follows on from *Darkness Yielding* in one other important respect: it engages with the power of the great biblical stories that shape the landscape of our faith. When encountering the Bible – no matter what our faith might be – we quickly become aware that the stories that figure so strongly in its pages are not only descriptive, but also prescriptive. These stories don't just tell us about what happened. They are stories that tell us what to do; how to behave, when to act, what to notice, and why. In living the stories in our lives, our inner world and the world around us is transformed. We often think we tell and retell stories, but the biblical stories *tell us*.

There is a real sense in which they are performative narratives for the Church and for all who follow Jesus in the way of discipleship. Indeed, the starting point for this book was a journey – specifically a pilgrimage to the Holy Land in 2013 – and the realization that for the early first-century witnesses, Jesus himself appears to them in (their) 'ordinary time'. He shares

xvi

their food, walks their roads and pathways, sleeps in the homes and villages and, in all respects, shares his 'ordinary' life with theirs. The truth of the incarnation is proclaimed by John's Gospel: the Word became flesh, and dwelt *among* us. This book is therefore rooted in the places that Jesus dwelt and the ordinary time he shared.

To that end, we might pause and reflect on how we know so much about the ordinary times and places of Jesus, and why this matters so much for our own spiritual pilgrimage today. And here, Christianity owes quite a lot to a woman by the name of Egeria. Sometimes called Aetheria or Sylvia, she was a Galician woman who made a pilgrimage to the Holy Land sometime between 381 and 384 CE. She wrote an account of her journey in a long letter, and circulated it to a group of women at home. Her long letter has survived to this day in fragmentary form taken from a later copy.

Indeed, Egeria's account of her travels may have been the first formal writing by a woman in western European culture. Yet we know little about her. To travel then, as a woman, and to be away for so long, indicates that she might either have been a nun or possibly a woman of significant personal wealth. But her work is of interest to us because she chose to dwell on the actual Christian sites that form the basis of pilgrimages today. She wrote about the places you could visit that we associate with the key events in the Gospels. And Egeria's writings show that from earliest times, Christians were already worshipping in and venerating the places where Jesus had walked and taught.

Egeria's journeys would be less easy today, ironically. And to some extent, therefore, *The Bright Field* is something of a 'binocular' book. We can't talk about the lens of the past, without the lens of the present also being brought to focus on our faith. The gradual partitioning of the Holy Land since 1948 has divided neighbours, relatives and friends. The Israeli West Bank Barrier – sometimes known, ironically, as the 'peace wall', and begun in 2000 – is but one tool that has enabled the annexation of land and settlements that once belonged to Palestinians. But this is not a fast-moving process. The gradual suffocation of Palestinians after the Israeli-initiated persecutions and violence of 1948 are now slowly squeezing out families and communities that had lived on the land for many centuries. Some are Christian, some are Muslim, some are mixed, but all are Palestinian.

It is not easy to see a way forward. Some call for a 'two-state solution' to the problem. Let Palestinians govern Palestine, and Israelis Israel. Others argue for a one-state solution. But whichever road is taken, what is clear is that many of the journeys taken by Egeria in the fourth century would be even more difficult today: roads to villages are blocked off; checkpoints forbid entry; communities that were once connected are now isolated. The promise of Isaiah – that every mountain would be laid low, the rough places made smooth, and the roads straightened – seems like a hollow prophecy for today.

I mention this because it seems to me that one cannot reflect deeply on sacred land, or sacredness within a landscape, without reference to the Holy Land. The ongoing conflicts are a powerful and painful testimony to the fact that that sacred landscape is by its very nature political, complex, contested. The very land that tends to feature in our churches – week by week in readings and sermons – is in a very real sense under threat. These threats pose real political issues for the people directly involved.

They also question the ways in which we read and interpret the scriptures, and the way we make sense of the sacredness of our own landscape. To reflect deeply on the holiness that is embedded in such a place is not to indulge in cosy spirituality, but to wrestle to the core with questions of theology and faith, of politics and identity. Perhaps this is inevitable. The time of the Crusaders, of Ottoman occupation or earlier centuries, reaching back to the Roman Empire, reveal a land that is abused and occupied. The history reflected in and by the Old Testament is not pretty either. Any holy land, perhaps – but especially *the* Holy Land – is always contested, divided, fought over and claimed.

However, this is only one of the dimensions or lenses through which the book is to be read, and can be used to reread the Holy Land. Although partly shaped by some of the current concerns shaping the Holy Land, and attentive to the endemic political plight of the Palestinians, the second lens of the book is predominantly spiritual and formational. The meditations, reflections and liturgies are primarily for personal use. The book is intended as a natural complement to *Darkness Yielding* (new 3rd edition, 2009).

So in the binocular approach taken to the crafting of this book, some of the meditations and reflections arise directly out of the present state of Palestine and writings on that, and some of my own recent visits. Others arise from exploring the depths of holiness to be found buried in more local soil. In this sense, the book has been prepared with pilgrims in mind – as a companion for those who might visit the Holy Land – as well as those who walk with Jesus day by day in prayer and discipleship, wherever they are. (Indeed, parts of this text were also prepared in the company of pilgrims from Newcastle Diocese during 2013, under the kindly shepherding of Bishop Martin Wharton, and with such excellent insights and talks provided by Peter Sabella, our Palestinian Christian tour guide. I owe my fellow pilgrims and Martin and Peter a profound debt for their hospitality.) As we walked and journeyed together, we fed on the word of God and feasted on the riches of the sights, sounds and senses of the Holy Land sites that we shared together.

In one sense, therefore, the collation of offerings in the book is a kind of 'meze', the Middle-Eastern tradition of lots of small dishes and platters of food, which can be eaten in any order and as an appetizer, or equally form something more substantial. 'Meze', then, is the defining motif here – and we encourage readers to try new things, to sample favourites and eat discerningly. But perhaps above all, to consume the writings in a way that allows space and time, and even lingering. Meze is for sharing with friends.

The idea of scripture and the interpretation of the Bible as a kind of 'food' is hardly new. The word of God is not only to be observed and learned, but also inwardly digested. Jesus, in speaking about his own body (Eucharist) in John's Gospel, invited his disciples to 'feed' on the word – and the Word made flesh. Nicholas King SJ goes one stage further in his recent translation of the Gospel of John and suggests that 'munch' is a better colloquial word for what Jesus had in mind when he used the word 'feeding'. He meant not merely opening our mouths and swallowing, but chewing, gnawing and savouring the flavours of something hearty and healthful.

These writings, then – like all meze – aspire to be broad, basic and balanced; but also serve as an appetizer that leads us into richer reflection and savouring. So in sharing and praying the food of God's word together, we hope and trust that readers might come to see something of what it is to feast on the Word of Life here and now, as surely as we feast with him at that eternal banquet in heaven.

Martyn Percy
Cuddesdon 2014

'The Bright Field' by R. S. Thomas

I have seen the sun break through
to illuminate a small field
for a while, and gone my way
and forgotten it. But that was the
pearl of great price, the one field that had
treasure in it. I realise now
that I must give all that I have
to possess it. Life is not hurrying
on to a receding future, nor hankering after
an imagined past. It is the turning
aside like Moses to the miracle
of the lit bush, to a brightness
that seemed as transitory as your youth
once, but is the eternity that awaits you.

PART ONE

Meditations for the Weeks of Trinity Season

I

Numbers

MARTYN PERCY

We are in the upper room on Mount Zion. The site, perhaps, of the Last Supper. St Mark's Syrian Orthodox Church is perhaps an alternative site, but most pilgrims identify with Mount Zion. So this is the place, therefore, that hosts the origin of the institution of the Eucharist. This is the site of Jesus' words to the disciples: 'one of you will betray me'. The site of Jesus washing his disciples' feet – another epiphany pointing to the suffering servant. The site of the coming of the Holy Spirit: the upper room where the disciples gather in fear, but then receive that which Jesus promised, as John records at the end of his Gospel.

Peter, our Palestinian guide, tells us that there are three grades of religious sites in the Holy Land. A grade one site is a place where Jesus was certainly present. The pools of Bethesda, the Mount of Olives, the Garden of Gethsemane – these are places where Jesus walked, talked and prayed. A grade two site is 'likely' to be the place that Jesus was present in – but we can't be sure; these are ambiguous spaces. We don't know the exact spot Jesus was born – only the name of the village and the sites 'traditionally' associated with his presence. And then there are grade three sites – places that we cannot be sure of at all. The Mount of Temptation is in a bit of a wilderness. But no one knows, or could ever know, if this was the mountain upon which Jesus was tempted. There are three sites for the dormition of Mary, the mother of Jesus – Gethsemane, Mount Zion and Ephesus. And a handful of possible sites for the death of the first martyr, Stephen.

The upper room is a grade two site. But there is much more to the room than any question mark hanging over its provenance. The space, like so much in the densely packed streets of Jerusalem, is rich in its liminality. The room is above King David's tomb, sacred to the Jews. The room was once a chapel of the Crusaders, but, after the fall of Jerusalem to the conquering forces of Saladin, became a mosque. Today it is neither a mosque nor a chapel. It is just a neutral, bare, open space – with a few pillars to support the ceiling.

But look more closely, and you can see the traces of its rich eucharistic history. A small representation of the Lamb of God can still be seen on the ceiling. And above a door there is the image of a pelican. Early Christians believed that pelicans fed and nourished their young with their own flesh and blood. A pelican, then, became a sign of Christ's intention in the Eucharist: feed on me, drink of me.

The upper room has, for many centuries, been a contested space – above David's tomb, so sacred to the Jews; a chapel, sacred to Christians; and a mosque, sacred to Muslims.

In the year 2000, Pope John Paul II came to Jerusalem and celebrated Mass in the upper room. A simple piece of modern art marks the moment. One tree stump, and three branches – the three symbolizing Christianity, Judaism and Islam, and all growing out of the single stump of monotheism. The branches sprout olive leaves, symbolizing peace. And the stump also carries a final surprise: images of grain and grape, the bread and the wine for which the room is remembered. Do this in remembrance of me.

But the room is otherwise bare. And it is in the bareness that we find the liminal. The first disciples waited there for the Holy Spirit; but now they are gone. They were sent out, as all Christians are. The Holy Spirit moves us out of the upper room and into the streets. The places to wash each other's feet are wherever we are called to serve. The places where we share bread and wine are where two or three are gathered. There he is, among us. The upper room is, quite rightly, an empty space – but full of meaning. Meaning, indeed, to be grasped; and then lived out as we wait for the Holy Spirit, stoop to serve our neighbour and share our faith in word, deed, sign and symbol. Do this, in remembrance of me. And with the ascension and then the first Pentecost, the whole world is now a grade one site; there is nowhere that Jesus cannot be.

2

Oak

JENNY GAFFIN

The oak stands resolute in the field.

Alone, the company it grew up in long since gone, it has come to play host to much life – the fungus around its roots, the moths laying eggs in its leaves, the lichens on its branches, the nesting birds, the insects, the small animals gathering to feed. From its highest branches to the depths of its roots there is so much colour, so much movement, so much busyness inspired and fed by this graceful tree.

This is a place to marvel and wonder. The mind cannot compute the minutiae or the breadth of such complex interwoven life. Nor can the imagination conceive of the changing humanity that, through centuries, has run its course here. Even now, this tree must witness some happenings – young people escaping the watching eye of family and friends; grieving people taking solace under the branches. Countless people must have argued and loved, hurt and hoped and aged as they came here through the years, until they came no more and the oak was left to wonder at their absence.

And I too take my turn through the seasons. In high summer, I envy the oak its resplendent vivacity. The breeze breathes life into every last leaf, and as I approach a frantic flutter of wings propels another creature to the safety of high branches. Insects race up and down, chasing or being chased, pursuing a course hidden from my most minute inquiry. And all has meaning, all has energy and purpose.

But as the months pass, when the abundance has gone, most of the creatures that fete and flatter this tree in high summer will prove themselves fickle, seeking out warmer climates and richer pickings. Only the few will remain, to suffer the cold and the lack in solidarity. And as winter deepens, this glorious tree will be stripped, its old, exposed body divulging the history of injuries and indignities it has suffered through the years – branches broken by high winds or careless human vandalism; holes bored into its bark by insect or bird; weakness inflicted by long-past drought.

Yet of course the oak has seen it all before. 'The thing that hath been, it is that which shall be, and that which is done is that which shall be done', go the ancient words, and the branches of the oak nod their stately assent. This tree has seen out countless cycles of life: the tough spring survivors battling for ascendancy, the born-again high expectations, the excited abundance of summer, the starved winter giving way once again to hard-won spring hope.

The oak will not be flattered by the youthful attentions of spring, nor disheartened by winter's deficit. Even in the harshest month, this tree will stand proud and receptive, upholding its ancient dignity. It is as if it made its decision long ago, injury and indignity notwithstanding, to offer up its body as host, welcoming and protecting without question those drawn to its outstretched arms; and it is strong in its hidden purpose.

So it is in harsh winter months that I most seek the counsel of this tree. I want to grieve with it in its bleakness; to believe with it in new life. Beginning as I am to bear in some small way the marks of time's passing, and wrestling in small part with the claim upon my life, I want to enter the roots of its resoluteness; to be strengthened by its endurance; to learn from its ancient generosity, as the youthful creatures prepare once more to claim their imagined entitlement, with such careless high spirit and such incessant demands.

'The thing that hath been, it is that which shall be, and that which is done is that which shall be done', insists the cherished text. Embraced by the ever-generous reach of these branches, wrestling with its wisdom, there is so much still to learn. The seasons will turn and turn again; there is time under the sun to listen and rebel, pray and acquiesce to such an ineluctable calling.

Reconciled long ago to that which is, and silently rejoicing in that which shall be, the generous branches of this ancient oak nod their fulsome concurrence to my still hesitant amen.

3

Depths

MARTYN PERCY

We are in a prison. One very like the one that Jesus would have been lowered into. The Church of St Peter in Gallicantu perches on the eastern slopes of Mount Zion. It is traditionally the site marking the spot where Peter denies Jesus. A stunning bronze statue outside the church matches the clean, pure and simple architecture of the building. This is no place for ornamentation. The church is bare – like the soul – before God. It is a place to sit and pray, unfettered by ecclesiastical clutter and religious imagery.

The church also sits over the site traditionally associated with Caiaphas, the High Priest who briefly imprisoned Jesus. The crypts and caves that are tunnelled out below are suggestive. Out of the depths I have called to you, O Lord. Why do you forsake me? Yet thou art with me.

It is commonplace, sometimes, to believe that when we encounter suffering or abandonment we have somehow failed God, or incurred his wrath. So that when we cry out for healing and deliverance, we are asking God to remove some pain or suffering that he has somehow permitted, or perhaps even bestowed. Surely, we reason, that if we had been really good, we would not really be suffering?

It is a fact that Jesus nowhere explains the origins of suffering. He heals, he consoles, he weeps, he loves. But he is not a philosopher who explains why bad things happen to good people. He does not at any point explain the origin of evil or the ultimate source of pain and suffering. What Jesus does do, however, is live and echo the psalms. He is the good shepherd. He is with us in the valley of the shadow. He does not abandon us in our pain, desolation and suffering. He walks with us. He hears us when we cry out.

The striking thing about the caves, cells and crypts below St Peter in Gallicantu is the crosses etched into the walls. Those who languished here for their faith did so with songs and psalms in their hearts. They made the sign of the cross to remind them that though sitting in darkness, and seemingly with little hope, they were not in fact abandoned. God was with them in the darkness.

It reminds us of a story Terry Waite tells of his imprisonment under Hezbollah in Lebanon. Moved from place to place to avoid detection, and frequently blindfolded and bound, he found himself one day bundled into the boot of a car. As he was being driven along, he sensed in the darkness another person, also bound and blindfolded. It was John McCarthy. 'There's not much room in this boot,' quipped Terry. 'There was a lot more until you got in,' replied John. They were to spend years in captivity. But what sustained them, partly, were the ancient hymns, collects and prayers of the Church that they had committed to memory, and the knowledge that, no matter how alone they felt, they were neither abandoned nor forgotten by God, and indeed all God's people, continually praying for them.

It seems for this reason alone, perhaps, that the site of the imprisonment of Jesus under Caiaphas, and the site of Peter's denial, should be so bound up with each other. Peter's desperation to avoid incarceration – or worse – is mirrored by Jesus' own imprisonment. One is jailed, while another walks free. A cause for a life full of remorse, perhaps, on Peter's part? No: this is Christianity – and the faith of the resurrection. The absolute triumph of God's total love and forgiveness. Peter's denial of Jesus will, in the end, be met at the lakeside by Jesus' renewed affirmation of Peter.

4

Carrion

JENNY GAFFIN

Carrion on the path side: an ugly reminder of nature's underside. Best avert your gaze.

In our villages and towns, death and decay is politely but firmly hidden, by a comfortable society with the wealth to deny its own most basic certainties and to mask its most shameful infirmities. Life insurance, package deals, designer funerals: our industrious society excels itself, turning even death into fashion and commodity, and hiding evidence of harm from sight.

We privileged few may shield ourselves, but nature has no such compunction. Out in the fields there is no escaping the detritus: from life cycles rounded to completion, or road kill flung over hedges, or creatures wounded by human or predatory aggression limping their way to a roadside grave. Everyday carrion, discarded in the field, argues the day-to-day expendability of life.

Strange then, that the Word should choose to become flesh; stranger still that from its very conception it spoke beauty. Womb to womb, the incorrigibly communicative John witnessed to two mothers-to-be, preparing the way for what was to come. Then as newborn, wordless and adored, flesh effused God's headlong love for humanity. So alive was word in flesh, so attuned to human longing, that its touch healed and its transient presence overturned worlds to the good. Words were freely forthcoming then, in parable and explanation, until finally on the cross, the torn inarticulate body spoke for itself.

Yet, it seems, even the Word shied away from such corruption, such decay. Mere hours in the tomb, and the stinking, mangled flesh was gone, replaced by enigmatic angelic appearances, a smattering of mistaken identities and the sweet smell of fresh possibility. Was this a physicality too far for the almighty? Did God, in repulsion, at the last opt out from this experiment in embodiment?

The faithful are quick to the defence, proclaiming Jesus' life, immersed in the ugliness of life and death. Jesus healed every kind of brokenness, cleansed all manner of corruption, even confronted the stench of Lazarus' decay and overcame it. Taboos were broken; societal decay was confronted and transformed. With a little help from a sympathetic commentator, good news is duly forthcoming: God is present and correct after all.

Perhaps. But then, what of the everyday human carrion, society's underside, discarded at the path side? Where is God in the thinly covered graves; the refugees abandoned to a living decay on the road; the war heroes drugged and emaciated on our streets?

Back in church, Sunday on Sunday, the bread is broken, the wine shared. The hurt is made visible, the brokenness confessed. Good people reconnect with the shock of betrayal, the scandal of violence, and declare anew their commitment to resurrection life. The Word revels in the wonder of healing and the astonishment of life impossibly reborn.

But far from the hallowed walls, Sunday on Sunday, week on week, everyday human carrion, torn and ignored, continues to argue the expendability of life. And even at the heart of the Eucharist it is possible to turn away. With a bit of modern artistry, bruised, torn body can be reduced to a wafer-thin imprint; traces of a bloodied past contained and glorified within bejewelled chalices. It is as if the rumour has got out that God could not quite go the distance, and generations of devoted followers have found sacred means to follow suit.

The church bells ringing out across the field summon us to our devotions and our choice. They, and I, declare with confidence that, against all the odds, the rumour is false: that the divine absence is no act of cowardice, but God's intentional rejection of such degradation – one final stand against the human scandal of flesh desecrated and cast aside.

But even with such confidence there is no denying that the evidence for the opposition is compelling. Outside the hallowed grounds of the church, on our pathways and our roadsides, in our streets and hastily hidden away in our cities, corrupted flesh, devoid of sacred word, cries its indignation at such flagrant disregard of its dignity.

And I wonder how many, like me, privileged onlookers, moneyed passers-by, hear in their cries disconcerting echoes of our own raw wounds – families' hazardous journeys into safety, soldiers' hidden cost, loved ones we wish we could provide for.

Ashamed, I too avert my gaze. Carrion on the roadside: I pray that I may atone.

5

Patience

MARTYN PERCY

Our scriptures have much to say about patience. Yet we assume all too often that it is a passive kind of waiting; a form of restraint in which we simply bide our time before we get the result we either wanted or didn't want. But patience is no such thing. It is being still before God, and realizing that in the waiting, all desires are known, transformed and reshaped. In the activity of patience – a virtue and a discipline – we discover that God does things with us in the space. Things gestate, germinate and grow; we find that we acquire a new wisdom. In the waiting, and in Godly patience, we discover new things that would not be seen had we just hurried by.

It may seem strange, but God can do some pretty good things with apparently unpromising material. Many seeds look like nothing in the hand. But what they need is time and space to grow, and a little bit of patient husbandry. What is needed is the wisdom to wait, attentively, for the signs. Of course, one cannot simply wait for ever. But in any case, we don't. For the scriptures assure us that *we wait in hope* – for what we cannot yet see, but what will be (Romans 8.25). There is a palpable longing for hope and change these days. Jim Wallis comments:

> Hope is the very dynamic of history. Hope is the engine of change. Hope is the energy of transformation. Things that seem possible, reasonable, understandable, even logical in hindsight ... often seemed quite impossible, unreasonable, nonsensical, and illogical when we were looking ahead to them. The changes, the possibilities, the opportunities, the surprises that no one or very few would even have imagined become history after they've occurred.
>
> Between impossibility and possibility, there is a door, the door of hope. And the possibility of history's transformation lies through that door ... Spiritual visionaries have often been the first to walk through that door, because in order to walk through it, first you have to see it, and then you have to believe that something lies on the other side. (Wallis, 1994, pp. 238–40)

There is plenty of hoping and waiting in the practice of Christian ministry. They are about a furtherance of that work that God began in us before we even knew it. Bishop Peter Selby suggests that this gestation – a pregnancy if you will – is all about the future hope:

> [W]hat love does do is make space for the unknowable possibilities which the future holds for those who know the history of love as revealed in the dealings God has had with God's people – patient, kind, ready to excuse, to trust, to hope, and to endure whatever comes ... We are to be towards one another as those who do not know or own each other's future, except that it is in the hands of the One who has proved trustworthy in the past. (Selby, 1997, pp. 64–5)

Love, then, does not end. It is attentive and watchful; hoping and waiting. It is proactive patience, not just passive. In waiting for God's time (*kairos*) we set aside our sense of time (*chronos*) so that God can meet us how we are, and change the what, why and where we are. Sometimes this can be frustrating – for we long for change. But God, in his wisdom, longs to reconcile all things, and so is prepared to wait – sometimes a very long time. And as the mystics say, God has only one weakness: his heart – it is too soft.

Knowing this, and practising God's time, requires a fusion of wisdom, virtue and discipline. It is often expressed and practised formationally in the phrase *feste lente* – make haste slowly. Sometimes the pause is more pregnant and profound than the action. Here is what Rowan Williams, reflecting on being in New York close to the Twin Towers as they collapsed, has to say about Jesus apparently doing nothing, when everyone wanted him to act, speak and judge there and then. But he does not. He pauses, writing in the dust:

> What on earth is he doing? Commentators have had plenty of suggestions, but there is one meaning that seems obvious to me in light of what I think we learned that morning. He hesitates. He does not draw the line, fix an interpretation, tell the woman who she is and what her fate should be. He allows a moment, a longish moment, in which people are given time to see themselves differently. (Williams, 2002, pp. 78–80)

It seems to me that the two great besetting sins of the Church these days are impatience and procrastination. The Church either moves too quickly, and then regrets the unforeseen consequences, or it moves so slowly or not at all, with all the activity and energy of a hibernating tortoise. And many in ministry – indeed, perhaps all of us – oscillate between action and inaction, impatience and procrastination. So you'd think that the art of ministry is all about striking the right note of compromise. But it really isn't.

Good ministry is, in the end, not finding the middle ground between action and inaction, or decision and indecision. It is about knowing your place before God, and being a person of character and virtue – 'marked' and 'formed', as it were, by Christ's life, and living out his goodness. It is about hope, love, grace, understanding, counsel, strength, depth, lightness, prayer, wisdom and humanity in the midst of it all. It is not about compromising between extremes; it is about living authentically in the midst of the place where God has set us.

Ultimately, a church without patience is a church without hope. And that is why, when Paul talks about patience, hope and charity – a wonderful trinity of virtues – we often focus on love, but underestimate patience and hope at our peril. We need to learn and relearn to be patient with God; and God, in his wisdom, will be patient with us. Because God is love: he believes and hopes all things for us and for his Church. It is always worth the wait. Patience is always rewarded – because we always wait in hope, and because God is good. And if you can be hopeful, patient and good – all shall be well.

Notes

P. Selby, *Grace and Mortgage: The Language of Faith and the Debt of the World*, London: Darton, Longman & Todd, 1997.

J. Wallis, *The Soul of Politics: A Practical and Prophetic Vision for Change*, Maryknoll, NY: Orbis Books, 1994.

R. Williams, *Writing in the Dust: A Meditation on September 11*, London: Hodder & Stoughton, 2002.

6

Rock

JENNY GAFFIN

In a field on the holy island of Iona, there is a plaque resting against a rock. It reads: 'Sitting silently, doing nothing, spring comes and the grass grows by itself.' The words are an invitation to slow down, to set aside daily preoccupations, and allow God and self space to be unencumbered.

It is counterintuitive, to say the least, for those of us of a workaholic persuasion, to entertain the possibility that the grass might grow without our intervention, to set aside aspiration and ambition and endeavour, to embrace the inactivity and the silence.

Yet, 'in returning and rest you shall be saved', says God through Isaiah, 'In quietness and trust shall be your strength.' There is a divine imperative to downing tools. So sit with me for a while. Let's take time and look about us and be still.

Not that there is much choice in this place. Beneath the oystercatcher's scream and the newborn grass, time slows and energy deepens. It is as if our whole being is drawn downwards, into the ancient rock beneath, melted and remoulded over untold millennia; its fierce powers endlessly destructive, remorselessly life-giving. I have lost track of the number of people who come to this place with plans to walk this distance, see that sight, only to succumb to the deep stillness of this island and pass their time here in rest and quietness.

Just over the water loom Mull's imposing peaks, dwarfing Iona. Out in the distance rise impossible rockscapes – the Dutchman's Cap perched jauntily atop the waves; Staffa, with its pillars of stone designed by a geometric genius with a few millennia on their hands; and far out, ghostly in outline, the ancient cliffs of Skye. Ambitious rock, flung by nature's forces into wild and fantastic sculptures, dares the foolhardy and the stoical to test their nerve against powers beyond their imagination.

The challenge to defy the limits imposed by the creator is one so many of us are hopelessly drawn to. There is something compelling about the toughness, the possibility, the pride.

What is it that brings us to the test? Vanity? Or maybe a not yet extinguished hope that what appears fragile and temporal is after all solidity and immutability in the making; that, through the alchemy of endeavour and prayer, transience can be transformed into eternity?

No wonder it was out there in the wild rockscape that Jesus fought his tempter, taunted by high expectation, and gifts as yet untested. Following ineptly in his footsteps, we weaker folk are bound to stumble. Most of us can be persuaded that with training, practice, a bit of creativity and a hefty dose of good old-fashioned tenacity, we can transcend divine injunction to the good.

What, after all, of the alternative? Willingly to subject self and all that is cherished and good to the vicissitudes of divine will? To return all to the destructive heat that will scarcely register the addition of one small ego in the melting pot? To embrace the very insignificance that, subjugated, drives our most enduring endeavour?

The rebellion is fierce. Yet even the rock we rest against now has finally submitted to its creator and ours. Its eccentric lines witness to the power that made us, to the extremity that could any moment unmake us, to the relentless forging of grace within our core. The rock's current formation is as precarious as our own fragile beauty, its presence as ephemeral.

Out at sea, the waves test their strength against the receding cliffs and the salt takes on the work of the master sculptor. Forces beyond our imagining battle it out for supremacy, putting our feeble posturing in its place.

So let us put aside high expectation for a while and deal gently with ourselves.

Spring will come, and the grass will grow without our stir.

And who knows, as we have sat here, how the gentlest touch of the Creator may have rested upon us unrecognized and unbidden, reshaping our energies and transforming us for some unknown purpose. Who knows what subtle changes have been wrought, what new depths of beauty have been forged within us, as, here in this field, we have leaned quietly into the presence of God, doing nothing.

7

Words

MARTYN PERCY

UN Resolution 242 will not mean much to most people. But on the definite article – 'the' – much hinges. The Franco-Israeli interpretation of the UN resolution (1967) is that Israel need only withdraw from territories occupied by Israel in the Six Day War. The Palestinian interpretation of the same resolution is that the definite article is used: 'the' means 'all'. But no 'the' can be taken to mean only 'some'.

Small words can make a mighty difference. And the reality of Israel-Palestine today is that lasting peace remains elusive while words and phrasing do more to divide than unite. As anyone in Northern Ireland or the Balkans can testify, words will mean little, if anything, unless backed up by a collective and trans-tribal will.

There is little sign of it in Israel at the moment. Peter, our Palestinian Christian tour guide, takes us through the different zoning systems that operate in the land. Here we are divided not by words, but by simple letters. Zone A is for Palestinians only; Zone B is mixed; Zone C for Israelis only. The divisions today are resonant with the Jewish and Samarian ones we find reflected in the Gospels. There are places you can go and people you can meet with; and places you can't go, and people who are to be avoided. Movement is restricted. Our Palestinian visitor tonight – a Christian – cannot travel freely from Bethlehem to Jerusalem. She needs a special permit to visit.

We listen to a talk in the evening from Sabeel, the Palestinian liberation theology centre. Stories of restricted movement for Palestinians, oppression and, almost daily, casual harassment pepper the conversations. Journeys that should take an hour can take several. People who live the wrong side of the dividing wall may find themselves divided from friends and neighbours. Gardens, groves and orchards are sliced in two by large concrete bulwarks.

We come to Hebron in the morning, and converge on the tomb of Abraham. One half can be seen through a mosque; the other half through a synagogue. Security is tight, barriers are up; the soldiers bristle in response to the tension you can clearly feel in the air. I wonder what Abraham must be thinking – whether he ever envisioned his land and his peoples to be so divided.

We meet Sami one afternoon – a Syrian Christian, who runs a tailors' business near the Syrian cathedral and the Maronite church. He was born in

1935, and has lived all his life in the city. There are only a handful of Syrian Christians left in Jerusalem now – perhaps no more than a thousand. Sami is nearly 80, and describes how he has held several different 'nationalities' as a resident of Jerusalem, yet somehow he still remains stateless.

His story is a reminder of how complex politics and history can be in Jerusalem. First, his father, Syrian-born, lived under Ottoman rule. Sami was born into a house that was shaped by both Turkish and Syrian Christianity. But under the British, and during the Second World War, he was simply treated as an Arab. Then he was under Jordanian control after 1948. But after the Six Day War (1967) he came under Israeli rule. And the Israelis now regard him as non-Israeli, and treat him as a Palestinian. He has held no passport for any of the nations he has ever been subject to. He remains a Syrian Orthodox.

And so I think of Abraham's resolution. A man who came from Canaan in response to the call of God, and lies buried in the cave of the prophets at Hebron. A man who resolved to live a holy life. A man who, through his resolve, is regarded as a pioneer of faith. I have not used the definite article here. For we cannot say 'the faith'. Abraham is a shared prophet, patriarch and pioneer of faith for Christians, Jews and Muslims. Shared. And, in sharing, one who points, perhaps, to how much else we might share, could we but set aside enmity, build trust and learn to live in peace.

8

Walls

MARTYN PERCY

Everywhere you turn in Jerusalem, there are walls and gates. Some are ancient, and would have been familiar to Jesus. But many are new. They are there for security; for dividing; for managing people; for making sure things don't get mixed up and too complicated. So, for the Western Wall, a queue for women and a queue for men. In Hebron, walls and barriers that keep Jew and Muslim apart. But venerate the memory and holiness of Abraham and Sarah. Though walls see to it that this cannot be done together.

At the numerous security gates, we are checked each time. And on each occasion the words of scripture resonate. I am the gatekeeper, says Jesus. I am the door of the sheepfold. Peter is given the keys to the gates of heaven.

We are standing in the plaza that looks on to the Western Wall – the Wailing Wall. The plaza is a flat space that accommodates thousands of people, but we are standing on the site of a small Moroccan Quarter, cleared after the Six Day War. The Moroccan Quarter would have been a maze of small streets, gates and low walls – as much of Jerusalem still is.

In the plaza today, security is relaxed, though I remember it was tight when I went before the Sabbath a few years back. It is the sheer absence of walls here, leading to the Western Wall, that is perhaps so stark. The plaza is, of course, not the holy place – merely the means of converging upon it. Yet the stark open space of the plaza is, ironically, the one with more meaning. Here you can stand and reflect on the lack of dividing walls. Here you can see the walls in the distance, and see that all our walls – no matter how high – never reach to heaven. There are mosques and churches peeping through the streets and alleyways. Spires, towers and domes are on the horizon. Everywhere you look, you see that for all the walls and gates, it is the open spaces that God also encounters us in. These are the spaces no one owns, and the places where we can meet together and begin to discover something more of God's purposes for humanity together.

We spend the morning in the Church of the Holy Sepulchre. In one sense, it is the heart of the Christian faith, for here is the site of the crucifixion and resurrection. The church is divided, of course, between several different denominations – each aisle and altar part of an invisible zigzag of ownership. One step to the left you are on Catholic ground; one step to the right, and you are on Orthodox territory. In recent times, the arguments about ownership have been bitter, even violent. God's sense of humour prevails, however. The master key to the church is in the possession of a Muslim, who locks and unlocks the church each day. Because the Christian denominations don't trust one another, guardianship has lain within the same Islamic family for centuries.

None of our walls reach to heaven; none of our boundaries and borders on earth, or in church, will be operational in God's Kingdom. Though they divide and separate now, they cannot prevail. We visit a section of the 'peace wall' in Palestine later that day, and we see a different barricade, covered in murals, and with one simple sign that says 'Hate can't last forever, and neither can these walls …'.

We move on to visit a UN Palestinian refugee camp. There are some more Banksy murals to see, but the abiding memory of the time spent there is of the conversations. It is the realization of the total absurdity of the situation that many still live with after decades of oppression. It is the relentless sense of hopelessness in such places – the impossibility of things improving, and of darkness being turned to light. But this is me talking. The people I talk with who live in the camp are different. Determined and angry, yes. But perhaps what is most striking is the resilience, cheerfulness and hope they seem to embody. They are not beaten. They are simply waiting. They live in hope. The poet Aino Makoto says that in a world where love, faith and peace can easily burn out, hope must stand strong for us all. Her poem 'The Four Candles' was written on 15 February 2004:

The Four Candles burned
slowly. Their Ambiance was so
soft you could hear them speak …

The First Candle said, 'I Am
Peace, but these days, nobody
wants to keep me lit.' Then
Peace's flame slowly
diminishes and goes out completely.

The Second Candle said, 'I Am
Faith, but these days, I am no
longer indispensable.' Then
Faith's flame slowly
diminishes and goes out completely.

Sadly The Third Candle Speaks,
'I Am Love and I haven't the
strength to stay lit any
longer. People put me aside

and don't understand my
importance. They even forget
to love those who are nearest
to them.' Waiting no longer,
Love goes out completely.

Suddenly ... A child enters the
room and sees the three
candles no longer burning. The
child begins to cry, 'Why are
you not burning? You are
supposed to stay lit until the end!'

Then The Fourth Candle speaks
gently to the little child,
'Don't be afraid, for I Am
Hope, and while I still burn,
we can re-light the other candles.'

With Shining Eyes the child
took the Candle Of Hope and
lit the other three candles.

Never let the Flame Of Hope go
out of your life. With Hope,
no matter how bad things look
and are ... Peace, Faith and
Love can Shine Brightly in our lives.

9

Wind

JENNY GAFFIN

Sunday morning in spring. There is new life in the air today: something has lifted, something sacred is restored.

I enter the church in holiness and marvel as good people, sacrificing the beauty of the morning to their obedient devotions, incline their heads in honest reverence and kneel to pray.

In scent and sound and glorious light, God is eloquent this morning, and, with impeccable antiphony, the people lift hearts and voices in reply. Voices crafted and tuned through the yearnings of the ages join in intimate harmony with their creator, and all is gratitude, all is praise.

Time passes, eyes down on the service sheet. Devout poetry gives way to solemn readings. Then the preacher perseveres. The preacher is me. *I* persevere, half listening in on words carefully prayed and prepared days before, hoping the congregation remains more attentive than their hapless priest. Startled and ashamed at my lapsed attention, I eavesdrop on my own inadequacies. I think I am talking about the Holy Spirit, or Jesus, or new life or something. But in truth I am distracted.

Because the wind is whistling round the church spire. I can hear it pushing against the doors, creeping in through the cracks in the side chapel windows, making the earnest folk shiver and draw their immaculate scarves close. The wind is in playful mood today. Tapping on the windows, flinging a little light rain against the roof, whistling a crazy descant, it teases the faithful huddled indoors, daring us to lose our concentration just a little, to forget our purpose just for a moment.

The wind is a mischief maker. While people and priest do our level best to uphold sacred decorum, it dances wild rhythms in the heavens, teasing the birds off course, glorying in its expansive virtuosity.

And this is the worst of it, this is my complaint: every decent gust of wind knocks five years clean off me. And I fear I am already more than a few gusts of wind too young for the succour and sense of some, and it is only mid morning. The dreaded moment is surely close, when the swell of joyful exuberance bursts out, brash notes disfiguring the immaculate harmonies of the morning.

We all do our duty, priest and people working as one: we fight the good fight, sing our devotions, honour the worthiness of the occasion. But I for one know I am beaten long before the final amen is sung and the cup of tea is empty, and the open door signals blessed release.

Out in the fields, the wind in my hair, like a child I laugh, shout, dance my joy. Prayer begun in dignified pianissimo, is blown into a wild and brazen crescendo. The rain in my face fizzes like champagne. And the long grass dances with me, moving this way and that, taking its cue from a Lord and leader that only a blade of grass with a comic turn would contemplate resisting.

My own comic turn mercifully over for another day, I finally concede defeat to the sublime mischief maker. Comprehensively beaten and too alive for sense, I giggle my adoration, throw up my hands in exasperated confession, and, forgiven and blessed, dance my way home.

But late into the evening, as energy fades and mindfulness returns, this is the question I ponder. Were the windblown variations on the morning's devotions simply a one-off performance? Has the mischief maker had its fling, and now departed in peace? Or was today a first shake-up, a summons, an invitation to the Church to move out of our perfect cadences, into something incomplete, reinvigorated, disconcerted, new?

One thing is certain. When the wind resumes that crazy descant, as surely as a child following the piper, my soul will answer its call. And as in my mind's eye I recall the faces of my fellow worshippers, and our shared struggle to keep our feet from tapping to this new beat, I know I am not alone. When that Spirit blows once more, we will join in its wild improvisation, and dance for good or ill into who knows what future.

But these are musings for another morning, as the wind blows gently into the ever-deepening sanctuary of night, and all finds its rest.

10

Waters

MARTYN PERCY

We are at the pool of Bethesda. This is a grade one site. Jesus was here, and he healed a man who could not enter into the waters by himself (John 5.1–9). The pool is now in the Muslim quarter of Jerusalem and can be accessed through the Lion Gate, also known as St Stephen's Gate – but in Jesus' day known as the Sheep Gate. The five colonnades (or porticoes) at the pool of Bethesda to which the Gospel of John refers are still visible.

Like so much else in the Gospel of John, the symbolism and metaphor is more important than the history. Only John mentions the pool of Bethesda, and the original Aramaic term on which the story of the healing turns is pregnant with meaning. 'Bethesda' means 'house of mercy' or 'house of grace'. But it can also mean the opposite: 'shame' or 'disgrace'. So the people at the pool are here for their healing – for the dreadful infirmities that render them not only invalids, but also unclean and untouchable. The pool is by the Sheep Gate. The shepherd of the lost is here for those who are truly lost.

Tradition had it – as the story in the Gospel of John confirms – that the waters awaited a 'stirring' or a 'troubling'. This was understood at the time as the water being touched by an angel; when the waters moved, the time for healing had come, and people quickly crowded in. The waters did indeed move regularly. And while this might have been the activity of a natural spring – waters and minerals bubbling up in due season – any potential geological explanation need not detain us here. Indeed, a geological account for the moving waters would take nothing away from the power of the story as a whole.

The man healed by Jesus had been ill for 38 years. Jesus heals him because, even in this place of invalidity, there is no help, hope or mercy. He cannot get into the water when it stirs and bubbles because others push past him. Not for the first time in his ministry, Jesus simply heals the most hopeless and marginalized. His gaze is upon the lost sheep; and here is the shepherd at the Sheep's Gate. Jesus heals the man instantly, too. The true spring – for Jesus is the water of life – need not wait for the natural stirrings in the waters. Jesus heals the man as he is, where he is, and now.

But there is something else about the pool at Bethesda that is rich in meaning. The church that watches over the site is dedicated to St Anne, the mother of Mary, the mother of Jesus. (Yes, the Blessed Annie, God's

Granny.) This is traditionally the site of Anne's birth, and so of a place where different waters have been broken: where there have been cries of pain and relief, and tears of joy at the arrival of a child. Bethesda is truly the house of mercy and grace. This is a place of risk and promise. Here is a place of birth and the new life that comes from another kind of water. The troubled and breaking waters that accompany each birth, the life that flows from Anne through to Mary, and that eventually gives us Jesus, is what gives Bethesda its meaning.

11

Corncrake

JENNY GAFFIN

It is illegal to imitate the call of a corncrake.

For those unfamiliar with this bird, and at the risk of delivering an ornithological lecture, the corncrake lives in tall vegetation in farmland and looks fairly nondescript – a little like a dull brown chicken. Sightings are rare, partly because so few are left and partly because of their innate shyness. But when the corncrake sings, it comes into its own. It has a raucous, rasping call that can be heard 1.5km away and can be repeated more than 20,000 times a night, mainly between midnight and 3am. That's good news if you're an avid bird watcher; bad news if you're trying to sleep in a caravan in one of the last remaining corncrake hot spots.

In the past, hunters perfected their corncrake impressions to lure the birds out of hiding, with such success that corncrakes, once the subject of Mrs Beeton's recipes, are now a protected species.

It was in conversation with a local man, expressing in no uncertain terms my murderous feelings towards these birds and their nocturnal habits after yet another disturbed night, that I was hastily and vehemently advised of current legislation.

Tired and fed up, this struck me as utterly ridiculous. There I was, in a rural community whose livelihood depends upon animals being bred and killed for human consumption, being told off for an idle threat of violence against a seemingly insignificant bird. We humans are a fickle breed: what we slaughter without compunction one minute, we pour tens of thousands of pounds into preserving the next.

Yet even as I chafed, I wasn't totally blind to the poetry. For love of a useless, unattractive and above all noisy little bird, rural landscapes have been transformed by farmers and conservationists working in partnership to recreate its habitat. As this shy corncrake suddenly finds itself valued, with its safety guaranteed and its land reinvigorated and protected, pilgrims who travel miles to see and hear it also catch a fresh glimpse of the extraordinary beauty of the environment that sustains it. A sacred and precarious landscape is rightly honoured anew, thanks to the corncrake's compelling if distracting ministrations.

Nonetheless, even the pleasure of knowing I was listening to a bird that very nearly faced extinction eventually wore off. So I was only too glad to travel in the opposite direction, many miles from the corncrake and its devoted followers. And with nothing more disruptive than traffic noise and car alarms to contend with at night, I was able to settle back into the altogether more predictable business of church life.

For all the undeniable absence of poetry, there is something innately comforting about the pragmatism of the Church of England. Over-idealistic draft policies are soon tempered by the realism of the finance bodies; fiery campaigns are diligently brought before the Lord in prayer then discreetly quenched and contained. At the heart of the Church, with a bit of imagination and elegance most problems can be solved, most radical ventures tamed and most human disasters made safe.

Yet even here, the voice of the corncrake haunts me.

Some challenges are not so easily answered. Some people are not so easily contained. It's not the serial correspondents to the *Church Times*, or the members of pressure groups, or those who come determined to change what they assume are my values, with tub-thumping biblical self-justifications. I honour their commitment to their chosen cause but they do not disturb my sleep.

For me, the real challenge comes from dignified individuals who approach tentatively, with achingly honest stories of costly integrity and exclusion and irreducible human complexity. And I dread these encounters. Their pain exposes the inadequacy of the Church and of its servants: the too-human fault lines in our hallowed walls, and the damage we collectively cause.

Calling out like the corncrake under the caravan, these unsettling voices demand that I and my colleagues make a choice: whether aggressively to block out the noise, or to allow their call to summon us to fresh engagement with those who have been legislated out of fullness of life. To leave the safety of our little cabin, to venture out into the unknown and listen, is to make ourselves vulnerable to people who, once protected and nurtured, might utterly redefine the landscape of the Church.

So the corncrake sings, keeping me awake at night once more, challenging me to imagine how different things might all be with just a few canonical changes here, a few tweaks to corporate perception there.

And for love of what might be, for the sacred transformation that could yet await, I welcome the intrusion. And I am grateful that it is illegal to imitate the call of the corncrake.

12

Size

MARTYN PERCY

On 10 June 1990 flight 5390 was on its way from Birmingham Airport to Málaga, Spain. The pilot, however, noticed something odd about his side window. It seemed to be buckling. He tapped it, only for the next sequence of events to happen in a flash. The window blew out; the cabin de-pressurized; the oxygen masks dropped; the plane lost height; the pilot was being half-sucked out of the window, and quickly lost consciousness. The co-pilot held on to his legs to stop him being sucked away. The first officer managed to perform an emergency landing in Southampton with no loss of life.

It was a drama, to be sure. But on that day, no one lost their life. The plane was taken to a height of about 2,000 feet, and made an emergency landing. In the investigation that followed, the inevitable question was asked: how does a passenger jet lose a window at 25,000 feet? The answer was deceptively simple. A cracked windshield had been replaced, but the screws to secure the window, although the right length and make, were slightly too thin; the thickness mattered, however. The difference was impossible for the naked, untrained eye to tell; but the millimetres in each case had nearly cost a great many lives.

I need not labour the point: size matters. Or, more accurately, proportionality counts. And when reading the scriptures, we often suffer from a curious kind of inflation when it comes to understanding the size and scale of the ancient world. We sing 'O Little Town of Bethlehem', but barely pause to consider that in Jesus' day 'town' meant something different. Bethlehem was not likely to be more than around 300 people when Jesus was born. So the 'Massacre of the Innocents' at Bethlehem meant that the number of infants slaughtered was perhaps a few dozen at most. This does not make it any better, of course. Indeed, the more insidious thing about the massacre is, arguably, that it would not have caused so much as a blip on the radar of the Judaean consciousness, let alone the Roman Empire. In a cruel, barbaric world, life was cheap. Later, when Jesus laments the fate of cities such as Chorazin, Bethsaida and Capernaum, we may be talking about communities not much bigger than around 3,000 people – a large village in today's currency.

When we consider our own theological education and formation, size, scale, proportions, dimensions, shapes, foundations and structures – each aspect matters to us in the architecture of our faith. Lest this all sound a tad too mechanistic, let us remember that in the business of formation for discipleship, we need to pay attention to size and scale, and also to inflation. As much as we need to be careful about what we construct, we also need to keep a critical eye on how we are constructed. In the building of our faith, as individuals and as churches and communities, we are not passive and inert material that is simply to be shaped around the perceived tradition, or even those power interests that might maintain such religion. We are, rather, to question, probe, examine and critique as much as we affirm and confess.

My sense is that Jesus counsels 'beware the doctors of the law' precisely because he understands deeply the way in which faith has been shaped – and it is a distorted shape. And it has been inflated too. The numbers are odd. Judaism has 630 commands. Christianity has but two – love the Lord your God will all your heart, mind, soul and strength; and love your neighbour as yourself. An inflated and disproportionate faith – in any religion – does not offer liberty and hope for followers. Rather, it suppresses the real issues and maintains the status quo. So Jesus, in his own attitude to buildings, size and scale, is something of a rebel; a disturber of constructions of faith and reality. Religion is always partly a question of size and scale, I think; how else do we get to talk about 'deep' and 'shallow' faith?

In *Prince Caspian*, C. S. Lewis writes of the young lost Lucy experiencing a visit from the great and mighty Aslan. As Lucy encounters her old friend, she perceives him to be somehow 'bigger' than she remembered:

'Aslan, you're bigger.'
'That is because you are older, little one.'
'Not because you are?'
'I am not. But every year you grow, you will find me bigger.'

This tiny shard of conversation contains a great deal of wisdom. The older we get, and the wiser we become perhaps, the more God increases. Wisdom, in other words, does not put God into perspective, and make God more comprehensible. The more we age, the more we realize just how much of God there is to unfold. Discipleship is about knowing that you can't know the infinite expansiveness of God, which is his wisdom. We can never know God fully; the more we devote ourselves to Jesus, the more we discover the inexhaustible nature of his love, grace, being. So size matters, yes. And scale too. Which is why we read the scriptures with such care and attention – for God will teach us, the more we gaze deeply into his word, about our size and scale – and indeed, the scales that will eventually weigh us.

13

Archaeology

JENNY GAFFIN

The pristine field hides a secret. For good or ill I do not know. Amid an untroubled walk through glorious wildflowers on this seemingly perfect summer day, I stumble for no reason, something unyielding underfoot.

'Nothing is hidden that will not be disclosed, nor is anything secret that will not become known and come to light,' says Jesus. Years ago, buoyed along by a spirit of adventure, I would have jumped at the chance to investigate, dreaming of hidden treasure below the surface awaiting my discovery, or a major archaeological find that could change history and make my name. Naive in my youthful optimism, I could only respond with excitement to such an opportunity.

But now I pause, uncertain. I have conducted more than a few burials in my time. I know that there are good, healthy reasons for yielding to the earth. What is dead must go one way, so that all that lives can be released to go another, and seek their salvation anew. The parting is life-giving and correct. With due solemnity and more than a hint of relief, we pile on the earth, flatten the grave and let the flowers grow. To prod around years later, to grubby what has been completed and sanctified, would be distasteful to say the least. Better, perhaps, to look around in that slightly embarrassed manner that we English have about us and pretend we never stumbled, that there was never anything there to fall over.

Perhaps. But as the therapists have long known, not all burials are healthy, nor is all that looks immaculate life-giving. Rumour and aching half-remembrance can break the surface unbidden, intimating buried life longing to find its fulfilment and seek its redress. Gently, in the presence of good people, excavation can release into new life, as, painstakingly, the soil is disturbed, and half-truths and self-imposed limits are nudged aside, and wholeness is restored.

The risks are huge. To uncover what has been carefully concealed, to exhume what time and forgetting has claimed for its own, is to risk bringing to light truths that could comprehensively shatter the peace of the day. It is to risk violating the self-declared sanctity of an institution or a human ego and, exposed, await the potent backlash.

And there are instances when the earth will simply not stay compacted, when the choice is taken from us. Terrifying moments, when the evidence breaks the surface against our bidding, when all that has been hidden, believed impotent, becomes suddenly and sickeningly visible and powerful, compelling engagement with a still-living, agonized past.

The too-public revelation and rancour; and, privately, the sorrow, the self-doubt and the longing: as the happenings of the past are laid bare, so too is the life of the present. Every one of us is exposed, individually and within the institutions we cherish. Our values, the stories upon which we base our lives, the glad forgetting in which we take refuge, our very reputations, all are open to be questioned.

'Nothing is hidden that will not be disclosed,' says Jesus. Hard to tell whether his words are a promise or a threat. In the unearthing, we re-enter relationship with what has been buried; with it, we are brought out into the light, visible, revealed.

Is it worth it?

I pause, uncertain, kicking at the dirt.

A large part of me wishes I had never stumbled in this field, never chanced upon what is buried. I want to collude with the beauty of the day, with the appearance of serenity of this stunning landscape: I want it to be real and all in all. I want to live as if it were true, to play my part in the upkeep of the illusion. But knowing what this moment intimates, with sinking heart I realize that the illusion is already broken.

Amid the fear and hurt of the immediate fallout, and the faltering journey into new possibility, may the rumours of resurrection prove to be true. As what lay buried is proffered to the light of day, may there be no brokenness that cannot be redeemed. May life in all its glorious fullness burst forth from the murkiest of tombs. May even the worst of the hurt be healed.

14

Time

MARTYN PERCY

What time is it? The question is not as plain and obvious as it sounds, when you are sitting in a café in Jerusalem. This is Monday for me. For my Jewish neighbours at another table, today is *Yom Sheni* – 'second day'. For my Muslim host who has just served Turkish coffee, this is *Ithnayn* – also the second day. So we all agree that this is the second day of the week. But on the month and year we are in, we would quickly discover that three religious calendars equate to three ways of telling time.

Christians, when they think about time, tend to make a distinction between *chronos* and *kairos*. *Chronos* is ordinary time. But it is also the time of judgement. Indeed, the English word 'crisis' means to 'judge' or 'weigh'. *Kairos* is God's time – the calendar that no one can see. But we live between these two times – all the time. Let me explain.

Like many parents, I suspect, I am awaiting exam results. Not mine, but my son's. Anxious? Well, a little. Despite it being the holiday season, many people spend the time between June and August on the cusp of anxiety and hope.

Woody Allen is perhaps not best known for his contribution to theology. But he has a nice line for all of us beginning a new job or challenge; or perhaps beginning to contemplate the start of a new academic year; or maybe just facing up to the end of the holidays. Or waiting for results ... How do we make God laugh? The answer: tell him our future plans.

One of the best-known psalms (23) captures the essence of assurance. God will be with us – through whatever shadows or valleys we walk. But we are not offered a detour. There is no way around the difficulties we face in life. Rather, faith offers a way *through* these things. So as we face the challenges and opportunities ahead, we step out in trust and hope. We don't know what our future looks like. As the poet Minnie Louise Haskins (d. 1957) put it, many years ago:

I said to the man
who stood at the gate of the year,
'Give me a light that I may tread safely
into the unknown.'
And he replied,

'Go out into the darkness
and put your hand into the hand of God.
That shall be to you
better than light
and safer than a known way.'
So I went forth
and finding the hand of God,
trod gladly into the night.

But living between *kairos* and *chronos* requires enormous reserves of patience, hope and love. And perhaps most of all, patience. I often admire the patience and composure of church leaders, who, when pressed to be assertive and directive on delicate or controversial matters, find the grace and strength to hold back. Some call this weakness, dithering or foolishness. But it seldom is. For such leaders, in practising hesitancy (or willed spiritual patience), allow the necessary space to develop which permits discussion and deliberation – and even ones that might call into question their own power, authority and leadership.

This is, of course, not a bad thing. Christians, like all groups of people, disagree. That's in the nature of meeting and belonging; whether it's in politics or just the local social club. The moral question for Christians is not 'why do we not agree?' (it is inevitable we sometimes won't), but, rather, '*how* do we disagree?' How do we conduct ourselves? With assertion, power and oppressive authority? Or with dignity, patience and humility?

We too easily confuse unity with uniformity. To belong to the Kingdom of God is not to be an elite member of a club for the like-minded. It is, rather, to be part of a communion that is groping its way to a common mind, but through an enormous range of diverse experiences, outlooks and values. If the Church can model the patience and humility that is needed here, there may be hope for our nations, communities and political parties – living and learning that unity is a higher and better goal than mere uniformity.

So, one prayer for time is this: may God grant me the serenity to accept the things I cannot change; courage to change the things I can; and wisdom to know the difference. But another goes like this:

Gracious God, grant us the grace to continue your work of reconciliation. Forgive us the sins that tear us apart; and give us the courage to overcome our fears and prejudices, and seek the unity which is your gift and will. Amen.

Note

M. L. Haskins, 'God Knows', in *The Desert*, 1908.

15

Wildflowers

JENNY GAFFIN

Churches up and down the country are solidly built and intended to last: architectural feats, constructed with the eternal glory of God firmly in mind; imposed upon the landscape, then sternly bequeathed to generations of Christians to come. They are grand monuments to confident faith, holding the collective memory of our small communities and our national life.

Standing at the altar, the light streaming through coloured glass, surrounded by people God calls into love, the heart opens in thanksgiving. Processing up the aisle, the organ commands praise, and the people obey. Then alone in the church afterwards, as the energy softens and the building settles down to rest, those last to leave are touched by God's tenderness and silent blessing. It is self-evident, even to the non-believer, that these places are special and sacred.

So why do my own prayers rise, only to feel as if they are netted in the elaborate tracery, or trapped by the all too solid stone? Ashamed, I wonder how many hours of my life and the lives of my colleagues have been spent, and are yet to be spent, worrying about the walls and the roof and the bell tower and the organ loft of this or that church; how much of our best creativity is yet to be poured into ever-more-elaborate fundraising schemes; how many nights' sleep will be lost in what must ultimately be a futile bid to keep the building intact.

Outside, the wild flowers grow, their roots clutching at soil like the fragile soul to its salvation. Unashamedly ephemeral, I envy the honesty of their endeavour. Tenacious and resilient in their moment of glory, they bestow upon future generations not the illusion of permanence, but the possibility of newness. There is no agonizing about significance; no second guessing the needs of tomorrow; no aspiration to timeless legacy. Here is generosity and humility in the extreme: a flamboyant celebration of life, and a complete and free acceptance of death. And here is sacrificial giving in its fullness: the shrivelled seeds flung into the wind, with utter trust, utter abandon.

Walking through the fields my heart at last bows in prayer, unencumbered, and I return inspired. To give of self with such abandon, to die with such grace: this surely is a poetic and beautiful response to calling, for the individual and for the Church.

But what of the practicalities? For the individual crazy enough to aspire to this level of faithful simplicity, no doubt all is manageable. Finances can be arranged; spirituality cultivated. But for the Church, the challenge is huge. Does this mean praying away cherished buildings in a bid to live and serve more nimbly, more freely? Surely it would be scandalous to sell or abandon the very vehicle, some would say, of our cultural memory and our hospitable worshipping ministry? And in our modern culture of investment and forward planning, could the Church ever justify pouring all its resources into the present moment, and failing to plan for its future?

Perhaps when all the musing and praying and meditating is done, the cost is after all too great. Perhaps the answer is to go back to God with a hefty dose of Anglican common sense, and explain how practicalities dictate that we must continue as we have for centuries, the wild flowers providing a pretty backdrop outside or extra stock for the flower arrangers within.

I don't know.

But I do know that out there in the fields, the wildflowers have become my icons; drawing me into new depths of freedom in prayer; and daring me to follow their lead, in embracing the life-releasing glory of anonymity and impermanence.

Back in the church I love so deeply, even as I worship I know that a part of its core and mine is dying and perhaps has already died. May what I take for shards of frustration, restlessness and disjointedness prove to be seeds of new life to be cast upon the Spirit, freely and with utter trust. And when the dying is done, may the new life be glorious in its honest ephemerality.

16

Maths

MARTYN PERCY

It would be obvious, I suppose, to say that the earthly life and ministry of Jesus – and his advocacy and augmentation of the Kingdom of God – is the measure against which we judge the Church. Jesus' ministry confounded his contemporaries, and it continues to disturb our sense of boundaries. He reaches out to the Samaritan woman and tells stories about good Samaritans, much to the annoyance of his potentially loyal Judaean audience. He embraces the widow, the lame, the ostracized, the deprived and despised, and the neglected. He befriends the sinners and sinned against. He takes his tea with tax collectors. Jesus heals nobodies; the Gospels, in nearly all cases, not able to name the afflicted individuals. The people Jesus reached out towards were excluded from the mainstream of society and faith. Jesus was no crowd-pleaser; he was, rather, their confounder. Jesus was a disturber of crowds. He did not seek their praise. He sought their commitment.

The Kingdom that Jesus preached, however, was more than just a creature of his adult imagination and inspirational prophetic vision. His childhood, I think, had probably taught him a thing or two about people, society and God. He grew up in occupied territories, so had seen the good and bad side of that coin – oppression traded off against organization. His childhood had included a sojourn in Egypt. And we know that by working in Joseph's trade – carpentry and building (in Greek, *tekton* means carpenter) – he had, by living in Nazareth, been exposed to the nearby Roman settlement of Sepphoris. This was a Hellenized community of almost 30,000 in Jesus' childhood, compared to the population of Nazareth, which boasted a mere 300. So Nazareth was a dormitory village supplying labour to a much larger cosmopolitan community nearby. It would have been full of Gentiles of every kind. So, from an early age, Jesus would have been exposed to a world beyond his native parochial Judaism.

The theatre at Sepphoris seated 5,000. It is almost certain that Joseph took Jesus. For Jesus, in his adult life, uses the Greek word 'hypocrite' quite a few times, which simply means 'actor' – one who is masked and playing a part. What is significant about this, I think, is this. Jesus' Kingdom of God project was, from the outset, supra-tribal. It reached out beyond Judaism to the Gentiles. Indeed, he often praised Gentiles for their faith, and often scolded the apparently 'orthodox' religion of his kith and kin for its insularity and purity. Jesus saw that God was for everyone; he lived, practised and preached this.

We see this in the healing miracles that Jesus wrought – to a Canaanite girl, a Samaritan woman or a Roman centurion's servant. To lepers, the blind, the demon-possessed; Jesus touches the untouchable, hears the dumb, speaks to the deaf and sees the blind. His healings are highly partial, being overwhelmingly directed to the marginalized and ostracized. It is there in parables too, with Jesus constantly teaching us about the least, the last and the lesser; God can't take his loving eyes off the people and situations we most easily neglect.

The ministry of Jesus is startling in its inclusivity. Consider, for example, the feedings of the 5,000 and the 4,000. It is customary, in a kind of lazy liberal and rather reductive way, to suppose that the Gospel-writers simply got their maths muddled, and were a bit confused about a single event. But in actual fact there may be good reasons to regard the two miracles as quite separate. The feeding of the 5,000 takes place on the western banks of the Sea of Galilee. The region was almost entirely Jewish, and the 12 baskets of leftovers symbolize the 12 tribes of Israel. What, then, of the feeding of the 4,000, and the seven baskets of leftovers? The event occurs on the eastern shores of the Sea of Galilee, and the region was almost entirely Gentile in composition. The seven baskets of leftovers correspond to the seven Gentile regions of the time (i.e., Phoenicia, Samaria, Perea, Decapolis, Gaulanitis, Idumea and Philistia). Moreover, the baskets in the feeding of the 5,000 (*kophinos*) are smaller than those mentioned in the feeding of the 4,000 (*spuris* – a basket big enough for a person, as with Paul in Acts 9.25). The point here is that the new manna from heaven will be distributed evenly, across all lands. There is plenty for all. The gospel of Christ is, in other words, radically inclusive: Jew, Greek, Gentile, slave, free – all shall be welcome in the Kingdom of God.

17

Twilight

JENNY GAFFIN

Some things are unthinkable in the full light of day.

With the sun blaring and the landscape clear for all to see, the Church lifts its heart in thanksgiving for the wholehearted obedience of the disciples, and celebrates those who answer the call without a backward glance. 'Let the dead bury the dead,' says Jesus, and 'follow me'. And where would we be if he hadn't? No sweeping saintly narratives of unquestioning and selfless devotion; no martyrdoms; no heroism.

But as light weakens and the lines of the landscape blur, the questions begin to nag.

What of the people in the story who don't leave father and mother, or home or possessions, or jobs or communities, to follow him? What happens to the shepherds biding their flocks that night who on hearing the song of the angels decide that their sheep take priority and they must stay at their watch? Or the shepherd in the parable who, on noticing that one of his flock is missing, decides to stay back and take better care of the remaining ninety-nine? How many would-be disciples did Jesus call out to at the lakeside before Simon and Andrew consented to become fishers of people? And how many people have heard the call to follow while in the arms of someone they love, and turned instead to hold their heart's desire ever closer?

There's no doubt the stories are troubling. Flocks of sheep that, a moment earlier, were protected and treasured are suddenly abandoned. The bread-winner of families is suddenly taken from their midst, without a word of explanation or a kiss goodbye. Partners and children are randomly aban-doned by newly converted disciples who, in their zeal to follow, are not even given the time to say goodbye.

So thank goodness that while the stories tell us to get up and go, the Church in its gentle wisdom finds ways to give us permission to stay. With the Mothers' Union we pray to share God's love 'through the encourage-ment, strengthening and support of marriage and family life'. We have permission to pray for breadwinners to do the decent thing; for children to grow up close and loyal to the parents who have nurtured them. With courage and good sense in equal measure, the Church celebrates the family and the disciples who leave the family; the tradesman and the zealous few who leave their trades to follow Jesus. Praise God for the generous plurality of his Church!

But, here is the question. What happens to those who can neither leave nor stay?

How many enthusiastic would-be disciples hear, and, not realizing the depth of their attachment to the dead they fail to bury, set out on the journey only to find themselves overwhelmed with loss and yearning and turn back to those they love? Do they become like Lot's wife, frozen in their indecision, unable to belong either to the past that they had almost rejected or to the future that they had almost embraced?

And what happens to the people who leave what is familiar through sheer necessity, hearing not the sacred invitation to a wondrous future, but only the deadening certainty in the pit of their stomachs that it is not safe or right to stay?

What of those who, trapped between tradition and modern life, amid the confusion of signs and symbols, simply cannot tell what is dead and needs to be buried, and what is life-giving and can lead into the future?

Walking the fields at twilight, with land and sky merging indistinguishably, and the eye no longer able to locate the horizon or interpret the shadowy presences in the deepening darkness, this is the question that haunts me.

Somewhere, estranged alike by the confident discipleship of the unquestionably heroic, and the respectability of those who find their God embedded in the comforts of tradition, and the generous contentment of those who have no reason to question, my heart is with the brave and hurting souls who inhabit the in-between place, with no way of telling their redemption.

Pioneers in this unknowable landscape, may the darkness prove itself gentle. And when the light returns, may the new horizons to which they are the first witnesses transform us all to the good.

18

Saints

MARTYN PERCY

There is a saint to celebrate for almost every day of the Christian calendar. Take Bartholomew and Monica. For most people, Bartholomew will ring some sort of bell – whether it is a hospital in London or a yellowy cartoon character who is simultaneously maddening and irresistible.

The tradition surrounding the original Bartholomew is that he brought the gospel to Armenia (where he is patron saint) and died a particularly gruesome death. Martyred, he was skinned alive before being beheaded. Christian art often pictures him in heaven, holding his own skin. And his patronage is also linked with hospitals and healing – like St Bart's in London.

He surfaces again in the Middle Ages. Because of responses to intercessory prayers made to him, he became well known as the saint to pray to for the healing of both body and soul, which is why the famous London hospital bears his name.

Yet partly what I most enjoy about Bartholomew is that we know almost nothing about him from scripture. It is as though the Bible is saying to us that not all the disciples who follow Jesus will gain a great reputation. So Bartholomew is called and named – but then simply vanishes into service and discipleship, and eventually martyrdom.

We can't all be a Bartholomew. Yet we must remember that all saints are basically normal folk. They just hand their lives over to God, and then watch God do something with that offering. So with Bartholomew, our prayer might be for healing:

> Grant, Lord, your healing grace to all who are sick, that they may be made whole in body, mind and spirit; and grant to all who minister to the suffering wisdom, skill, sympathy and patience. Amen.

What then of Monica, the mother of St Augustine of Hippo? She died in 387 CE and is perhaps best remembered for the way in which she mentored her son, who in turn became not only one of the great gifts to the Church, but also to western civilization. Augustine, perhaps more than any person of his age, did the most to establish faith as a key element in the shaping of public life.

Saints come in all shapes and sizes. Granted, it is easy to be humorous with hagiology – the study of saints. There are saints for travellers, sore throats, children, pets and television. Their benefaction leaves nothing untouched. Yet to focus on their patronage misses their point. Saints serve a far more serious purpose in life, and we ignore their function at our peril.

But why remember Monica? I think one answer might be that for everyone who performs and achieves on the world stage, there are many more who are unsung heroes, working hard behind the scenes. Normally, someone like Monica would hardly merit a footnote in history. Yet it is only through the patience and love she showed that Augustine gained the courage and wisdom to become the kind of person and leader the world needed at the time. Sometimes when we look behind the great leaders and saints who dominate the foreground, we can see some evidence of an even greater work of love and service in the background. The invitation is to look with care, and see beyond the immediate.

Almighty God, grant us the grace, wisdom and courage to follow your saints in faith and hope and love. May our lives reflect your greater light, and so illuminate your world with all virtue, godliness and truth. Amen.

According to one Jewish tradition, we are all in the hands of God. But it is the righteous souls who 'glow like sparks in the stubble'. It is an enchanting image. Saints, rather like the embers of a fire, continue to give off light and heat, and may still illuminate life. But they are also thrown out of the fire into the world. They are on loan there, setting light to life, but illuminating us with their wisdom and holiness. Although they are dead, it is because of their deeds that they are not forgotten. But their lives – sacred, selfless and sacrificial – still speak to us today, and ask us what we think life is really worth living for.

To answer this, you have to look into your heart and ask some searching questions. What random and costly acts of kindness and generosity will you perform today? Can you love and serve others – putting all before yourself – and yet not count the cost? Can you, at the same time, radiate warmth, peace, openness and hospitality? Can you be a beam of God's light and warmth in a world that is sometimes dark and cold? Can your friends and colleagues say, hand on heart, that to know you is to somehow have been touched by the presence of God?

All saints, like all souls, are basically normal folk. They just give their lives over to God and watch God make the ordinary into the extraordinary. There is no better way to live. As another prayer puts it:

Set our hearts on fire with love for thee O Christ, that in that flame we may love thee and our neighbours as ourselves.

19

Shepherd

JENNY GAFFIN

Some years ago, I fulfilled a childhood dream of working alongside a real-life shepherd on a sheep farm on Iona. Sheep are fascinating animals, both in themselves as creatures and because of the place they occupy in our Christian heritage, with ministers regularly described as shepherds looking after their flock.

For those of us who live in town at a respectable distance from the nearest muddy field, it can be very easy to idealize the life of a shepherd, imagining a carefree, simple life. It's easy to imagine Jesus the good shepherd – and the church leaders who emulate him – as a gentle pastoral person looking after an occasionally wayward but basically benign flock. But for those of us who have spent time shepherding real sheep, the image conjured up is rather different.

Within a few days of my time on the farm, I had the blisters and bruises to prove just how difficult it can be to tend to the needs of animals that frankly have their own ideas about what is good for them, and that can run faster, think more quickly and act more spontaneously than I can. And the means that shepherds use to contain, control and maintain the health of the sheep can often appear to be really quite brutal. Sheep are strong animals, and holding them down to inject them with antibiotics, or pinning them upside down to trim their hooves, or forcing them into small pens in order to tag and treat and sheer them, turns regularly into a full-blown wrestling match that isn't always won by the shepherd. After six months of being thrown to the ground, run off my feet, stamped on and humiliatingly outwitted by these creatures, I had come to honour the profound love being described in the image of the shepherd that motivates someone to go through all that and still be willing to love and nurture and even sacrifice their own life in the service of their flock.

'My sheep hear my voice. I know them, and they follow me,' says Jesus the shepherd. And he isn't kidding. They know his voice from times of stress and danger, as he shouts instructions to them and does his best to keep them together and safe. They know his voice in playful times, as he relaxes and enjoys his work. They know his voice from times of sickness, as he gently nurses them back to health. They know his voice in the wind and the wet and the baking heat of summer. The relationship between them is hard won, and they trust him and listen to his voice because time and time again he has led them through the toughest of times, into new life.

This is so important, because if it's easy to idealize the relationship between shepherd and sheep, it's also far too easy to idealize and romanticize the relationship between a priest or bishop or lay leader and their human flock. It's worth remembering that very few priests fit the pretty image of the serene shepherd sitting on a hillside. I know I don't. And in my experience, very few congregations ever manage to behave quite like the benign, passive flocks that we've all seen depicted. And I for one am glad of that. To me, it's not only important but positively life-giving that, like a priest, the 'flock' dare to be curious and strong and independent-thinking.

But that does mean that there is a certain rough-and-tumble to church life, locally and on the national stage, as many passionate people try to use the best of their skills and insights, and pull in different directions all at once. We really aren't a million miles from the true reality of the shepherd, and there are times when all of us get hurt – clergy, lay people, bishops included. Yet, if we listen closely, the shepherd's voice calls out to us through it all. And we know the shepherd's voice when we hear it, because that same voice of love and challenge, inspiration and forgiveness, has guided us through many a tough time, and will guide us now.

So let's listen attentively to the voice of the good shepherd, speaking to us in word and in our Holy Communion and in our fellowship with one another; calling out to us in joyful times and in the challenges we face. And let's delight in the gentleness and the robustness of our fellowship, trusting that our shepherd is here in our midst, leading us into fullness of life in this world, and eternal life in the next.

20

Wilderness

MARTYN PERCY

Jordan and Israel are divided by little more than a small river. In the summer season at key points, you could wade across. The muddy water is not deep, and the river not wide. The River Jordan runs on from the beautiful fresh water of the Sea of Galilee, which teams with fish and bird life. The sea, in turn, is fed by the high and mineral-rich Golan Heights.

But the surrounding countryside of the River Jordan, as it gently ambles south, is unmistakably wilderness and desert. There are few places to hide from the intense heat of the sun, and the ground is rocky and unforgiving. This is John the Baptist country. This is real wilderness – locusts and wild honey would be a feast in such a barren place.

The wilderness features strongly in biblical narratives. Wildernesses are often places of encounter and wrestling, but also of escape and refuge. I think of Jesus in the wilderness, making ready for his ministry: the ultimate retreat, with no distractions, but plenty of discerning and testing. I think of Elijah, who fled Ahab, and went to the brook of Cherith, near the River Jordan, to be sustained. The story is told in 1 Kings 17, where Elijah is fed with bread and meat – but by 'ravens', we are told. It is a puzzling story, until we realize that many Bible commentaries mention that scholars dispute that Elijah was fed by *ravens* and instead think the word in 1 Kings 17.4–6 ought to be translated *black Arabs* or perhaps *Orbites* (i.e., inhabitants of Orbo). This makes much better sense of the story. This would mean that Elijah was fed by the indigenous Bedouin of the land, which makes perfect social sense, both in the light of Arabian hospitality and also their likely (superstitious?) reverence for a holy man. It also makes sense of Elijah's next meeting: in Zarephath, where a widow would care for him. This is yet another encounter in the wilderness where Elijah is faced with God using apparently unclean or alien agents to feed and sustain his chosen people. As is so often the case in the Bible, God works through the channels we least expect, often confounding our sense of expectation: and our theology and ideas of purity.

For Elijah, this confounding continues all the way to his hiding place on mount Tabor. It is here that Elijah hopes God will speak to him dramatically and clearly. But as 1 Kings 19.11–13 says,

Then the LORD said: Go out and stand on the mountain before the LORD; the LORD will pass by. There was a strong and violent wind rending the mountains and crushing rocks before the LORD – but the LORD was not in the wind; after the wind, an earthquake – but the LORD was not in the earthquake; after the earthquake, fire – but the LORD was not in the fire; after the fire, a light silent sound.

When he heard this, Elijah hid his face in his cloak and went out and stood at the entrance of the cave. A voice said to him, Why are you here, Elijah?

The Hebrew phrase translated as 'a light, silent sound' is not quite right. A better phrase might be 'the thick silence'. And sometimes this is indeed how God speaks to us in the wilderness. More often than not, we don't get clear directions in response to our desperate petitions, let alone for our most childish prayers and pleas. We get the 'thick silence'; the response that says, in the wilderness, look around you and see what God has already provided. God often wants us to see that his provision is to be found in the places that we distrust, or even despise. Or that our future – as we imagined it – is what God will give us if we keep asking for that. God has other plans, sometimes; other futures for us to embrace. This is the lesson for Elijah in the wilderness, and often for us too, when all seems barren and beyond redemption.

What God asks for, then, is that we are open in heart and mind in the wilderness, and not clammed up and bitter – as Jonah became for a while, and as Elijah might have become. Being open is the key. But to imagine that being open-minded is the way forward is to miss the point. Being open to God's grace and abundance is not simply a matter of being more liberal in our thinking. Rather, being open leads us to a richer place of generosity. If we can learn to receive from the people we would rather disdain, God will teach us not only of his generosity, but also something of how we, in turn, might become open and generous through his grace.

So what would it mean to be generous and open? Bruce Barton wrote this short piece, 'There are Two Seas', in 1928. It was also reprinted in the *Reader's Digest* in 1946:

There are two seas in Palestine.

One is fresh, and fish are in it. Splashes of green adorn its banks. Trees spread their branches over it and stretch out their thirsty roots to sip of its healing waters. Along its shores the children play as children played when He was there. He loved it. He could look across its silver surface when He spoke His parables.

And on a rolling plain not far away He fed five thousand people. The river Jordan makes this sea with sparkling water from the hills. So it laughs in the sunshine. And men build their houses near to it, and birds their nests; and every kind of life is happier because it is there.

The river Jordan flows on south into another sea. Here no splash of fish, no fluttering of leaf, no song of birds, no children's laughter. Travellers choose another route, unless on urgent business. The air hangs heavy above its water, and neither man nor beast nor fowl will drink.

What makes this mighty difference in these neighbour seas? Not the river Jordan. It empties the same good water into both. Not the soil in which they lie; not the country round about.

This is the difference. The Sea of Galilee receives but does not keep the Jordan. For every drop that flows into it another drop flows out. The giving and receiving go on in equal measure.

The other sea is shrewder, hoarding its income jealously. It will not be tempted into any generous impulse. Every drop it gets, it keeps.

The Sea of Galilee gives and lives. The other sea gives nothing. It is named The Dead.

There are two kinds of people in the world. There are two seas in Palestine.

Note

B. Barton, 1928.

21

Reception

JENNY GAFFIN

Shortly after I got my first ever mobile phone, I fell in love.

Soon after meeting this man, I went on a walking holiday in the hills. To my dismay, I discovered there was no mobile phone reception whatsoever in the valleys. But on the hilltops, and occasionally on a slope, my phone registered just a bar or two. So my holiday took a delightful turn. As I neared the top of a hill, my phone beeped to tell me that word had arrived from the love of my life. And on the way down the hill, praying that reception would last just a few seconds longer, I texted my reply.

In this way, I learned the truth that prophets down the ages have always known: if you want to reach out to the divine, climb a hill.

The novelty of the romance passed, but entrenched habits die hard. I confess I have lost track of the number of hours I have spent when I was supposed to be communing with the Almighty, perched on a mound in a field out in the middle of nowhere, guiltily waving my phone in the air, desperate to catch just a few words of news from people back home.

And let's not pretend that I'm alone.

I know, and you know, how hard it can be to cut off completely. Let the fields be ever so pretty, let the hills be ever so remote, the instinct to switch on the phone, just in case, will always win out in the end. There is a moment of triumphant relief when the device of your choosing registers a bar or two of reception, and life is connected once more.

Does this count as treasure in a field? Or is it a worthless distraction, a kind of fool's gold?

A part of me – the worthier part – wants to argue for the folly, the triviality, even the spiritual impoverishment, of such a find. The imposed de-clutter, the enforced detachment, frees the heart to choose to love and serve again. The emptiness of the space imposes honest self-appraisal, and con-fession uttered from the deepest place of lack. There is an absolute quality to availability to God, which must be practised and practised again without distraction if the soul is ever to be trained in the art of detachment and full-ness of presence.

Yet surely the purpose of such communion with God is, ultimately, to reach out afresh to those around us. After all, Adam in the first idyllic field had all the opportunity he needed to engage face to face with his creator, but in the end he could not cope with the aloneness. God had to gift him with companionship in order that human life in all its depth and richness could begin. As a race, we are hardwired for connectivity, and, as a faith, our first commandment only ever comes to completion in its outward-looking partner.

Out there in the fields, nature, as ever, is one step ahead of us. Reports suggest that all manner of bird species, from blackbirds to starlings, are mastering the sound of mobile phone ring tones and incorporating the digitalized music into their song. Is their distorted song a harsh play-back of our noisy self-absorption? Is this nature's way of rebuke? Or is it possible that the nature in which we seek our God is more at peace with our compulsive extroversion than we are?

As phone and birdsong combine, it strikes me that there is a profound synchronicity between the yearning for connection with God we express in our return to the natural world, and our longing for connectivity with one another. The search for reception in the remotest places stems from one and the same impulse that drove Moses up the hill all those centuries ago, to return with the ultimate hardware, the building blocks for human and divine relating.

So, unashamed, I delight to hear my phone beeping in my rucksack as I once again roam the fields in search of my God. At peace, my heart opens in expansive generosity, ready to receive.

22

Touch

MARTYN PERCY

St Thomas is often dubbed the Patron Saint of Doubt. Indeed, the phrase 'doubting Thomas' has entered into our lexicon of cherished national epithets. Who would want to be Thomas – the man who could not trust his own eyes? This is a pity, as the subtlety of John's Gospel intends to convey Thomas' faith, not his doubt: 'blessed are those who have *not* seen, yet believe' is not a word of chastisement to Thomas. It is, rather, a word to us all who will not see Jesus after he has ascended. We normally take this passage to refer to those Christians born after the ascension – all of us, who have to make do with our imaginations, stained-glass windows, icons, Franco Zefferelli and our favourite paintings – Caravaggio, Botticelli, Rembrandt or Da Vinci, to name but a few. But this is a rather lazy assumption on our part. For John is not talking about those who (literally) could not have seen Jesus; he has, I suspect, something else in mind.

What, then, does Thomas' testimony now have to say to us? I suspect that John's Gospel is trying to say something to us about seeing and touching, and about our role in holding people in the liminal, dark and uncertain places of life. In the Gospel of Mark, we read that Jesus 'leads a blind man by the hand'. This is a gentle, tender image – as most of us would take a blind person by the arm, and walk side by side. But 'leading by the hand' has an edgy feel of risk about it. But Jesus does it anyway, for even in his hand we are safe to move forward. Even though we cannot see, his hand is enough for us – for all of us.

Closer inspection of the gospel narratives surrounding Thomas suggest that we should perhaps be less inclined to remember him as a person of doubt, and instead focus on the depth of his profound faith. Thomas is, according to John, one of several who have not yet seen the resurrected Jesus. Yet for Thomas, sight is not enough. Perhaps he already knows that our sight can be faulty and our eyes can sometimes deceive us. So what Thomas wants is a deeper encounter; something tactile that shows that there is a relationship between the tortured and crucified person he loves, and the person who now stands before him. In this sense, hands start to play a significant role in the encounter. Thomas must see the hands of Jesus for the mark of the nails. And he must touch the wound in Christ's side with his own hands.

Touch, then, not sight, becomes the dominant theme of this encounter. And it reminds us that touch can carry so much more weight than words or sight. That what is seen and heard is sometimes not enough – for we ache for embrace: to be held, and to hold. Interestingly, so much of our ministry is about holding and touching. Even for clergy, and perhaps especially in the first few years of priesthood, one becomes aware of just how crucial touching and holding can be. Cradling a child at baptism; joining hands at a wedding; holding the dying and comforting the bereaved; the breaking of the bread; the anointing with oil: these are all 'touching places' where words are not enough. Here we need holy hands touching the wholly ordinary.

Bill Vanstone, the great Anglican spiritual writer, used to say that the Church of England is like a swimming pool: all the din and shouting comes from the shallow end. It is too easy to say that St Thomas is the patron saint of doubt; too superficial to dismiss him as someone who would not walk by faith, but by sight. But his testimony is richer and deeper, for in his persistence for the truth, he establishes the real connection between the physical Jesus and his torture, and the resurrected Christ. Touch is the key. Yes, the voices of the deep often go unheard; gestures in the twilight often go unnoticed; only connect. Touch.

For Thomas, as the disciples gather in the house, it is feeling and touching the suffering of Jesus – not just seeing it – that allows him to confess 'My Lord and my God!' And this is where Christian ministry begins – in having the courage to touch and be touched by the wounded yet risen Christ, so that we can embrace all those who may still be in the darkness, and for whom seeing and hearing will not be enough. We are called to behold and be held by Jesus, so we might hold others for him.

23

Fog

JENNY GAFFIN

The autumn fog lies thick on the fields. The clarity of summer is a distant memory. Perhaps it was an illusion.

Heavy, I force myself to walk, weighed down by the density of the day. And as I walk, the uncertainties deepen and proliferate. Cherished landscapes are estranged in the ghostly half-light. Direction becomes uncertain, and distance unclear. Fearful in my disorientation, I stop still, engulfed in the bleakness of this day. The carefully mapped path is gone. There is no obvious way.

Out here today, you and I are as invisible as the veiled landscape. Relieved, I allow my guard to drop. Too much of life revolves around visibility, around clarity of word and deed and confident expressions of faithful certainty. Just for a short while, there is no one watching the minutiae of the performance, no one testing the creed.

Here and now, I gladly lay down all that I carry. No one's credibility is in the balance. Not mine, not yours, and not our Lord and Saviour's. Just briefly, with gratitude, I can let God go. It has the feel of a much needed interval in a high octane play: down time from an impossible drama in which everything is at stake – nothing less than the salvation of the whole world.

Somewhere, invisible yet imminent, I sense that the relief is shared. In this mist-bound hiatus, none of us has to play our part, not even the hero of the whole story. None of us needs to squeeze ourselves into the carefully crafted images of holiness or pronounce the immaculately rehearsed lines. Back stage and off duty, the soul is at last free to imagine and to wonder, to marvel at the strangeness of so much that is taken as gospel in the clear light of day.

But as the fog deepens so too does the darkness of the imaginings. What if my prayers and yours, the prayers of our people, rise to fall again, buoyed up only by the fervour of our own wishful thinking, going nowhere? What if the best insights of our collective studies only ever lead us back into the depths of this same fog, uncertain as to whether God is elusive as the great mystics teach, or just plain absent? In the heaviness that in these moments too easily engulfs my soul, I for one cannot tell which is the more real – the joyful summer clarity, or the darkness that now enshrouds its true or imagined memory.

Does it matter? Do we really need to know?

Today, swamped in deepest fog, the overwhelming reality is of the darkness, with its absolute power to disorientate and disenfranchise. To deny its force would be one dangerous folly too far.

But even now, straining to see through the fog as through a glass darkly, uncertain of the most immediate surroundings, there is no denying that it was a beautiful story which swept us along in the clear light of day. As dramas go, it has it all: sex scandals, high betrayal, obscene levels of suffering and an ending so unexpected in its twist, so overwhelming in its hopefulness, that no one would ever have the audacity to predict it.

The story presents an eloquent hypothesis; an improbable hypothesis for sure – a rash one even – but one unrivalled in its defiant positing of the absolute reality of light, of the untainted purity of awaiting love, from within the depths of such murkiness, such dense undermining fog.

Here, fog swirling, path indiscernible, there is a choice to be made. Wayward to the last, I opt into the hypothesis. To the blank face of the unperturbed darkness, I dare to offer up my most joyful thanks, and present the very best of my love and my time for duty: an act not of intellectual certainty, nor of piety or moral or theological conviction, but of unadulterated audacity.

And somewhere out there, invisible yet imminent, perhaps even at the heart of the God whom I have today set free, I sense that my defiant love and joy has met its match.

24

Journeys

MARTYN PERCY

The queue is long and seems not to move. We are in Bethlehem, and the line that snakes its way through the Church of the Nativity has already spilled out in the warmth of Manger Square. The grotto in the church is the focal point for worship. A silver star set into a marble floor marks the place where Jesus was born. I wait patiently for my turn – perhaps a few brief prayers and a moment of silence before the momentum of the queue pushes me on.

But as we are about to step down into the grotto, the queue suddenly stops. There is no explanation. But after ten minutes of stillness, it then suddenly becomes clear we cannot enter – not until the midday office is complete. Half an hour later, my moment comes. In the midst of the pressing throng I kneel before a space; a place of birth that is the beginning of Christian faith. There is nothing to say or do at the point; simply to be still, and to remember that God, in his goodness and tender mercy, came to us as a baby, so that shepherds and others could gaze, level-eyed, upon the face of God. 'The glory of God revealed in the face of Jesus Christ' is how Paul expresses it in 2 Corinthians 4.6 – in the face of a newborn infant, we gaze on God's own countenance.

The Holy Land is full of surprising journeys. The descent from the Paternoster Church, where Jesus taught the disciples how to pray, leads you inexorably down the Mount of Olives and to the Garden of Gethsemane. On the way, you pass the Dominus Flevit Chapel, where Jesus wept for Jerusalem. The plain geography also guides our theology. The simplicity of the Lord's Prayer leads us to look upon the world differently, and must also be linked to the agony of the prayers of Jesus in Gethsemane.

In the afternoon we head out to Nablus. We go by another way – as the wise men did to avoid Herod – to avoid a sticky checkpoint. Our guide explains that sometimes the longer routes turn out to be the shorter journeys. We meet Father Ibrahim in Nablus, an Anglican priest doing some wonderful work in a city choked with the congestion of too many people trying to fit into too small a space. Ibrahim introduces his assistant – a bright young Muslim woman – and together they serve food and talk about their common problems. In Nablus, it matters not if you are Christian or Muslim – only that you are Palestinian. Long ago, St Philip came to Nablus where he taught and baptized (Acts 8). Today, the vision of the church is for education and building partnerships in the community.

The next day we head out to the Church of the Annunciation. And this is where one can start to connect the womb to the tomb. To connect Mary's 'yes' to Jesus' 'yes'. To realize that for the journeys Jesus will make, his mother must also travel – Nazareth, Bethlehem, Jerusalem and more besides. Pilgrimage is movement. Following God in the footsteps of Jesus and Mary is movement. God, it seems, keeps us nomadic. But he also makes his home among us, and dwells with us.

The archaeology is telling. The monuments, churches and chapels themselves all speak of God's presence, as one would expect. But it is the new evidence of early Christian graffiti that is perhaps the most moving of this journey today. 'God was here' is what it says – and perhaps one surprising aspect of early Christianity was that worshippers felt able to scribble on pillars and walls that God had touched specific places. In the Church of Annunciation, a pillar was recently found dating from the late first or early second century that simply says 'Hail Mary'. In the former house of Simon Peter – now a ruined church and synagogue – Peter's name has been found scrawled into the stone. It seems that within 30 years or so of Peter's death, Christians already revered this site enough to put Peter's name to it. We stand above the ruins, and look down on a room where Jesus must have slept; a space where he must have eaten; a room where he may have healed Peter's mother-in-law.

This is what 'Emmanuel' means here. God abiding with us is now no longer an affirming theological construct. At Capernaum, we come face to face with the reality of Christ's presence in our midst. He ate, slept, chatted in this place; in the space, God dwelt with us. Here. We move on down the coast from Capernaum, and one suddenly realizes that Magdala and Tiberias are close. The place where Jesus walked on the shore and called the disciples is at hand; the rock on which Simon Peter is commissioned can be seen and touched. The Lake of Galilee stretches out before us. But above all else, it is the closeness of these places that is striking. It is the realization that our longest journeys are not physical, but spiritual. That the journeys and breaks Jesus undertakes are not just of historical interest. They are invitations. Walk with me, they say. Abide in this place, as I have abided with you. Come, let us journey.

25

Foxhole

JENNY GAFFIN

I have come to love this place. I love the contours of this land, its chang-ing moods through the seasons, the history it holds of life deeply lived, of time with cherished friends and transformative encounters. Here in this place I feel as rooted as the hedgerows; as connected as the horizon to the land. It is extraordinary how in so few years this place has, very deeply, become home, its logic and grammar embedded within me as surely as any birthright.

'Foxes have holes, and birds of the air have nests but the Son of Man has nowhere to lay his head.' These are brave words. But is it really possible to uproot, to transplant self to another field at will, to flourish amid all that is temporary, provisional? Can the human psyche survive the repeated wrenching apart of deeply nurtured relationships; the disorientation of the strange; the distancing imposed by the dread of further parting?

It is a challenge willingly embraced by the courageous few – armed forces' personnel and their families, religious ministers, journalists, travelling com-munities. But it is also an unwanted gauntlet imposed on too many more, through war or personal misfortune or natural disaster: and the trauma of radical dislocation reverberates through the generations, resurfacing in inexplicable longing for a land never visited, or in the startling recognition of self in a language never spoken.

Of course Jesus himself lived on the road, the perfect embodiment of holy itinerancy. But as weary fellow travellers are fond of reminding me, Jesus only made it into his fourth decade. And in truth that is not so far from today's reality: people living homeless on the streets can expect to die 30 years younger than those of us who are rooted and sheltered in flats and houses. There is no glamour to complete and perpetual transition. Quite the opposite: there can be the appalling threat of total destabilization, of enduring suffering, and loss unredeemed.

Yet for millennia, the Jewish people have been on the move. Sometimes at will, rejoicing; but too often through sheer force of necessity, journeying between lands and across cultures, becoming multilingual, versatile. And through the centuries of exodus, of travel, of change, of grief and violence and daring new beginnings, they have distilled an extraordinary wisdom into one audacious and entirely portable commandment: love.

This hallmark of pilgrim faith is manna refined and proffered through the centuries: to partake of it, en route to wherever and whatever might be next, is to share expansively and wholeheartedly in each stopping place, re-rooting no matter how deep the longing for the place left behind. To break this bread at each stopping place is to enter into fresh sacred covenant with strangers even as the voices of loved ones lost still echo in the ear. It is to trust that in this place, in this moment, God has already arrived ahead of us and only awaits our joyful acquiescence.

Loving nomadically, grand plans of permanence or ownership or status are put firmly out of place, the captivity they mask exposed and rejected. Freed from such encumbrances, full and glad acceptance of the gift of this moment, this person, is more than just a possibility: it becomes imperative, the source and sustenance of new life, as at each turn we invest deeply of time, talent and self in the most unlikely soil and, to our astonishment, grow. All this, knowing that in the fullness of God's time, the exodus will happen again, and the now-cherished field must be left behind.

Rooted immovably in the heart attuned to its own transience is the certainty that when the time of parting arrives, it will be love that infuses the grief with thanksgiving, and love that enables the road ahead once again to come alive with hopeful possibility.

So here in this cherished place, bag in hand, I will give thanks. I will not envy the fox its carefully dug hole nor the birds of the air their nests. Love, portable and resilient, is itself the rootedness; another change of scene can only deepen the truth of it. So now, together with the Son of Man, and in the most excellent of company, I once again turn my face to the road.

PART TWO

Readings and Reflections for the Weeks of Trinity Season

COMPILED BY
GEOFF MILLER

26

The Seed and the Fruit

Bible passage: Galatians 5.22

In his lectures *The Seed and the Fruit: Christian morality in a time of transition* (1953), delivered at McGill University in 1951, Leslie Hunter concentrated on the need to state the morality arising from the gospel in plain terms and in colloquial speech. He summarized his theme in an initial parable:

> As the threats of war and the cries of the dispossessed were sounding in his ears, Western Man fell into an uneasy sleep. In his sleep he dreamed that he entered the spacious store in which the gifts of God to men are kept, and addressed the angel behind the counter, saying: 'I have run out of the fruits of the Spirit. Can you restock me?' When the angel seemed to be about to say no, he burst out, 'in place of war, afflictions, injustice, lying and lust, I need love, joy, peace, integrity, discipline. Without these I shall be lost.' And the angel behind the counter replied, 'We do not stock fruits, only seeds.'

Prayer

Lord Jesus Christ,
alive and at large in the world,
help me to follow and find you there today,
in the places where I work,
meet people,
spend money,
and make plans.
Take me as a disciple of your kingdom,
to see through your eyes,
and hear the questions you are asking,
to welcome all others with your trust and truth,
and to change the things that contradict God's love,
by the power of the cross
and the freedom of your Spirit.
Amen.

Notes

Reading: *Strategist for the Spirit*, ed. Gordon Hewitt, Oxford: Becket Publications, 1985, p. 135.
Prayer: John V. Taylor, *A Matter of Life and Death*, London: SCM Press, 1986. Used with permission of the Estate of the late John V. Taylor.

27

Love: Some kinds of love

Bible passage: 1 John 4.7

There are some kinds of love which keep us like children, childish, which restore or reinforce relationships of dependence. There are some kinds of love which set us free, and which enable those who were once helped, to take responsibility for themselves.

Loving your neighbour as yourself means seeing him or her as your equal, wanting to give to him, but also accepting that you should receive from him too. It means establishing a relationship between equals; it means complete mutual interdependence.

Prayer

Lord you have taught us
that all our doings without love are nothing worth:
send your Holy Spirit
and pour into our hearts that most excellent gift of love,
the true bond of peace and of all virtues
without which whoever lives is counted dead before you.
Grant this for your only Son Jesus Christ's sake.

Notes

Reading: Newsletter of the French Protestant Industrial Mission.
Prayer: Collect for the Second Sunday of Trinity, *Common Worship: Daily Prayer*, London: Church House Publishing, 2005, p. 435. *Common Worship: Daily Prayer* copyright © Archbishops' Council 2000. Used by permission.

28

Joy: An empty tomb

Bible passage: John 19.41

In my mind's eye the sun was shining, fresh, tentative, even hesitant
But growing stronger, more sure of itself;
ochre, orange brilliance lightening up the moment.
And the garden,
the garden smelt of dew-dampened, heavy-headed,
shy flowers.

Yet I think the women in tearful panic
and Peter and John in their frantic haste
would have taken little note.
(They are, after all, still nailed to Friday!)
No, I can't imagine they stopped to savour the moment,
to think of the millions who would follow,
in eager anticipation, their every step to the
open, now empty, tomb.

Thank God they did not pause,
did not leave us in baited-breath
suspension,
but took us with them to the empty grave!
Surely this is the sun-kissed, flower-fragrant birthing-place of salvation.
For only the Messiah could be born in a grave!

Prayer

Lord, may every day be a day of resurrection
but may it be especially so today.
Give me to taste again the frantic eagerness of finding an
   empty tomb
and a risen Lord.
Let me smell the freshness of a life richly blessed
and then in your grace
give me the naive simplicity
and loud energy
to tell my world of the
greatness of the
victory of your love.
Amen.

Note

Poem and prayer by Geoff Miller.

29

Peace: Wildpeace

Bible passage: Matthew 5.9

Wildpeace

Not the peace of a cease-fire,
not even the vision of the wolf and the lamb,
but rather
as in the heart when the excitement is over
and you can talk only about a great weariness.
I know that I know how to kill,
that makes me an adult.
And my son plays with a toy gun that knows
how to open and close its eyes and say Mama.
A peace
without the big noise of beating swords into ploughshares,
without words, without
the thud of the heavy rubber stamp: let it be
light, floating, like lazy white foam.
A little rest for the wounds –
who speaks of healing?
(And the howl of the orphans is passed from one generation
to the next, as in a relay race:
the baton never falls.)

Let it come
like wildflowers,
suddenly, because the field
must have it: Wildpeace.

Prayer

May your kingdom come, O God,
with deliverance for the needy,
with peace for the righteous,
with overflowing blessing for all nations,
with glory, honour and praise
for Christ the only Saviour.

Notes

Reading: Yehuda Amichai, *The Selected Poetry of Yehuda Amichai*, University of
  California Press, 1996.
Prayer: *Common Worship: Daily Prayer*, London: Church House Publishing, 2005,
  Psalm 72. *Common Worship: Daily Prayer* copyright © Archbishops' Council
  2000. Used by permission.

Forbearance: A different hilltop!

Bible passage: Mark 9.2–3

If there had been any idealistic sentimentality in the message Jesus preached in Galilee it would have culminated gloriously in that moment of transfiguration on the mountain top. There the disciples could have been satisfied with a splendid apotheosis of the messenger of love and simplicity. And down in the valley a lunatic boy and a whole lunatic world would have remained unsaved. The sentimentalist Peter would gladly have remained there – and he spoke for a large part of the Church in all ages. But the mind of Jesus was set upon a different hill, and he took them down to start the journey towards it.

Prayer

Lord God,
you have called your servants
to ventures of which we cannot see the ending,
by paths yet untrodden,
through perils unknown.
Give us faith to go out with courage,
not knowing where to go,
but only that your hand is leading us,
and your love supporting us;
through Jesus Christ our Lord.

Notes

Reading: John V. Taylor, *Weep Not For Me*, Geneva: WCC Risk Series, 1986, pp. 30ff. Used with permission of the Estate of the late John V. Taylor.
Prayer: *Book of Lutheran Worship*, Minneapolis: Augsburg Publishing House, 1978, pp. 137, 153.

31

Kindness: A sample of Galilee

Bible passage: Mark 6.47–48

Joseph Meehan was born cruelly handicapped and known to the world as the 'crippled boy'. Here his friend invites him to go fishing on Loch Derravaragh.

> Easter beckoned next bringing real relief at the thoughts of Peter's invitation ... The day with the Nicholsons was a sample of Galilee. The boat navigated by Peter's father chattered serenely while Peter trawled for fish. The sky was overcast, rain just managed to hold off. Joseph sat among his friends and felt as one of them. Lonely days were but a dream; now he never looked back, never looked forward, never asked for tidings of joy. Now his cup was huge and his purse was no longer empty. Life was letting him thumbsuck for comfort for now, city-festered, french-horned-boldness yelled fire in his findings.

Prayer

Holy God,
when our memories blot out your kindness
and we ignore your patient love,
remember us, re-make us,
and give to us poor sinners
the rich inheritance of Jesus Christ our Lord.

Notes

Reading: Christopher Nolan, *Under the Eye of the Clock*, London: Pan, 1987, p. 95.
Prayer: *Common Worship: Daily Prayer*, London: Church House Publishing, 2005, Psalm 106. *Common Worship: Daily Prayer* copyright © Archbishops' Council 2000. Used by permission.

Goodness: Feasting on grace

Bible passage: John 1.16

Perhaps a novel but creative spiritual discipline to practise would be:

To **fast** from grumpiness and meanness of spirit and
to **feast** on seeing the good in others, even in ourselves.
To **fast** from complaining and living life in the negative and
to **feast** by enjoying, nourishing and, yes, treasuring all that
we have been given.
To **fast** from seeing things in the minus and
to **feast** on the 'more than' abundant grace of God.

Feasting on God's grace is easier than you may think for it is available in
bucket loads!

Prayer

Gracious God, your love for us is
at the same time outrageous and yet naively profound,
It is
exhilarating and challenging in equal measure.
Coach me in its crazy ways that I may share its shockingly beautiful effect
on me but also on my world.
Amen.

Note

Reading and prayer by Geoff Miller.

33

Faithfulness: A bishop's advice

Bible passage: John 21.15

Moral endeavour as well as moral complacency may lead us off the true road. Christianity does not begin with an alarm clock and a cold bath. It begins – the Credo becomes an operative faith – with a profound obeisance at the foot of the Cross ... You and I, therefore, are more likely to meet the Lord of life in our failures than in our successes because they throw us back on the mercy of God and the power of his Holy Spirit, instead of allowing us to trust in our own powers. The dynamic ... of the Mission of the People of God is therefore an unutterable thankfulness which can only be confessed in a dedicated life and a courageous confidence that God glorifies Himself through human weakness. On our side, the readiness is all.

Prayer

Father,
if the hour has come
to make the break,
help me not to cling,
even though it feels like death.
Give me the inward strength
of my Redeemer, Jesus Christ,
to lay down this bit of life
and let it go,
so that I and others may be free
to take up whatever new and fuller life
you have prepared for us,
now and hereafter.
Amen.

Notes

Reading: Leslie Hunter, Bishop of Sheffield (1939–62), From *Strategist for the Spirit*, ed. Gordon Hewitt, Oxford: Becket Publications, 1985, p. 139.

Prayer: John V. Taylor, *A Matter of Life and Death*, London: SCM Press, 1986. Used with permission of the Estate of the late John V. Taylor.

34

Gentleness: A bowl and a towel

Bible passage: John 13.5

The worker needs his tools,
Whether it's hammer and chisel or brush and palette it matters little.
Artist or artisan, professional or labourer, you are lost if you've got
   nothing to blame.
But what tools do you need to build a kingdom?
Would an orb and crown be any use to change hearts and minds?
Can you refashion a people with your hands?

Bring me a bowl and a towel!
Some jobs are surprisingly done better on your knees
because you can more easily get to the hard to reach parts:
Those nooks and crannies that harbour the dirtiest bits.
Let me sit at your feet and show you what love can do.

Prayer

Tender God,
gentle protector in time of trouble,
pierce the gloom of despair
and give us, with all your people,
the song of freedom and the shout of praise;
in Jesus Christ our Lord.
Amen.

Notes

Poem: Geoff Miller, 'A bowl and a towel'.
Prayer: *Common Worship: Daily Prayer*, London: Church House Publishing, 2005,
   Psalm 57. *Common Worship: Daily Prayer* copyright © Archbishops' Council
   2000. Used by permission.

35

Self-control: How to cure a fanatic

Bible passage: Galatians 5.22–23

And if you promise to take what I'm about to say with a big pinch of salt, I can tell you that, in principle at least, I think I have invented the remedy for fanaticism. A sense of humour is a great cure. I have never once in my life seen a fanatic with a sense of humour, nor have I ever seen a person with a sense of humour becoming a fanatic, unless he or she has lost that sense of humour. Some of them have a very pointed sense of sarcasm, but no humour. Humour contains the ability to laugh at ourselves. Humour is relativism, humour is the ability to see yourself as others may see you, humour is the capacity to realise that no matter how righteous you are and how terribly wronged against you have been, there is a certain side to life that is always a bit funny. The more right you are, the more funny you become. And, for that matter, you can be a righteous Israeli or a righteous Palestinian or a righteous anything, but, as long as you have a sense of humour, you might be partially immune to fanaticism.

Prayer

Lord, make me laugh. I'm not asking for a raucous belly laugh or even to be tickled pink. A wry smile or a gentle titter will do. Just enough to exercise some underused facial muscles, to ward off cynicism, to widen my perspective and pump prime some hope.

Lord, spread a little more laughter in the world too – am I asking for too much? Not a flippant or cruel comedy. Not a disparaging smug smirk or a laughing 'at' but a laughing 'with', a delight in life, a twinkle in the eye, a camaraderie of smiles.

Lord, I hope you can laugh as well – indeed I'm relying on it! I hope you can, at least sometimes, at our strange ways, our inconsistencies, inadequacies and eccentric mannerisms. I even hope that you will graciously smile on some of the fine messes that we manage to create and help us see a way through.

For if humour really is the antidote to fear, failure and fanaticism then your world could do with an extra dose – right now!
Amen.

Notes

Reading: Amos Oz, *How to Cure a Fanatic*, London: Vintage, 2012, p. 73.
Prayer: Geoff Miller, 'Make me laugh'.

36

Go Easy on Yourself

Bible passage: Romans 7.4–5

Soul self; come poor Jackself, I do advise
You jaded, let be; call off thoughts awhile
Elsewhere; leave comfort root room; let joy size
At God knows when to God knows what; whose smile's
not wrung, see you, unforeseen times rather – as skies
between pie mountains – lights a lovely mile.

Prayer

We have strayed from thy ways like lost sheep ...

Lord, to be honest I find it hard to say I'm sorry for the petty misdoings, little slips and minor misdemeanors that seem to be the life-blood of confessions. I can't help but think that you have better things to be bothered with than such irritations. Is this an arrogance on my part, or perhaps a conceited humility that assumes that my life is too insignificant to count?

And there is no health in us ...

Yet I know that I stand in shameful solidarity with humankind in all the shortcomings that bring pain and struggle to so many and wilful destruction to a bountiful world.
I also know that if the gospel we proclaim is even a shadow of the truth, then you have a tender love for even the insignificant like me – even with my false modesty!

O Lord, have mercy upon us ...

And I cannot escape the fact – nor do I really want to – that to you not only do I, and countless others, matter but we can, with your grace, make a difference and contribute to a wholeness beyond our wildest dreams.

Lord, have mercy ... please!

Notes

Poem: Gerard Manley Hopkins (1844–1889), 'My own heart let me more have pity on'.
Prayer: Geoff Miller, 'There is no health in us!'

37

Generosity

Bible passage: Luke 7.37–38

The alabaster jar

The world had already taken so much from her.
It had lifted her skirt and
exchanged her dignity for the wide eyes of fear,
replaced her self-respect for the bowed head of shame.
Yet she still had much to give –
So much!
All around her there was the sweet smell of generosity:
An aroma of uncomplicated adoration.
Gentle hands lovingly prepared beautiful feet for the hard road to the hill.
At long last the fragrance of freedom hangs in the air.

Prayer

How generous is your goodness, O God,
how great is your salvation,
how faithful is your love;
help us to trust you in trial
and praise you in deliverance;
through Jesus Christ our Lord.

Notes

Poem: Geoff Miller, 'The alabaster jar'.
Prayer: *Common Worship: Daily Prayer*, London: Church House Publishing, 2005,
Psalm 66.*Common Worship: Daily Prayer* copyright © Archbishops' Council
2000. Used by permission.

38

Daydream

Bible passage: 1 Corinthians 13.9–10

One day people will touch and talk, perhaps, easily,
And loving be natural as breathing and warm as sunlight;
And people will untie themselves as string is unknotted,
Unfold and yawn and stretch and spread their fingers,
Unfurl, uncurl, as seaweed returned to the sea.
And work will be simple and swift as a seagull flying,
And play will be casual and quiet as a seagull settling;
And the clocks will stop, and no one will wonder or care or notice,
And people will smile without reason, even in winter, even in the rain.

Prayer

Almighty God,
you have made us for yourself,
and our hearts are restless till they find their rest in you:
pour your love into our hearts and draw us to yourself,
and so bring us at last to your heavenly city
where we shall see you face to face;
through Jesus Christ our Lord.

Notes

Poem: *ASJ Tessimond: Collected Poems*, ed. Hubert Nicholson, Tarset: Bloodaxe, 2010, p. 48.
Prayer: Collect for the Seventeenth Sunday after Trinity, *Common Worship: Daily Prayer*, London: Church House Publishing, 2005, p. 441. *Common Worship: Daily Prayer* copyright © Archbishops' Council 2000. Used by permission.

39

The Superabundance of God

Bible passage: John 2.10

So this is the mystery of worship as perfect service. God has done everything that needs to be done, and requires no assistance or praise; yet in Christ he embodies perfect service as the praise of his glory; thus it is possible for God's people to live lives – eternal lives – of service, made possible by grace not by need, in which obedience is perfect freedom. This is the life to which God's people aspire when they engage in worship. In worship they pray for the full, evident and complete coming of God's reign. They affirm the superabundance of God – more creativity, life, love, compassion, forgiveness, strength, grace than they can possibly imagine or need. They seek to imitate the God-filled service of God embodied in Jesus. And they pursue the gifts of attention and joy; the presence and engagement, the completeness of offering and receiving gifts that can only deepen over eternity. In these ways the perfect service of worship in the kingdom expresses the superabundance of God.

Prayer

Spirit of God,
Lord and giver of life,
moving between us and around,
like wind or water or fire,
breathe into us your freshness, that we may awake,
cleanse our vision, that we may see more clearly,
kindle our senses, that we may feel more sharply,
and give us the courage to live
as you would have us live,
through Jesus Christ our Lord.
Amen.

Notes

Reading: Samuel Wells, *God's Companions*, Oxford: Blackwell Publishing, 2006, p. 38. This material is reproduced with permission of John Wiley & Sons Inc.
Prayer: John V. Taylor, *A Matter of Life and Death*, London: SCM Press, 1986. Used with permission of the Estate of the late John V. Taylor.

40

Small is Beautiful

Bible passage: Romans 8.19

When you thrust a shovel into the soil or tear off a piece of coral you are godlike, cutting through an entire world. You have crossed a hidden frontier known to a very few. Immediately close at hand, around and beneath our feet, lies the least explored part of the planet's surface. It is also the most vital place on Earth for human existence.

Prayer

We thank you for the integrity and diversity of all living creatures. Enlarge within us a sense of fellowship with our brothers and sisters, the animals with whom we share the earth and who love the sweetness of life. Grant us compassion in our dealings with all creatures great and small.

Notes

Reading: E. O. Wilson in the Foreword to David Liittschwager, *A World in One Cubic Foot*, University of Chicago Press, 2012.
Prayer: Taken from *Praying the Earth*, 2nd edn, Newcastle Diocesan Environment Task Group; Copyright © Newcastle Diocesan Board of Finance, 2011.

41

Risk!

Bible passage: Revelation 3.20

The door

Go and open the door.
  Maybe outside there's
  a tree, or a wood
  or a magic city.

Go and open the door.
  Maybe a dog's rummaging.
  Maybe you'll see a face,
or an eye,
or the picture
  of a picture

Go and open the door.
  If there's a fog
  it will clear.

Go and open the door.
  Even if there's only
  the darkness ticking,
  even if there's only
  the hollow wind,
  even if
    nothing
      is there,
go and open the door.

At least
there'll be
a draught.

Prayer

O Living God,
we who are partly living,
scarcely hoping,
and fitfully caring,
pray to you now
to make us fully alive.
Give us the vitality, awareness and commitment
that we see in Jesus Christ,
through the power of his death and resurrection.
We ask this in his name.
Amen.

Notes

Poem: Miroslav Holub, *Poems before & After: Collected English Translations*,
   Tarset: Bloodaxe, 1990.
Prayer: John V. Taylor, *A Matter of Life and Death*, London: SCM Press, 1986.
   Used with permission of the Estate of the late John V. Taylor.

42

Anam Cara

Bible passage: John 15.15

In everyone's life, there is a great need for an *anam cara*, a soul friend. In this love, you are understood as you are without mask or pretension. The superficial and functional lies and half-truths of acquaintance fall away. You can be as you really are. Love allows understanding to dawn and understanding is precious. Where you are understood you are at home. Understanding nourishes belonging ... the *anam cara* is God's gift. Friendship is the gift of God ... Jesus as the Son of God is the first Other in the universe ... He is the secret *anam cara* of every individual.

Prayer

The Sacred Three
My fortress be
Encircling me
Come and be round
My hearth and my home.

Notes

Reading and prayer: John O'Donohue, *Anam Cara: Spiritual Wisdom from the Celtic World*, London: Bantam Press, 1997, pp. 36–7.

43

The Dilemma

Bible passage: Romans 12.4

When Harold Fry nips out one morning to post a letter, leaving his wife hoovering upstairs, he has no idea that he is about to walk from one end of the country to another. He has no hiking boots or map, let alone a compass, waterproof or mobile phone. All he knows is that he must keep walking. To save someone's life.

It is a journey of encounter and there is in every encounter a lot he reflects upon ...

He had learned that it was the smallness of people that filled him with wonder and tenderness, and the loneliness of that too. The world was made up of people putting one foot in front of the other; and a life might appear ordinary simply because the person living it had done so for a long time. Harold could no longer pass a stranger without acknowledging the truth that everyone was the same, and also unique; and that this was the dilemma of being human.

Prayer

Thank you
scandalous God,
for giving yourself to the world
not in the powerful and extraordinary
but in weakness and the familiar:
in a baby; in bread and wine.

Thank you
for offering, at journey's end, a new beginning;
for setting, in the poverty of stable,
the richest jewel of your love;
for revealing, in a particular place,
your light for all nations ...

Thank you
for bringing us to Bethlehem, House of Bread,
where the empty are filled,
and the filled are emptied;
where the poor find riches,
and the rich recognize their poverty;
where all who kneel and hold out their hands
are unstintingly fed.

Notes

Reading: Rachel Joyce, *The Unlikely Pilgrimage of Harold Fry*, London: Transworld
    Publishers, 2012, p. 158.
Prayer: Kate Compston, in Janet Morley (ed.), *Bread of Tomorrow*, London: SPCK/
    Christian Aid, 1992, p. 51. Reproduced by permission of SPCK.

44

Finding the Hidden Christ

Bible passage: Matthew 25.44

How to hide Jesus

There are people after Jesus.
They have seen the signs.
Quick, let's hide Him.
Let's think; carpenter,
   fisherman's friend
   disturber of religious comfort.
Let's award Him a degree in theology,
A purple cassock
And a position of respect.
They'll never think of looking here.
Let's think;
His dialect might betray Him,
His tongue of the masses.
Let's teach him Latin
And seventeenth century English,
They'll never think of listening in.
Let's think;
Humble,
Man of Sorrows,
Nowhere to lay his head.
We'll build a house for Him
Somewhere away from the poor.
We'll fill it with brass and silence.
It's sure to throw them off.

There are people after Jesus.
Quick, let's hide Him.

Prayer

Jesus, don't let us hide you.
Please break cover, break out into my world
   and do it now!
Force open my eyes to see you in every encounter,
   in every person,
      in every place.

Notes

Poem: Steve Turner, *Up to Date*, London: Hodder & Stoughton, 1976.
Prayer: Geoff Miller, 'Please break cover'.

45

A Simpler Way

Bible passage: John 1.14

There is a simpler way to organize human endeavour. It requires a new way of being in the world. It requires being in the world without fear. Being in the world with play and creativity. Seeking after what is possible. Being willing to learn and to be surprised.

The simpler way to organize human endeavour requires a belief that the world is inherently orderly. The world seeks organization. It does not need us humans to organize it.

The simpler way summons forth what is best about us. It asks us to understand human nature differently, more optimistically. It identifies us as creative. It acknowledges that we seek after meaning. It asks us to be less serious, yet more purposeful, about our work and our lives. It does not separate play from the nature of being.

This world of a simpler way is a world we already know. We may not have seen it clearly, but we have been living it all our lives. It is a world that is more welcoming, more hospitable to our humanness. Who we are and what is best about us can more easily flourish.

Prayer

Lord, help us to go barefoot,
to walk a simple way
a way of fun and laughter,
a way that enjoys the best in others
a way that practises the art of the possible and pleasant.
The way of the learner and the optimist,
the naive believer that things can be different:
Simple, straightforward and open to your future.
For the sake of the Christ who simply lived through simple love.

Notes

Reading: Margaret J. Wheatley and Myron Kellner-Rogers, *A Simpler Way*, San Francisco: Berrett-Koehler Publishers, 1996. Reprinted with permission of the publisher. Copyright © 1996 Margaret J. Wheatley and Myron Kellner-Rogers. All rights reserved www.bkconnection.com.
Prayer: Geoff Miller, 'The simple way'.

46

This Is Where I Am

Bible reading: Luke 9.57–62

Not everyone is able to walk, but most people can, which makes walking one of the most easily available spiritual practices of all. All it takes is the decision to walk with some awareness, both of who you are and what you are doing. Where you are going is not as important, however counterintuitive that may seem. To detach the walking from the destination is in fact one of the best ways to recognize the altars you are passing right by all the time. Most of us spend so much time thinking about where we have been or where we are supposed to be going that we have a hard time recognizing where we actually are. When someone asks us where we want to be in our lives, the last thing that occurs to us is to look down at our feet and say, 'Here, I guess, since this is where I am.'

Prayer

God of Pilgrimage
be with me on my journey
    Through this life;
guard and defend me,
shelter and feed me,
challenge and inspire me,
teach me and lead me,
and when my days are ended
welcome me home at last
to rest in your love for ever.

Notes

Reading: Barbara Brown Taylor, *An Altar in the World,* Norwich: Canterbury Press, 2009, p. 56.
Prayer: Author unknown, from *A World of Blessings,* Norwich: Canterbury Press, 2000, p. 341.

47

The Need for Roots

Bible passage: John 15.1

Simone Weil's classic book *The Need for Roots* was written in the early months of 1943 in London, the same year of her death. Shortly after her arrival in England in 1942 she had been asked by the Free French in London to write a report on the possibilities of bringing about the regeneration of France. The report is this book and it was published in 1949; it calls for the recovery of spiritual roots before it is too late:

> Uprootedness is by far the most dangerous malady to which human societies are exposed, for it is a self-propagating one. For people who are really uprooted there remain only two possible sorts of behaviour: either to fall into spiritual lethargy resembling death, like the majority of the slaves in the Roman empire, or to hurl themselves into some form of activity necessarily designed to uproot, often by the most violent methods, those who are not yet uprooted, or only partly so.

Prayer

Crown us, O God, but with humility,
and robe us with compassion,
that, as you call us into the kingdom of your Son,
we may strive to overcome all evil
by the power of good
and so walk gently on the earth
with you, our God, for ever.

Notes

Reading: S. Weil, *A Matter of Life and Death*, London: SCM Press, 1986, p. 33.
Prayer: *Common Worship: Daily Prayer*, London: Church House Publishing, 2005, Psalm 21. *Common Worship: Daily Prayer* copyright © Archbishops' Council 2000. Used by permission.

48

Hospitality

Bible passage: Hebrews 13.2

Silently and openhandedly, welcome the guests that providence sends to your table. Besides a meal, you offer them a space of calm and peace and your prayer can only be nourished by these contacts. Think of all that Jesus did, said and revealed while at meals and of his promise that his followers should all eat and drink one day at his table in his kingdom. In this broken world, God sees the table as a sacred thing. A forgotten treasure for you to rediscover and cherish.

Prayer

In the name of the Sacred Trinity we,
who have found in this place a home,
bid you welcome.
With the Father's love we open wide our doors.
In the name of his Son we invite you to enter.
Empowered by the Spirit we extend
our friendship.
May we welcome you as Christ himself
and through God's good grace
may you see Christ in us.
Amen.

Notes

Reading: *A City Not Forsaken: Jerusalem Community Rule*, London: Darton, Longman & Todd, 1985, p. 33.
Prayer: Geoff Miller, 'A Newcastle welcome'.

49

A Community of Faith

Bible passage: Acts 2.43–47

Lord, if I thought you were listening I'd pray for this above all: that any church set up in your name should remain poor, and powerless, and modest. That it should wield no authority except that of love. That it should never cast anyone out. That it should own no property and make no laws. That it should not condemn, but only forgive. That it should be not like a palace with marble walls and polished floors, and guards standing at the door, but like a tree with its roots deep in the soil, that shelters every kind of bird and beast and gives blossom in the spring and shade in the hot sun and fruit in the season, and in time gives up its good sound wood for the carpenter; but that sheds many thousands of seeds so that new trees can grow in its place.

Prayer

Lord, take the shoes off this Church
not only physically, outwardly, actually,
but inwardly also.
Lord, take the shoes off this Church –
the shoes of pride and fear,
complacency and factionalism.
Lord, take the shoes off this Church
that the quality of its worship may touch
the whole life of this people:
And to this end, put the shoes on this Church that it may
    go out to serve all men and women everywhere, Lord.

Notes

Reading: Philip Pullman, *The Good Man Jesus and the Scoundrel Christ*, London: Canongate Books, 2010, p. 200.
Prayer: John Carden, 'Lord, take the shoes off this Church', CMS (c. 1987).

50

A Last Word: A silent and a shocking blessing

Bible passage: Mark 10.13–14

A silent blessing

I am still in the side chapel, asking God to meet me in the Eucharist. 'Aren't you sick of blessings,' he asks, 'like children on Easter morning who eat all their chocolate eggs at once? When you expect titillation, what are you saying about your relationship with me? Isn't my quiet presence enough?' … 'Your children have bikes and when they want newer and better bikes, you say, "There are children who have no bikes. Be content with what you have," You are like a child always asking for toys. Why do you always want blessings? Sometimes you go into your children's bedroom when they are asleep. You touch them, bless them and pray for them. They receive a blessing but never know it. In the morning when they are squabbling over who has eaten the last of the favourite breakfast cereal, you and I are aware of the blessing they have received. The fact that they don't know about it doesn't diminish its power.'

Prayer

A shocking blessing

May God bless you with discomfort at easy answers,
half truths, superficial relationships,
so that you will live deep within your heart.

May God bless you with anger at injustice,
oppression and exploitation of people,
so that you will work for justice, equity and peace.

May God bless you with tears to shed for those who suffer from pain,
rejection, starvation and war,
so that you will reach out your hand to comfort them and change their
pain to joy.

And may God bless you with the foolishness to think that you can make a
difference in the world,
so that you will do the things which others tell you cannot be done.

Notes

Reading: Geoffrey Howard, *Dare to Break Bread*, London: Darton, Longman &
Todd, 1992, p. 11.
Prayer: Source unknown, from *A World of Blessings*, comp. Geoffrey Duncan, Nor-
wich: Canterbury Press, 2000, p. 102.

PART THREE

Sermons and Homilies for Ordinary Time

51

Water into Wine

MARTYN PERCY

Bible passage: John 2—11

I don't really like wedding receptions very much. By and large, there are very few I have been to that I have really enjoyed. My own, obviously. But others? If I'm honest, they belong to my own personal Room 101 – in they go with caravans, any kind of camping holiday, semolina, junket, coconut … and most hymns. So it is a bit odd to be reflecting upon this particular wedding reception.

The idea that God uses fairly unpromising or unusual material to further his purposes should not surprise us. In the Gospels, even miracles begin with ordinary, simple things. A child's packed lunch – a very ordinary thing – needs to be prepared, packed, lugged up a hillock and then offered before anything can happen to help feed 5,000. To catch fish, someone needs to build a boat and make some nets. The miracle of the wedding at Cana in Galilee – a story rich in analogy and symbolism – is no different. But it is also packed with a telling litany of detail that should make us reflect a little more on our own place within God's world. Most people remember the story of the wedding of Cana in Galilee for the end result – an absurd amount of very good wine produced at the end of a feast in which, presumably, many have already had quite enough, and won't be riding their donkey home.

But consider this. For the miracle of the wedding of Cana in Galilee to happen at all, two people have to take the risk of falling in love and declare that they want to spend the rest of their natural lives together. To make water into wine, several people have to draw and fetch large amounts of water. To make the huge jars which carry the water, and later the miraculous wine, someone has to dig the clay, stoke the oven, mould the clay and fire it. And someone has the final headache of organizing a Jewish wedding and hundreds of guests. Without these 'base', ordinary materials, there is no miracle at Cana. We all have our part to play in the transformations and miracles that are wrought of God.

And so it is with the Church. The Gospel today reminds us that base, and perhaps rather unpromising, materials, when offered to God, become transformed. Ordinary bread becomes the body of Christ; ordinary wine his blood. And yet it is important to remember that these materials remain as they are, even as they are transformed. It is important to face this, because in a church that is sometimes obsessed with being pure and holy, we need to remember that there is no version of Christianity that does not have a local accent. Every type and form of Christianity is incarnated within its local culture – its time, its space and its life.

The story of our faith is, in other words, a story of common, local water into wine – the transformation of what is base; but it draws out the very best of what that life or material is, to a new and redeemed status. Put another way, it is the blessing of reality. Our faith is just that. It is the taking of ordinary people – with their own special and unique qualities – and beginning to see that they can become instruments of God's blessing to us. It is sacramental; the ordinary made extra-ordinary.

But, lest you need reminding, the ordinary remains, and for good reasons. God is reminding us that it is here that he meets us – in the plainest things: bread, wine ... and people. Even wedding receptions. This is, of course, a very Anglican definition of miracles. If you like, 'doing something quite interesting with something fairly ordinary'. For most Anglicans, such miracles occur with regular frequency in the vicarage kitchen, or study or church room – God uses them all.

This is why the apostle Paul's well-known phrase is so vital to remember: 'his power is made perfect in our weakness'. We do not belong to a religion where power finds expression in perfectionism. Rather, we look for the God who is incarnate; who comes to the world and is found in human form. God uses our weaknesses – the foolish and base things of the world – to work his changes. But whereas we look for perfection, God looks for the weakness – he is drawn to it, because he seeks not only to change it, but to work through it.

As the mystics say, if God has a weakness, it is his soft heart – he cannot resist a challenge. There would have been people at the wedding in Cana, therefore, who would be sipping the wine, but perhaps not agreeing with the steward's verdict that the groom had 'saved the best until last'. You can perhaps imagine others muttering: 'Well, he says it's good, but personally I don't care for these new fruity Mediterranean wines myself. Give me a good claret any day, or perhaps a nice dry Burgundy.'

What, then, are we to make of the miracle of the wedding of Cana? There is a sense in which we are often invited to look at these stories in ways other than the literal. 'Miracles', you see, are not descriptions of events, but interpretations. You have to look for the meaning; you have to find the point; you have to discern the leaven in the lump.

Perhaps the first thing to say is that the story itself is a vehicle for a host of analogies. The performance of the miracle has something to say about the necessity of renewal; that the Church is to be the new wine. That in Jesus, the time of celebration has arrived. And that the Kingdom of God, now dawning, is a place of plenty. So often in the Gospels, the meaning of a miracle is on the inside of the story, and not the outside.

Second, the miracle is also a reminder of God's absurd abundance. His love and grace is not measured out – in ration-book tokens, as it were. It is there for all in ridiculous, stupefying and intoxicating quantities. His love flows, flows and flows. This miracle speaks of his extravagant love and generosity. It says that even at a wedding reception, God lavishes his love on those whose gaze is wholly elsewhere. They are saying, 'Ooh, I don't think much of Mary's outfit – those colours really don't work; blue is so last season.' Yet this is the time; the new wine is here, and it is being served now – even to those who don't notice. Ten lepers are healed. Only one bothers to say thanks. But the other nine don't lose out. So it is with the wine; all may drink (and be merry), just as God's love and grace is for all. But only a few will notice that their taste buds have been tickled, and then read the label.

Third, the miracle at Cana in Galilee is a definite echo of the resurrection story. The miracle at the wedding takes place on the third day. Out of the dry earth – whether a pot or a hewn-out grave, it matters not – new wine flows where there was nothing before. What was thought to be water is now wine; this is the carpenter's son. Jesus is himself the new wine; the best of God saved until last. Down the ages the prophets have come – and gone. But the word of the Lord is now rare. It is not often that his people sense the voice of God through his anointed. All that was centuries ago. So just when you thought the party was all over, and about to end in a whimper, not with a bang, there is an unexpected coda from God. All is not finished. Actually, the party has really just started.

Fourth, the miracle invites us to consider how God uses ordinary material today, not just bread and wine, but people too – like you and me. But how does God make the ordinary into something that brings transformation, grace, extravagant excess, lavish (even foolish) love?

In her book *Travelling Mercies*, Anne Lamott describes seeing a miracle at church, and it is one that rather surprises her. She relates how a member of the congregation, a man named Ken, was dying of AIDS – his partner having already died of the disease. She writes:

There's a woman in the choir named Ranola who is large and beautiful and jovial and black and as devout as can be, who has been a little stand-offish toward Ken ... She was raised in the South by Baptists who taught her that his way of life – that he – was an abomination ... But Kenny has come to church almost every week for the last year and won almost everyone over. He finally missed a couple of Sundays when he got too weak, and then a month ago he was back, weighing almost no pounds, his face even more lopsided, as if he'd had a stroke. Still, during the prayers of the people, he talked joyously of his life and his decline, of grace and redemption, of how safe and happy he feels these days.

So on this one particular Sunday, for the first hymn, the so-called Morning Hymn, we sang 'Jacob's Ladder' which goes, 'Every rung goes higher, higher' while ironically Ken couldn't even stand up. But he sang away sitting down, with the hymnal in his lap. And then when it came time for the second hymn, the Fellowship Hymn, we were to sing 'His eye is on the sparrow'. The pianist was playing and the whole congregation had risen – only Ken remained seated, holding the hymnal in his lap – and we began to sing, 'Why should I feel discouraged? Why do the shadows fall?' And Ranola watched Ken rather sceptically for a moment, and then her face began to melt and contort like his, and she went to his side and bent down to lift him up – lifted up this white rag doll, this scarecrow. She held him next to her, draped over and against her like a child while they sang. And it pierced me. (1999, pp. 64–5).

So the miracle of Cana is also just like the miracle of Zarepheth; small acts of hospitality and preparation are the foundation for God's good grace. If you want to see a miracle, you can help to make one. Make a pot; fetch some water; arrange a wedding; do all the ordinary things you normally do. But do these things with open eyes, open hands and open hearts. And ask God to transform the ordinary; offer yourself, and ask God to use your ordinariness, and perhaps your weakness. And just as God pours out his spirit, so will you also be poured out, in the most surprising and abundant ways, for his sake, and for his glory.

Note

Anne Lamott, *Travelling Mercies*, New York: Anchor Books, 1999.

52

Wise and Foolish Virgins

MARTYN PERCY

Bible passage: Matthew 25.1–13

I think it was Alan Bennett, in one of his *Beyond the Fringe* sketches, impersonating a religious education teacher, who posed this question to his pupils: 'Now boys, would you rather be in the light with the wise virgins, or in the dark with the foolish ones?' Most lads manage a titter at this point. But titter ye not. Even though it's a kind of Frankie Howard humour – more *Up Pompei* than *Footlights* – the point is well made: where do you stand?

In most modern translations, the Greek for 'virgin' has been replaced with the more sanitized 'bridesmaid'. A pity, really, as the Greek is clear. It is the same word used for Mary, the Mother of Jesus, in Matthew 1 – *parthenos*. The Parthenon is the temple on the Athenian Acropolis, and dedicated to the Greek goddess Athena, whom the people of Athens considered their virgin patron.

So, no mention of bridesmaids. Except that bridesmaids were usually virgins, and this parable, as so many do, plays on our expectations and assumptions. More of that in a moment. But let me begin with the bridegroom, who almost certainly would have carried a lamp or a torch as he approached the house at midnight. Recently I was staying in a friend's house and there was a fridge magnet on her rather large fridge with a reproduction of Holman Hunt's *The Light of the World*. The caption on the picture read, 'Jesus is coming', and underneath, 'Quick, look busy!'

This parable is a bit more sophisticated than that, but it picks up that constant Advent theme in Jesus' teaching about being ready for the coming of the Kingdom. The imagery speaks of a bridegroom who could arrive at any moment, and who expects to find the virgin-bridesmaids ready to accompany him to the chamber or the house of the bride. The virgin-bridesmaids have a pivotal role in the ceremony. They march with the groom. They need to light their way, and his, and the streets for others to follow.

The parable has a twist. The foolish ones don't have enough oil, and there isn't enough to share. So they have to go on a late-night shopping spree to get some more. And while they are queuing at the cash-only two-for-one offer on lamp oil at their local supermarket, the groom has taken the remaining virgin-bridesmaids who were prepared, and they have gone off to the bride's house and chambers. The consequence of being unprepared is devastating. The remaining foolish virgin-bridesmaids now have some oil, but no idea where the bridal party has gone ... and they are too late for the banquet, even if they catch up. When they get there, breathless and illuminated, the door is shut. It's too late. The meaning of the parable is, for once, fairly plain. And for pastoral practice, there is scriptural warrant to read the riot act to all late bridesmaids: don't be late, because we'll start without you.

Like so many of the parables of this kind – and here we have a banquet, invitations, and so forth, but also a rallying call to *be ready* – they seek to remind us that all that we have is ultimately God's. That what we are about to be involved in does not belong to us. We are guests of God at his table, not the caterers. We run to his timetable; we must just be ready.

The parable connects to others that Matthew offers. Like the preceding parable of the steward, we are not owners but tenants, stewards entrusted with the things of God's creation. And with this stewardship comes respon-sibility, the responsibility to be ready to welcome our master and to treat all that has been entrusted to us well. This is not a call to inactivity: the servant is meant to run the household as a faithful and prudent manager. He is not meant to sit up all night every night, but simply to be able to respond when the knock comes and to show things in good order, well managed. Yet he is to know that it is ultimately not his but his masters.' A master is not to be feared but to be respected.

And in the parable that follows the wise and foolish virgins – the parable of the talents – similar issues arise. This is about stewardship and savvy investment. The parable of the talents is, in some sense, about the conse-quence of not even trying. The three servants are each given a quantity of money by their master before he departs for a long spell abroad. One gets five talents, one two and the last one.

We are not told why the division is uneven; it is easy to imagine good reasons based on age, experience, aptitude. Each has been entrusted with some of the master's money and two make the most of this opportunity, thinking about how the money can be used to grow the resources that have been entrusted. But one is uncertain of the whole enterprise, and buries what he has been given. Eventually the master returns and the servants are called to account. The first two are proud of their endeavours; they have used what they had well and they have double to give to their master. He is delighted, and each is praised for being faithful over a little and promised that he will be entrusted with a lot. Enter into your master's pleasure, they are told. So far, so good.

However, the last servant comes with a self-righteous attitude to his own indecision. There is a certain posturing, and even justification for inaction: 'I knew you to be a mean and unfair master,' he says, 'and I was afraid so I hid the talent and here it is returned just as it was given.'

The master is far from impressed. Even if he can be considered a hard master the servant could at least have got interest on the money (this is quite a sneering comment as usury was forbidden). Instead it is a rejection of the gift and opportunity given, it is returned unused. Fear and mistrust had paralysed the last servant. The ending is harsh. The one who didn't try has the gift he didn't want given to someone else, and he is dismissed into the darkness.

So, darkness awaits those who lack foresight, imagination, preparedness and faithful stewardship. Jesus is on a bit of a roll here: three parables that seem to push in the same direction. These parables are a call to take seriously the way that we live in our world, conscious that we will all at some time be called to account for how we have cared for and responded to all that God has given us and called us to. This has implications for our dealings with the world and our discipleship. It is a call not to take short cuts and believe that we can make it all right in the end; we do not know when we will be called to account.

These parables, of course, remind us that it is not just in terms of finances that we should keep our house in order. The fact that the virgin-bridesmaids could go to the late-night convenience store to buy more oil is not the point. In counting on that, they missed the wedding banquet. So, the parable says that all aspects of our living should be open to God's scrutiny. Be ready, therefore.

I was often told as a teenager to keep short accounts with God. Forgiveness is on offer; but don't put off being in a constant state of readiness to meet your maker. Don't delay making things right. This parable is a call to eager, righteous living; and we need to consciously think about what that means for us within the different spheres of our lives. How can we do our best to be sure that we are living our Christian lives not in terms of our own comfort and time frames, but in terms of the things Christ is calling us to right here and now.

So, back to the question where we began ... why virgins? Of course, this is not a parable about virgins at all. A pity, perhaps; but that's life. The parable is not about sexual fidelity either. It is simply about wisdom and foolishness. The foolish are those who made little preparation and took their place at the banquet for granted. They burnt their lamps in the day – so there is nothing left for the burning of the midnight oil. The foolish ones are all spark but no oil. Foolishness is a failure to read the situation; and it makes rash assumptions about entitlement. The foolish are distracted, take their eye off the game and then expect to be rescued by the others. But there is simply not enough midnight oil to share.

Wisdom, on the other hand, as is so often the case in the Bible, is about knowing your place before God, and is linked to the virtue of humility. We get the word 'humility' from *hummus*, meaning earth or earthed. The wise virgins have their feet on the ground. They do not expect, of right, to be at the wedding banquet. They assume that they need to be prepared. The lessons for the world could hardly be more pertinent. If you use up your precious resources and exhaust your social capital, you'll be screwed – politically, economically and socially. And virgins no longer.

The analogy for all of us could hardly be more telling. Be prepared, always. Pace yourself. Live by Advent – expect the unexpected. Take nothing for granted. Be wise and humble. Take your holiness and purity seriously. Don't live in a constant state of fear, or take your future for granted. Live in a constant state of readiness, because there is a wedding banquet ahead. And if you have oil and spark, we need you to light the streets, so many may find their way to the celebration.

53

Pilgrimage

ROWAN WILLIAMS

Bible passage: Luke 1.46–55

If you don't usually go to evensong or sing worship songs, the word 'magnify' isn't instantly going to communicate much; it simply means what a magnifying glass does – making things look bigger. Actually, this isn't such a bad start to understanding what 'magnify the Lord' means. When Mary sings the Magnificat, she wants to make God look bigger, to draw attention to the greatness of God, as we do when we sing it. But the words used in the ancient languages are more robust – they really mean making something greater in fact, not just making it look greater. And this would be an odd thing to say in relation to God, since we can't do anything to make God more than God is. Yet in those languages the words are regularly used to mean praising, whether praising God or praising other human beings. And perhaps we should think of that as suggesting that when we praise someone or something else we make them bigger in the sense of giving them more room: *we* step back, we put our preoccupations and goals and plans aside so as to let the reality of something else live in us for that moment, find room in us. Real praise is about forgetting myself, even my feelings, so that the sheer beauty and radiance of something beyond myself comes alive in me. It isn't literally increasing the volume of what we're looking at and absorbing; but it is a moment in which what I am begins to turn into what I'm looking at, so that it lives in me as well as in itself.

Well, if that's how we are understanding the word, Mary's soul 'magnifying' the Lord is exactly what we would expect – because she has just handed over her whole existence, body and soul, to give room to God. She has literally allowed something – someone – beyond herself, beyond her furthest imagining – to come to life in her. She is not only saying words that make God look greater; she is performing the most extraordinary and the most utterly self-forgetting action a human being could perform, making room for the life of the everlasting Word of God in her own flesh. She is still emphatically the human woman Mary; but she is also the one in whom the presence of God is growing moment by moment in the long, mysterious and subtle process of pregnancy. Because of her yes to God, there is through her freedom a new release of God's presence and power in the human world.

There is more room for God, because the usual obstacles to God's work, in self-preoccupation and fear and resentment, have been overcome in Mary's unswerving willingness to absorb the vision God has given.

And so she says also that 'he that is mighty hath magnified *me*'. As she gives room to God, God makes her greater. What could be a more vivid illustration of how wrong and silly it is to think that God and humanity are somehow in competition? As if the more God there were, the less humanity there could be. But when Mary gives room to God, God gives room to her: her humanity blossoms into its fullest glory. Learn to give God room and you realize that what has to be cleared away to make room for him isn't your real humanity but all that has stopped you being human, all that makes you less than you could be. On the far side of the terrible, forbidding, draining business of letting go of your expectations, your safety and your possessions lies more not less of life.

For centuries, Christians have kept coming back to the idea that what happens in Mary is what has to happen to some degree in each of us. She, uniquely and once for all, says a yes so complete that her entire material life is changed by the coming of God to her; God's everlasting gift of himself that is the Son, the Word, emerges from her to begin that life which will change everything in creation. But we are called to the same job, to give God room so that we may be changed, so that the eternal Word will live in us and speak and act in love to others. Only so are we 'magnified', given our full dignity and splendour – not by rushing around in panic defending ourselves and standing on our dignity, but by being still enough to reflect and absorb the light flowing from God the holy Trinity, something so wonderful that it can put into perspective the fears and pettinesses that we think are real life, and silence us for a moment, letting true life in.

Hilary Wilson tells us about her experience of living in a number of communities of people with serious learning difficulties and challenges, especially in the L'Arche community in Liverpool, in her book *My Life Together* – a title that already tells you quite a lot! In the course of it she summarizes the path to Christian unity by adapting what another writer said about Christian prayer: we need to learn the three Rs – relate, relinquish, receive. And this sounds like a translation of what 'magnifying' God should be, and a hint about how we are 'magnified' in the process. One of her most moving stories is the testimony of a mother describing what it was like to come to terms with having a brain-damaged daughter – the shattering of expectations first, and the learning to live from day to day; then the unexpected relations made possible by the new challenge, the contacts with people you'd never otherwise meet; then the discovery of the reality and beauty of the child, growing into an adult, giving the parent what could not have been predicted. Gradually the fear of 'Who'll look after her when we're gone?' is overcome as a whole world of fresh relations opens up. And the final *normality* of the mother lies in learning to be a friend to this child who had seemed destined to be in profound ways a stranger. Relate, relinquish, receive: two lives 'magnified' as there is a slow absorption of the difficult reality that is also compellingly beautiful; dignity discovered and celebrated.

We are mostly very fearful, whether we call ourselves believers or not, of a God who will somehow take away from us what we most cherish. The unbeliever cannot manage to get out of his or her head the idea that God is an unfriendly alien, and that people who believe in God become less than properly human, boring at best and dangerous at worst. It would be easier to persuade them otherwise, of course, if we Christians were a bit more convincing in our witness to the fact that humanity blossoms where room is given to God, and that the half-life is ultimately the life without faith. Mary says to us in her song that when God is magnified, humanity is magnified also. Mary's Son is the only fully human being there has been, because he is wholly and utterly alive to and in God the Father. The gift of his Spirit which we celebrate at this season is poured out so that we can be always growing into his life.

So we must say to each other, 'Don't be afraid of magnifying God, being still and open to give him room; don't be afraid of the letting go and the risk God asks from his friends.' This is the deepest wellspring of all in our learning how to reverence human dignity, to magnify one another also. As Mary magnifies the Lord, she also celebrates the Lord's honouring of the poor and feeding of the hungry, and his disappointing of the prosperous and self-satisfied. At a time when we are forced to confront daily the images of wilful human blasphemy against the image of God in others and the all too frequent refusal to confront and acknowledge the scale of the offence against human dignity, we need to hear Mary's challenge; she sings for the insulted and injured everywhere – in Iraq and Zimbabwe and her own Holy Land. And she calls us in her Son's name not only to be still and let God flower in us but to let God's justice work in us and through us also, as we seek to make room for each other with love and respect in our tormented and petrified world.

A magnifying glass is also a burning glass. Mary gave birth to a child who would one day say that he had come to cast fire upon the earth. In magnifying the Lord, she gives room for the Spirit to descend, to come upon her, to work in every moment of the life of her Son, to fall upon the disciples in tongues of fire. When God is given room, the Spirit begins to burn, to consume what holds us back from our own joy. We are called to look beyond the immediate danger to the longer hope and possibility that Mary's words speak of, to the promise that by the fiery Spirit of Mary's Son the face of the earth may be renewed and the glory of God's children revealed.

So it is, finally, the Spirit that will carry us through those three Rs. Relate – be in the company of God and God's friends to be reminded of what faith is; relinquish – let go of what stops you being human: fear and prejudice and the longing to be known to be always in the right; receive – welcome with gratitude and reverence what God gives you through each other, through friend and stranger. Magnify the Lord and the Spirit overshadows you. And the Lord will magnify us, will glorify his creation, give us room in his love and the love of each other, as we find life together in the Body of Mary's Son.

Note

A sermon delivered by the Archbishop of Canterbury, Dr Rowan Williams, on the occasion of the National Pilgrimage to the Shrine of Our Lady of Walsingham, Walsingham, Monday 31 May 2004.

54

The Woman at the Well

MARTYN PERCY

Bible passage: John 4.1–42

In some respects, this is one of the most fascinating encounters we have in the Gospel of John. Laden with playful subversive conversation, the encounter teases the reader with its meanings and inferences. The early verses of the story set the tempo. Jesus, we learn, is accused of baptizing with water – a charge that is false, because it is his disciples and those of John who have been doing this. So Jesus starts to retreat to Galilee, where we are treated to a story about water and wells that never run dry. But before he can get to Galilee from Judaea, he must pass through Samaria – he has to cross a region that is, by definition, a place of taint and compromise that is normally to be avoided. But Jesus does not need to pass through Samaria; he could have chosen the route that follows the Jordan Valley, and avoids Samaria. So John, in stating that Jesus 'had' to pass through Samaria, is not making a cartographical point; Jesus chooses this route in the same way that the Son of Man 'must' suffer (Mark 8.31) – the accent is on Jesus' obligation to a deeper path that remains concealed from most of those who follow him. This is why Jesus arrives at the town of Sychar (4.5–6), where he then sits at Jacob's Well (thereby linking Jesus with the Patriarchs), with John telling us that Jesus is 'tired'. It is the sixth hour – a resonance, one suspects with John's later declaration in John 19.13–14, where Pilate declares to the crowd, 'Here is your king'.

And it is here that the Samaritan woman enters the story. The time of day for entry is critical, as it suggests her marginality. Water is traditionally drawn at dusk or early in the morning. But the sixth hour is noon, when the sun is at its hottest, suggesting that this woman's company is questionable; she is something of an outsider within her own community. The woman is also unnamed, which can be interpreted as a cipher for 'undesirable', or even 'sinner' – the latter term having more of a social than ethical significance in the first century. What is startling, therefore, is Jesus' direct address to her: 'Give me a drink.' Furthermore, notes John, the disciples have all left to buy provisions: there is no mutual hospitality between Jews and Samaritans. This means that Jesus and the woman are alone.

On a superficial level, this request can be read as a preliminary gesture of reconciliation. Jesus asks something of a Samaritan, and a woman. In so doing, there is a hint of equality in the conversation. Jesus needs her help, and he asks for it. But this gesture is, of course, met with astonishment: 'How can you ask anything of me, a Samaritan?' And the response from Jesus only serves to widen her eyes, for Jesus states that if she knew who she was talking to and what God gives, it is she who would be asking for water – 'living water'. Or more accurately, in the Greek, this is 'running water' – the kind that echoes that which *flows* from the rock in the desert from the staff of Moses. John is, in other words, making a contrast between the still, perhaps even stale, water of the well and the water of life that Jesus speaks of. This is a water that, literally, brings life.

The conversation, like the depth of the well, goes another stage deeper at this point. The woman's question becomes laced with rhetorical tropes: are you greater than Jacob? Where do you get this living water from? John turns the woman's astonishment into curiosity – she wades into the deeper waters of the conversation. And again, the conversation turns on what, to us, must seem like a staged artificiality, to draw the woman in even deeper. Jesus says: 'Anyone who drinks from this well will be thirsty again ... but whoever drinks the water I give will never thirst again.' Bearing in mind that there are no witnesses to this conversation, and that the disciples' arrival at verse 28 causes the woman to depart, we have to assume that the nature of this encounter is staged, even as it may be rooted in an actual event. But this need not detain us, since it is reasonably clear that the Gospel-writer intends the reader to be drawn into the conversation – even seduced by it – as indeed the woman is, to an extent.

The mention of 'seduction' is not accidental here, for in verse 10 there is a playful and, it must be said, highly ambiguous reference to 'a spring of water gushing forth'. The Greek term used here is not easy to gain a fixed meaning on, partly because the word is rarely used of water, but more properly of animals or humans. The term literally translated means 'leap' or 'well' up, with connotations of release and liberation. This is a term more commonly associated with ecstasy, and yes, even the erotic. Water that 'leaps up' is capable of being read as a cipher – an interpretative key for the next phase of the story, which will overshadow the liminality of the discussion about the woman's marital relationships, which in turn infers something about the religious status of Samaritans and their actual attachment to Judaism. This is about the movement from *bios* (basic life) to *zoe* – lively life. The movement of the water from still to gurgling is significant.

Of course, it is possible to read this phase of the story in a slightly less steamy way. One could, for example, simply take the leaping water to refer to wisdom as the 'fountain of life' (see Proverbs 13.14) – but I suspect that John intends us to read this story as a contrast between *eros* and *agape*. This is about sensual and earthly desires not being sated in the way that they expect, but being met by deeper and more fulfilling wisdom that transforms the very nature of human existence. So the woman, for the moment, plays ball: 'Sir, give me that water so I will never be thirsty and never have to come back here to draw water' (v.15). The basic, earthly desires and hungers are being both met and set aside in this question. But the encounter has another twist, for the response from Jesus is not 'OK', but 'go call your husband'. It seems a very curious request in response to the woman's 'yes', but I suspect that this hinges on the encounter being rooted in the transformation of all desires.

Up until this point, there is a sense in which the passage can be read as playful, or even (possibly) mildly flirtatious. Jesus is alone with a woman at a well (a deep hole, that brings forth sustenance and life), but the conversation quickly turns to being one about releasing fountains of water that will bring new life, satisfy deeply, and for ever. It is not, then, a great surprise that the conversation in the encounter moves from one of slight seduction into interrogation: 'I have no husband,' replies the woman. And Jesus replies by stating that she has had five, and the man she now lives with is not her husband. We need to pause here at this point, and be reminded that at no point does Jesus explicitly suggest the woman is sinful. There could be many reasons why she has had five men and is on her sixth. This may not be her fault.

To lose a few husbands, we might say, may be considered unfortunate in a peasant agrarian context; but I suppose to lose five must be marked down as downright careless. Perhaps this is what John intends – the woman is a cipher for Samaria – and the multiple partnerships are seen as a reflection of the alleged Samaritan dalliance with polytheism. Nonetheless, what we have here from Jesus is challenge, not condemnation. Moreover, the invitation extended by Jesus seems to centre not on repentance, but on a particular conversion of desire.

This reading makes some sense of the continuing exchange. The woman perceives Jesus to be a prophet, and he in turn suggests that worship in the future will neither be in Jerusalem nor on the mountain: believe me, 'the hour is coming'. This leads to a parenthesis from Jesus on spirit and truth – not here as opposites to material and falsity, but more as a sign of completion. The further mention of 'hour' in verse 17 also alerts the reader to a foreword to the Passover, which will ultimately obviate the need for worship to be located in a physical place; spirit and truth will prevail. It is no surprise, then, that this insight leads to the key epiphany in the text, the woman's confession and Jesus' response:

The woman said to him: 'I know that the Messiah is coming, the one they call Christ. When he comes, he will explain everything to us.' Jesus said to her, 'I am he, the one speaking to you.'

This is (intentionally) one of the most uncompromising statements in the Gospel: 'I am he' echoes Deuteronomy 18 – 'the Lord your God will raise up a prophet like me from among your own people. You must listen to the prophet ...' But before the narrative can develop further, the story is interrupted by the return of the disciples. A subplot is allowed to develop, with Jesus not eating the food the disciples have brought him, and then lecturing them about 'real food', just as he talked to the woman about real water. But the woman leaves the story at this point, abandons her bucket (a sign, therefore, that such material desires have been superseded) and returns to her community to recount her tale.

The story ends as it began – with a tale of an unexpected encounter, with themes of taint, surprise and boundary-crossing redolent in the text. A group of Samaritans now come to see Jesus, prompted by the unnamed woman. This in turn prompts an excursus from Jesus about the harvest – a cipher for God's abundance, but also judgement. It is now obvious (if also perhaps puzzling to the disciples) that Jesus, throughout this encounter, is making a profound series of political statements about the nature of the Kingdom and the Messiah. We can summarize these briefly.

First, it is God who, in Christ, comes to the Samaritans and engages with them on their own territory and in their own idiom and dialect. Remember, this was not the obvious route for Jesus to take to get to Galilee – he chose to deviate and allowed himself to be distracted. Second, the message to the Samaritans is not 'become a Jew like me', but rather 'there is a time when tribal boundaries will cease to matter', and genuine faith will not be about which party, sect or denomination one belongs to, but instead be about 'spirit and truth'. Third, the striking particularity of the story is its radical inclusiveness. As is so often the case in the Gospels, Jesus is fraternizing with people that raise questions of taste, discernment and even purity. But Jesus is not interested in such outward judgementalism. He is not interested in why this woman has been married five times, and John does not tell us. Perhaps she had to have a sequence of Levitical marriages, all arranged, and now lives with the only man she has loved. Perhaps all five have died. It is not implausible in a developing, poor country. The point is, Jesus does not ask, and he does not judge. And nor should we. This is all about grace – new outward signs of an invisible change. The woman leaves her bucket; that says it all.

55

The Word and the Work of God

ROWAN WILLIAMS

Blessèd were the chosen people
out of whom the Lord did come;
blessèd was the land of promise
fashioned for his earthly home.

These are words that may be familiar to some who have experienced worship in the Anglican tradition. One of the great Marian hymns of modern Anglicanism, 'Ye who own the faith of Jesus', reminds us of what the feast of the Conception of the Blessed Virgin Mary is all about: God has prepared for the coming of Christ.

The birth of Jesus is not something that happens, so to speak, by God dropping his Word out of a clear sky. It is indeed the beginning of something radically fresh, a new creation. But at the same time it has been coming to birth since the very beginning of creation. The Word who was in the beginning with God is always moving towards Bethlehem to be born, and God prepares the way. God prepares through the graces and gifts of the first covenant; through the lives of the holy people of that covenant; and above all in the birth and the life of the Virgin Mary. God is – all the time – making a space into which his Word incarnate may come.

Remember the imagery of the Jesse tree that you sometimes see in stained-glass windows. In my old diocese of Monmouth it was represented in the parish church of Abergavenny by an enormous wooden sculpture of Jesse fast asleep. During the Middle Ages, a great branching wooden sculpture grew from that sleeping figure showing all the saints of Jesse's line culminating in the Virgin. We could say that if you cut through that tree at any point it would be the same sap flowing, the same life, the life of God preparing a space for his incarnate Word to come.

It is sometimes a help in reading the odder portions of the Old Testament to think that wherever we cut through the history of the covenant God is at work, however unlikely it seems on the surface. This bit of ritual regulation in Leviticus or that bit of unedifying tribal history in Judges is all part of the same story, the same making space for the Word incarnate. In Romans 8.28–35, 37–40) our attention was directed to God's choice before all ages, not only of the path *towards* the incarnation but of the path *beyond* the incarnation: the path of holiness into which *we* are drawn. Those called according to God's purpose are the ones he chose to become true images of his Son. We are part of the same history of God's work in the human heart, God's work preparing and then honouring that space he has made for his Son to become flesh. In other words, the feast of the Conception is a feast of God's faithfulness, a feast of a God who keeps his promise.

If we ask a bit more about the nature of God's promise we might perhaps turn to the very end of St Matthew's Gospel where Jesus makes the greatest promise of all to his disciples: 'I am with you always to the end of the age' (Matthew 28.20). Approaching that with the Feast of the Conception in mind, we can be confident that this is a promise that Christ keeps. He is with his disciples; he is with his friends to the end of the world. And just as in the stranger and less edifying bits of the Old Testament we can discern God making his way towards Bethlehem, so even in the stranger and odder bits of our lives as Christians, both individually and together, we can discern a God making his way towards full presence and free grace.

Jesus has promised that he will always be with those he calls his friends (John 15.15): those he calls to himself in baptism and establishes with him as sons and daughters of his eternal Father. And so we, who share baptism in the name of the Father and of the Son and of the Holy Spirit, may be confident that Jesus has promised to be with us – to be with the *other* who shares that baptism, however unlikely, however difficult that other may be. And when we are tempted to talk of an 'ecumenical winter', tempted to focus our attention only on the stresses and conflicts between communions of Christian churches, it is worth remembering that our God is a God who keeps his promise and that he has promised to be with us. He has promised to be with that unlikely, difficult Christian stranger with whom we strive to enter into dialogue every bit as much as he has promised to be with us, equally strange and difficult as we are going to seem to some of our brothers or sisters.

The history of the Church – like the history of 'the chosen people out of whom the Lord should come' – is not a uniform history of holiness, success and edification – not then, and not now. But this is the human family in which Jesus has promised to be present. And when we celebrate a God who is faithful to his promise our hearts are renewed in hope and understanding together. In our meetings, in our discussions, and, yes, even in our conflicts, just as in the history of the people of the first covenant, so now God is deeply and invisibly making a space into which the life of his Son may come.

When we pray, when we open ourselves to God, we open ourselves to a depth that is already given in our own hearts, open ourselves to that relationship already given in our baptism whereby we are able to call God 'Abba, Father!' because we are brought into the fellowship of the Son. We open our hearts in silence to that depth so that we may become more aware not only of Jesus who has promised to be with us and in us, but so that we may become more and more aware of Jesus who has promised to be in and with our Christian neighbour, our brother and sister. Without that dimension, ecumenical relations are always going to be a matter of mere politeness. With that dimension an element of Spirit-filled and Spirit-fuelled hope enters in.

The God who keeps his promises is the God who is already making his Church one, the God who is already alerting us to the one, Jesus, who has promised to be faithfully present in the neighbour and the stranger. God began to prepare the way from the very first beginnings of creation. God began to prepare the way in the covenant with Abraham, in the Exodus, in the anointing of King David; above all, on the very eve of the incarnation he prepares the way in the holy life of the Virgin Mary. And, as in the body of Mary Christ grew, silently and secretly for nine months, so now in the history of our Church, in the life of each person seeking to be a believer, Christ grows silently, unseen, yet powerfully and faithfully.

Our call to holiness is a call quite simply to let that promise and that faithfulness take us over, permeate every aspect of our being, shape our relationships with one another – *within* our own Christian families, *between* our Christian families. And as we grow into that divine faithfulness, as that holy promise shapes our lives, we learn to say with greater and greater clarity and conviction the words from Romans: 'Not any power or height or depth nor any created thing can ever come between us and the love of God made visible in Christ Jesus our Lord' (Romans 8.30).

There could be no more powerful affirmation of the promises of God, the faithfulness of God, what God achieves in that history whereby he prepares the way for his incarnate Son, and what God is achieving silently and secretly now, even as we speak, even as we pray.

The vision that I believe we are called to today in the relations between our Churches – between us as individuals, and with God in his wider world – is a vision of Christ keeping his promise, and our calling is to turn away from everything that makes us blind to, or insensitive to, that promise, so that divine faithfulness may be the rationale and the inspiration of all we do and say together.

In the life and the childbearing of the Blessed Virgin Mary that promise first, and once-and-for-all, came to fruition in our history. In our lives and our prayers that promise continues to move towards our own particular Bethlehems, our own particular future as sons and daughters of the everlasting Father. The Spirit moves in us; the Spirit is bringing Christ to birth in us; the Spirit is directing our hearts, our eyes and our ears to one another, and to the Christ who has promised to be there. And no created thing can ever come between us and the love of God made visible in Christ Jesus our Lord.

56

Gestation

MARTYN PERCY

Bible passage: Matthew 13.31–32

My favourite Christmas cracker joke is unquestionably: 'Why did the mushroom go to the party?' Answer: 'Because he was a fun guy'. Be that as it may, in apparently one of the most innocent and understated phrases from the Gospels, Jesus tells us most of what we probably need to know about our future ministry. He suggests that the Kingdom of heaven is like yeast that is mixed in with bread. Yeast? That microbe fungi? That discardable and forgettable material that is, oddly, the key to so much of our lives? It would seem so. (One presumes Jesus said this without obvious humour, although I bet he managed a wry smile.)

For yeast is what ferments the wine and beer; and it makes the dough rise to make the bread. It is the tiny, insignificant catalyst for our basic commodities and the formation of our communities. The leaven in the lump; the difference between bread and dough; juice and wine; refreshment and celebration.

The word *yeast* comes from the old English word *gist* or *gyst*, and ultimately from an Indo-European etymological root simply meaning *yes*. But that 'yes' also grew to mean to *boil*, *foam* or *bubble*. Put another way, yeast is the ingredient that turns the passive into active; the flat into flavoursome; the ordinary into the extraordinary.

But yeast is, as I say, small. Moreover, it is lost and dispersed into the higher purposes to which it is given. And when Jesus talks about the Kingdom of God as yeast – and our ministries too – he is not advocating the concentrate in a jar: yeast for the sake of yeast. No. In Jesus' imagination, we are invited to get lost. To lose ourselves in something much bigger.

But not pointlessly. Rather, in 'dying' to our context, we activate it. We become the catalyst that brings flavour, strength, depth, potency and growth. Without yeast, there is no loaf; just dough. Literally, we die to ourselves for growth: we are what makes bread for the world.

But this does not mean we have to die or dissolve. Funnily enough, God wants us alive, not dead. Indeed, the more alive the better. So the notion of our Christian ministry is not that we are the yeast, per se; but rather that we offer a yeasty ministry. It is about being the agent of transformation that is often small, or even unseen. It is about being immersed so deeply in the world and the local church that the depth of growth is often unquantifiable.

Baking bread, if you have ever done it, is rewarding work and very therapeutic. But it also offers us a rich analogy for what Christians are about. The writer John Paul Lederach offers a rich meditation on our calling to be yeast. Consider this. The most common ingredients for making bread are water, flour, salt, sugar and yeast. Of these, yeast is the smallest in quantity, but the only one that makes a substantial change to all the other ingredients. Lederach says you only need a few people to change a lot of things. Quality changes quantity. I want to consider three things here – about character, gift and virtue in churches, and why size does not matter very much. It is quality that counts, not quantity.

Small things, then, make a difference. Tiny spores of yeast change the mass. So yeast, to be useful, needs to move from its incubation and be mixed into the process – out of the church building and into everyday life. Christians, like the proverbial manure, do the most good when they are spread around. But yeast also needs to grow – it requires the right mix of moisture, warmth and sugar. And it initially needs covering and cultivating before it is ready to do its work. Only then should the yeast mix with the greater mass. In bread, it is kneaded into the dough; it requires a bit of muscle. It also requires someone else to light the fire to make the oven. Bread, in other words, is not just about the yeast, but about a context – one of feeding, desire, need and the skills of others. The fun guy goes to the party; but he did not organize it. He responded to an invitation.

In talking about small fungi that produce change and growth, Jesus is asking us to imagine his Kingdom – one in which tiny spores mixed into the social mass can make a massive difference. But sometimes, as I say, this is about losing one's self within a bigger picture. So, small things matter. The mustard seed is minute. But what is planted can, in the end, play host to so much and so many. The mustard seed reminds us that God can do some very promising things with the apparently negligible. That is why Christ enjoins us to let him get on with the gardening – because we'd tend to overlook the small things and assume they don't matter. But this is where God is different, for here he sees potential and hope.

So we have no mandate to try and divide the ingredients that God has given us and put them back in the cupboard. We are, rather, to add life and leaven to the mix. So, let us get on with the business of being God's yeast. We must not be afraid of what is to come, for there is no need for fear. We must get stuck into the mix; be kneaded in. Watch the dough rise; the juice turn into sweet wine. It is in giving that we receive. And in dying that we are born to eternal life. Unless the grain of wheat falls, it cannot bear much fruit; but when it falls, it yields more than a hundredfold.

We can be the yeast that is kneaded in to make the bread, that we may all become one. But we must let God set the pace; the bread rises in time; the wine matures only when it is ready. As one hymn puts it:

The reign of God, like farmer's field,
bears weeds along with wheat;
the good and bad are intertwined
till harvest is complete.

Like mustard tree, the reign of God
from tiny seed will spread,
till birds of every feather come
to nest, and there be fed.

Though hidden now, the reign of God
May, yet unnoticed, grow;
from deep within it rises up,
like yeast in swelling dough.

The reign of God is come in Christ;
the reign of God is near.
Ablaze among us, kindling hearts,
the reign of God is here!

Delores Dufner OSB

57

The Absurdity of Grace

MARTYN PERCY

Bible passage: Matthew 20.1–16

And so we come, today, to another misnamed parable. Usually known as 'the labourers in the vineyard', this story is perhaps better titled as 'the grumbling, productive loyal workers'. 'That's not *fair!*' is a wail that nearly every parent dreads but knows well. Children develop a very keen sense of justice early on, especially when their own deserts are at stake. In a society that is conscious of fairness through industrial disputes, payment and differentials, waiting lists, public anger about fat cats and inflated bonuses – surely in a just society rewards should be distributed according to merit and pay related to work? It would appear in this parable that the complainants have a very strong case, and most members of any church congregation would agree with them. But as with nearly all of Jesus' parables, there is more to the story than meets the eye.

Clearly, the vineyard is a workplace. In Palestine, as with other agrarian economies, the window for harvest is short and, in particular, the grape harvest comes just after a season of heavy rain. So, the vineyard owner needs the maximum number of workers for the minimum amount of time. The workers themselves are day labourers, the most insecure, powerless and exploited of all, they are hired by the day and paid at sunset. So an idle day is a hungry day, for the wages described in the parable are only just enough for a family to live on.

The parable introduces some surprises even before we get to the end. As the sun sets, the labourers line up for their pay, and this is where the trouble really begins. For a start, the men who were hired last are paid first, and to their great surprise they get a full day's wage. Those who have been at work all day rub their hands: obviously they're going to get a day's work and a bonus! But of course they don't, it is the same wage for everyone, irrespective of how hard they have worked. No wonder the cry comes, 'That's not fair'. Well, that's the story, but what does it mean?

One standard way of interpreting the parable was to focus on the equality of pay. In other words, the vineyard owner is acting mercifully by making sure that all have enough money to feed and clothe their family. John Ruskin, more than a century ago, wrote four articles in the *Cornhill*

Magazine, which were eventually published as a book with the title *Unto This Last* – which is a quotation from this particular text in the parable. Ruskin's exposition of the parable was an eloquent attack on the economic theory of his day. Ruskin, as you will probably remember, was an associate of F. D. Maurice and Charles Kingsley (also author of *The Water Babies*), so Ruskin's exposition has a close association with early Christian socialism – New Labour before there was even Old Labour. Ruskin, in his exhortation, pleads for a sort of minimum wage, describing the parable as offering a pattern for the Christian care of the underprivileged and the powerless.

Whatever you think of that interpretation, it certainly has some merit. But there are deeper meanings in the parable that lie even beyond this social and political exposition. In this respect, it is useful to distinguish between what is fair and what is generous, and the relation between earnings and needs. The parable makes a delightful play on our own childish conceptions of fairness in relation to the vineyard, which I take to be a cipher for the Kingdom of God. And here's my point. The generosity and the justice of God are so abundant that it is in the end deeply *unfair*. The parable is aimed at the sort of people whose conscious rectitude makes it difficult for them to allow God to be generous to those who have done less well.

In other words, here's a parable that questions our motivations and our reasoning. Do we really feel that we have 'earned' God's favour? Invariably we do. So once again, we have a parable that sides with the lazy, the publicans and sinners, those who have done less well and worked less hard. It is a terrible parable for the Church – but that's salvation for you, isn't it? In the war between Jesus and the Church, the Church is ahead on points, but it is a war it cannot win. God will open his Kingdom to whom he chooses; all are invited. You are not the gatekeeper.

The Gospels offer extreme cases of this. The dying thief on the cross is an obvious example. He could not have worked in the vineyard for more than a few seconds, let alone an hour, yet on the cross, for the most minimal confession, he is promised paradise. Had the disciples still been around to witness this exchange shortly before the death of Jesus they must have wondered to themselves what on earth the point of giving up everything and forsaking all for the Kingdom of God had been. Had they not been with Jesus for three years? Had they not abandoned their jobs? Had they not left behind their families, even leaving the dead unburied? Of course they had. So how come, then, that Jesus is offering precisely the same – no more and no less – to a man who has been committed to a lifetime of violence and crime. Precisely. It isn't fair, is it?

The parable gets right under the skin of the real motivation for being part of the Church, and following Jesus. And the interesting thing that the parable suggests is that in Christ's scheme of salvation, the rewards and bonuses scheme is rather 'flat'. In other words, salvation does not come in half measures – you cannot be half saved; you're either welcomed into God's

Kingdom or you're not. You can't be half ordained. Salvation doesn't come in fractions. You cannot be half baptized. You either receive the Eucharist or you don't – sacraments are not divisible. And so the parable, as so many do, comes back to haunt the Church. Instead of policing the borders and the boundaries of God's Kingdom, acting as passport control or immigration officers, we are invited instead to gather up everybody – as many as we can – to share in precisely the same fortune that all of us already enjoy, and have known for years.

The parable takes us back in to the parable of the prodigal son, and asks whether we are enjoying the feast, celebrating with the younger son who was dead but is now alive, and has been miraculously resurrected – that's what the party is for – whether we are bitter and resentful towards the older brother, believing that the party and celebration is undeserved. This parable is in fact terrible news for the Church, for it points to the foolish abundance, the ridiculous generosity of God towards those on whom he bestows his favour. Mercy and grace are infinite, and all shall receive the same. It is the same salvation for the bishop of 50 years' ministry, the churchwarden who has put 25 years of hard graft, blood, sweat and tears into keeping a church going, as it is to the tiniest child who is baptized right at the end, or indeed to those in the middle, who stumble around in their half belief, perhaps even barely caring about the inheritance that has been bestowed upon them. In all of that, this parable asks, do you as the Church rejoice at God's abundance, or seek to limit it or control it?

We can't be saying 'no' to anyone yet – because God's 'yes', his invitation to all, is still there. What better way to end, then, than with the words of F. W. Faber's surprisingly inclusive early Victorian hymn:

There's a wideness in God's mercy,
Like the wideness of the sea;
There's a kindness in his justice,
Which is more than liberty.

There is no place where earth's sorrows
Are more felt than up in heaven;
There is no place where earth's failings
Have such kindly judgement given.

For the love of God is broader
Than the measure of man's mind;
And the heart of the Eternal
Is most wonderfully kind.

But we make his love too narrow
By false limits of our own;

And we magnify his strictness
With a zeal he will not own.

There is plentiful redemption
In the blood that has been shed;
There is joy for all the members
In the sorrows of the Head.

There is grace enough for thousands
Of new worlds as great as this;
There is room for fresh creations
In that upper home of bliss.

If our love were but more simple
We should take him at his word;
And our lives would be all gladness
In the joy of Christ our Lord.

58

Faith and Fear

ROWAN WILLIAMS

Bible passage: Job 38.1–11

It is so difficult to accept that we're not in charge. And to be told that we're not in charge usually feels humiliating; it sounds like denying us our right to make the decisions that suit us. That's why this Bible passage isn't the easiest to get our minds around. Here is God telling human beings that they mustn't dare imagine that they can understand the universe he has made: he seems to mock our weakness and to leave us helpless. Confronted by the terrible suffering of Job, God seems not to care. All he wants to say is that there is no answer to suffering and that he alone sees how it all fits together.

We might well feel like protesting. No: we're not completely helpless; we may not have been around when the pillars of the earth were laid and the stars sang and the heavenly host shouted for joy, but we can shape our environment in some ways and make it more friendly to human beings. 'We plough the fields and scatter/The good seed on the land.' And surely it is rather important not to think we are helpless just at the moment when we need to work out the best steps to take so as to avoid environmental disaster. There really are things we can do, and it doesn't help to think we are all doomed.

Indeed, to say 'we are all doomed' would be to get the meaning of the biblical passage slightly off-key. God is not telling people to step back from acting and making a difference. It is more that he is saying you can make a difference only when you give up the idea that you can predict everything and make everything work just to suit the decisions that you and people like you want to make. This world is not there just for you. It is a wild and diverse world, often threatening, sometimes just baffling; but it is a world that the stars and the angels look at with overflowing joy, a world that is both regular in all sorts of ways that we can grasp by observation and science, and also unpredictable, a world where you can work out some of how things work, yet are still left always on the frontiers of deeper and stranger realities. It is a world you can make some sense of, yet also a world where you will never finish questioning and exploring.

Much of our environmental crisis comes from the half-hidden assumption that the ideal position for us humans is being completely in control, being able to make nature do whatever we want it to. Yet if we are ourselves part of nature, not some mysterious extra, standing outside the natural processes of our environment, we can hardly expect that our own plans and desires, which are just one little part of the working of the universe, should be able to dictate what happens in the whole of that universe without upsetting the balance of things. The hard challenge is acquiring a sort of 'feel' for that balance – which means being able to look long and hard about what we think we want or need, what we take for granted about what makes a good life, so that we don't just expect God's world to reorganize itself entirely around what we happen to think will make us safe or happy.

In a way, this means learning to relate to the world around us in something of the same way we relate to other people. We know a bit about how they work, we can learn how to work with the grain of someone else's personality, we can make a difference to how a relationship goes, yet there is always a dimension of strangeness and mystery in another person, and we have to approach that with respect, ready to go on learning and exploring. I wonder whether this is why St Francis used to refer to the things of the physical creation as members of the family – Brother Sun, Sister Water and so on. He saw the universe around him as a set of relationships in which he had a share. The objects he encountered each day were part of a great complex circle of life in which he as a human being had a vital and unique role – but not the role of sole manager and proprietor.

In other words, he wasn't afraid of not being in charge. And that fearlessness is expressed in so many aspects of his life – in the risks he took in reaching out to outcasts and people with dangerous diseases, in his insistence on living simply and relying only on other people's charity, even in his courageous acceptance of pain and death – '*Sister* Death', not a terrifying thing that denied human dignity but just another feature of this astonishing and uncontrollable world. He had learned the great lesson of Jesus Christ himself, that the biggest difference is made by those who are strong enough and secure enough to let go and to forget the dreams of total power.

We are not going to get very far in responding to the desperate problems of our environment – climate change, deforestation, the limited supplies of fossil fuels and so on – if we cannot take at least a small step along the road St Francis took: recognizing that we are a part of the whole, not the owners of a property, that we have to think of the life of the world around us as a sort of family life, with all that this means in terms of patience and not trying to control everything or bend it to our own agenda. Francis found a deep and mysterious joy in accepting all this. Perhaps he caught an echo of what the poet of the book of Job imagines – the stars and the angels shouting for joy as God unrolls his endlessly diverse, inexhaustible world. And without the echo of that joy, we shall never make the right kind of difference in the world. May God help us hear the stars singing – and then perhaps we shall be better able to work out how we live on this extraordinary planet without killing it and killing each other.

59

One, Holy, Catholic, Apostolic

SAM WELLS

Bible passages: Acts 2.1–21; John 14.8–17

What is the difference between a motto and a mission statement? A mission statement commits an organization to do something, whereas a motto expresses a reality you believe to be true whether you do anything about it or not.

The Church has a motto. It is tucked neatly into the Nicene Creed: 'We believe in one, holy, catholic and apostolic church' – or *una, sancta, catholica et apostolica*, if you like your mottoes in Latin. You can see every dimension of this motto displayed in the Pentecost story in Acts 2, the moment we often call the birthday of the Church. This tight-knit group of disciples surrounded by tongues of fire shows all four of these characteristics, sometimes known as the four marks of the Church. We see the Church as one, when it says, 'They were all together in one place.' We see the Church as holy, when it says, 'A tongue [of fire] rested on each of them. All of them were filled with the Holy Spirit.' We see the Church as catholic, in other words as embracing what today we often call diversity, when it says, 'There were devout Jews from every nation under heaven living in Jerusalem,' and when the large crowd says, 'How is it that we hear, each of us, in our own native language?' And it goes without saying that we see the Church as apostolic, because this moment is the sending out of the apostles that all subsequent mission looks back to.

One, holy, catholic and apostolic? If only. It is just as well this is a motto not a mission statement, because if it were a mission statement we would all be fired. All Christians have experience of church being few or even none of these things. Church congregations may work hard at being one, holy and catholic but endlessly defer to sub-committees, reviews, reports and bureaucracy, and lose all the simplicity and urgency of the first apostles. Sometimes people dedicated to holiness and to faithfulness to the early Church are unable to be patient and understanding and remain one, or are apparently incapable of embracing the diversity of the rainbow of God's nations. A church may seem to flourish and embody the unity, diversity and mission of the Acts of the Apostles, but holiness is let down by human fragility and failure.

Yet, we continue to love the Church. There may be many things wrong with it, but we remain held by its mystery. The Catholic philosopher Gabriel Marcel made a distinction between a problem and a mystery. A problem is something you can stand outside and walk around. It is something you can usually solve by technical skill. A broken window is a problem; you can solve it by fixing a new one. Often a problem can be solved using a technique developed by somebody else. But a mystery you can't solve. A mystery you can't stand outside. You have to enter it. A mystery is something you can't just look at. It absorbs you into it. Someone else's answer probably won't work for you. You have to discover your own.

The Church is a mystery, not a problem. Some may approach it as a problem and try to offer you a solution. There are countless conferences every year offering techniques of church growth or training in family systems theory. But there isn't a simple solution that solves it. And that's because it's a mystery. The Church is the best idea anybody ever had: dynamic unity, profound godliness, gregarious diversity, historic identity. You can't beat that. It's a fabulous combination. But it frequently becomes a monster, or a mess. It's a real mystery.

One author who describes this mess is the British novelist Rose Macaulay. She spent a lot of her life on the edge of the Church, partly because of its mysteries and partly because of her own. Her semi-autobiographical novel *The Towers of Trebizond* describes a journey around the Middle East in the 1950s. In it she tells the story of a woman named Laurie, caught between the eccentricity of the characters she meets and her own irreconcilable loves. All the while Laurie is wrestling with the absurdity of the Church. Her Middle Eastern travels bring Laurie to Bethlehem, and, while in that little town of poignant beginnings, she reflects on what's so terribly wrong and yet so completely right about the Church, long ago and today. Bethlehem epitomizes the contrasts and mysteries of the Church she knows so well. This is what she says:

> [The Church] grew so far, almost at once, from anything which can have been intended, and became so blood-stained and persecuting and cruel and war-like and made small and trivial things so important, and tried to exclude everything not done in a certain way and by certain people, and stamped out heresies with such cruelty and rage. And this failure of the Christian Church, of every branch of it in every country, is one of the saddest things that has happened in all the world. But it is what happens when a magnificent idea has to be worked out by human beings who do not understand much of it but interpret it in their own way and think they are guided by God, whom they have not yet grasped. And yet they had grasped something, so that the Church has always had great magnificence and much courage, and people have died for it in agony, which is supposed to balance all the other people who have had to die in agony because

126

they did not accept it, and it has flowered up in learning and culture and beauty and art, to set against its ... incivility and obscurantism and barbarity and nonsense, and it has produced saints and martyrs and kindness and goodness, though these have also occurred freely outside it, and it is a wonderful and most extraordinary pageant of contradictions, and I, at least, want to be inside it, though it is foolishness to most of my friends.

This is the mystery of the Church as described by someone who knows it as well as she knows herself, and loves it the way you long for something or someone unique that lingers just out of reach. What Laurie is saying is that the Church has been one, but it has also been divisive. It has been holy, but it has also been sinful. It has been catholic, but it has also been narrow. It has been apostolic, but it has also been forgetful. And yet amid what she calls its 'wonderful and most extraordinary pageant of contradictions' she sees a place even for her, despite all her confusions and despair.

The biggest difference between a problem and a mystery is not just that a problem can be solved, while a mystery can't. It's that a problem is something you can walk away from, whereas a mystery becomes something that absorbs and engulfs you in such a way that your life depends on it. That's what *The Towers of Trebizond* is fundamentally about. One night Laurie is troubled by a dream. In the dream she is wrestling with whether she will finally be drawn into the Kingdom of God or instead remain profoundly conflicted on the periphery. The fabled Black Sea port of Trebizond in northern Turkey becomes for her a vision of the new Jerusalem. She sees ethereal Trebizond, and she imagines herself on the doorstep of heaven.

> Then, between sleeping and waking, there rose before me a vision of Trebizond: not Trebizond as I had seen it, but the Trebizond of the world's dreams, of my own dreams, shining towers and domes shimmering on a far horizon, yet close at hand, luminously enspelled in the most fantastic unreality, yet the only reality, a walled and gated city, magic and mystical, standing beyond my reach yet I had to be inside, an alien wanderer yet at home, held in the magical enchantment; and at its heart, at the secret heart of the city and the legend and the glory in which I was caught and held, there was some pattern that I could not unravel, some hard core that I could not make my own, and, seeing the pattern and the hard core enshrined within the walls, I turned back from the city and stood outside it, expelled in mortal grief.

By talking about the 'pattern' that she can't 'unravel' and the 'hard core' that she can't make her own, Laurie seems to be echoing Gabriel Marcel's distinction between a problem and a mystery. If the Church is a problem, Laurie is never going to solve it, but remain gloomily outside it looking for the solution. Yet the Church isn't a problem. The Church is a mystery, and, as she says, it is 'magic and mystical, standing beyond my reach yet I had to be inside, an alien wanderer yet at home, held in the magical enchantment'.

My experience as a pastor has taught me that most churchgoing Christians are more like Laurie than we generally care to admit. Our view of the Church is stretched between our thrill at the 'magnificent idea' and our horror at the 'incivility and obscurantism and barbarity and nonsense'. And our view of ourselves is similarly stretched between our longing for certain answers and clear solutions to problems, and our recognition that, like Laurie, we are complex and compromised people knee-deep in complicity with fallible commitments and flawed convictions.

So how do we regard the Church, without lapsing into bitter cynicism or escaping into lofty idealism? How do we eagerly seek the Church's renewal, even while we know we can't *fix* it? Well, I suggest we translate the Church's motto, one, holy, catholic and apostolic, into four questions. When faced with a new development, a change in leadership, a moral quandary, a pressing crisis, these are the four questions to ask – four questions to make us one, holy, catholic and apostolic.

First, the unity question: is our church making us one with one another? Second, the holiness question: is our church making us one with God? Third, the catholicity question: is our church as gloriously diverse as God's world? And fourth, the apostolicity question: would the first apostles recognize us?

Almost every church is strong on one of these questions. One of the reasons the Church is so divided is because various different parts of the Church differ on which of these questions is the most important one. We all have our favourite and we're all liable to focus on one to the exclusion of the others. But the truth is, they are all *equally* important. The difficult part is not saying yes to one of them, it is saying yes to all of them at the same time.

How can you tell the Holy Spirit is at work in the Church? When the people are drawing closer to one another, when they are being drawn closer to God, when the Church is becoming as gloriously diverse as God's world, and when it is looking more and more like the early Church, so the first apostles could immediately recognize it. That's what the Holy Spirit did at Pentecost. The Holy Spirit embraced the full diversity of humanity and made people one with one another and one with God. That's what the Holy Spirit does today. That's what the Holy Spirit alone does. That's what we're praying for when we call on the Holy Spirit.

One, holy, catholic, apostolic. Never be persuaded that you have to choose one out of the four. Always seek all four together. One, holy, catholic, apostolic. It is a magnificent idea, and it is a pageant of contradictions. And, in the power of the Holy Spirit, it is a mystery that, once you enter it, will absorb your whole life.

Note

R. Macaulay, *The Towers of Trebizond*, London: Collins, 1956.

60

Healing Two Women

MARTYN PERCY

Bible passage: Matthew 9.18–26

There is a dimension to the healings of Jesus which places his ministry in sharp contrast to many of today's healing movements. It is the notion that there is some sense in which Jesus takes on the suffering and affliction of the individuals he cures, such that it becomes part of him. This view would not have been strange to the early church Fathers, whose progressive move towards a richly incarnational theology required them to conclude that what was not assumed could not be redeemed. So, Jesus risks social ostracization when he dines with Zacchaeus, consorts with sinners and receives women of dubious repute into his company, precisely in order to take on their brokenness, as well as take on the taboos of society that maintains structures that divorce the secular and sacred.

As Janet Soskice has pointed out, it is no different in the healing miracles themselves. Noting the story of the haemorrhaging woman in Luke 8.40–56 (cf. Mark. 5.21–43; Matthew 9.18–34), she points out that what is striking about it is Jesus' willingness to touch or be touched by an 'impure' woman.

Although modern readers of the text may find this aspect of the narrative difficult, the significance of Jesus' action should not be underestimated; '[she] defiled the teacher which, according to Levitical law, she would have done for she was in a state of permanent uncleanness, polluting everyone and everything with whom she came into contact'. Her poverty – 'she had spent all she had' – is a direct result of her affliction.

Modern readers struggle with this text – but are we so far on? The Independent Television Commission only lifted the ban on TV ads for 'feminine hygiene' products for England in 1985 – and then the 9p.m. watershed applied. The ban was not lifted in Northern Ireland until much later. Indeed, the origins of the Samaritans lie in our squeamishness in relation to menstruation. Chad Varah, a young curate in a Lincoln City parish, found himself conducting the funeral of a child on unconsecrated ground because she had committed suicide at the age of 13. Why? Because she had started bleeding. These 'hang-ups' are in our lifetime.

So, the stories of these healings are remarkable, perhaps especially of the older woman. Jesus seems to have gone out of his way to affirm her. Yet

Jesus, apart from healing her, also seems to challenge the social and religious forces that have rendered this woman 'contagious'; he calls her 'daughter' in all three accounts, and all three evangelists stress the woman's faith.

Interestingly, the Synoptic accounts of the haemorrhaging woman are all paired with the raising of Jairus' daughter. Again, the issues of impurity (touching a corpse) and of menstruation occur: the girl is 12, and her untimely death clearly prevents her from entering womanhood. Jesus declares her 'not dead, but sleeping', and his touch, resulting in his defilement, raises her.

There are other features of this story that we should note. The Greek term for 'daughter' is conferred on the woman from the crowd. Jairus' daughter is also addressed as *pais*, meaning 'child'. The pairing of these two stories seems to turn everything around. A woman becomes a daughter once more; and a daughter who was losing her life in childhood has her health restored, so she can now enter womanhood. We might also allow ourselves a little further speculation with the intertwining of these two stories.

What precisely is the relationship between Jairus and the bleeding woman? Remember, Jairus is the synagogue ruler, and would therefore have an instrumental role in policing its precincts, keeping the impure and undesirable out. So now we have a story about immediacy and patience. The woman has waited for 12 years – and probably been excluded from worship for the same period of time. One of the subtle yet blunt exercises of power is to make people wait, or be kept waiting.

If you are in power, people wait to see you – or you keep them waiting; it is the powerless who wait. For that appointment, the letter, the news, the interview – waiting is a form of powerlessness. Jairus has kept this woman waiting for years, but he wants Jesus, for his daughter, *now*. What does Jesus do? He gets distracted by an apparently pointless brush with a member of the crowd, and keeps Jairus waiting – and too long as well. Where is the lesson in this? This is a miracle with a moral.

My reading of the healing miracles in the Gospels suggests three things in this case. First, that touching and embracing the afflicted, in the widest possible sense, is critical to Jesus' ministry. Second, that judging the cause of sickness, or naming it as 'sin', has no place in Jesus' ministry. Third, that (somehow) inculcating the sickness itself into the body of Jesus was important. So Jesus becomes the untouchable here – but in touching others, he restores them to their community. His healing is social, physical and spiritual.

So, we are now in a position to understand the significance of Jesus' encounter with the two women, and their 'healing', or indeed, why Jesus bothered with lepers. When, in the midst of the dynamics of this particular understanding of the relationship between an 'impure' body and the social body, Jesus reaches out and *touches* the unclean and declares them healed, he has, in Crossan's words, 'acted as an alternative boundary keeper in a way subversive to the established procedures of his society'. Jesus subverted the social order that had declared such people outcasts. Jesus made possible a new community that refused to be founded upon the exclusion of the other.

61

Lepers

MARTYN PERCY

Bible passage: Luke 17.11–19

Here are some recent headlines from the *Daily Mail*, the self-appointed national guardian of morals, the middle class and all things decent:

Benefit Cheats Gets Legal Aid
Immigrants Jump Housing Queue
Asylum Seeker Lives in Luxury – at Tax-payers Expense.

The *Daily Mail* is what I normally describe as a 'tut' paper. If every page doesn't make you 'tut', the journalists are not doing their job.

But you might wonder what this has got to do with the Bible passage. Well, it is simply this. If there was such a thing as the *Galilee Gazette*, *Nazareth Times* or *Jerusalem Observer*, then the headline – with the 'tut' factor – might well have been 'Jesus Heals Lepers' and it might have added, 'And They Are Samaritans Too!' A good Judaean reader would have tutted. Samaritans? That lot? No good, low down, tainted, spongers, half-castes. If Jesus wants to heal, why does he not start with decent folk like us: the ones who deserve it, and have been waiting in line for a bit of a break? But Samaritans?

Looked at like this, we are immediately confronted by the potential for the inner meaning of this miracle – or indeed any of the healing miracles. But it is all there in the text, if you just look. The ten lepers are probably all Samaritans – the ostracized of a community that is itself already ostracized: the unloved of the unloved. But Samaritans they almost certainly are: for Jesus is between Samaria and Galilee, and the only recorded 'thankful' leper is a Samaritan – who, even though a leper, is unlikely to be with those who are not of his kind. So Jesus' miracle is amid despised, foreign folk, who are triply tainted: wrong faith, wrong ethnicity, wrong disease. A good Judaean would do more than 'tut'; they would choke on their kippers as they turned the page.

Of course, Jesus hardly ever heals his friends, and rarely ever heals anybody with any significant social or moral political status. In nearly every case, the healings of Jesus are directed towards those who are self-evidently on the margins of society, or who have been excluded in one way or another from the centre of social, political, moral or religious life. Not only that, the friendships that Jesus made also suggest that he was more than willing to share his time and abundance with this same group of people. This observation is not particularly interesting in itself, but it does start to raise a question about what the healing miracles were for, if they are in effect 'wasted' on groups of people who appear to be unable to make a significant response.

Moreover, these folk – more 'tutting' here – turn out to be profoundly grateful; even thankful, like today's example. A thankful Samaritan? That's rubbing salt in the wound.

Jesus consorts with the *wrong* sorts of people in the eyes of the righteous; he's not in church, but down the pub. Moreover, Jesus seldom gets any return for his investment in 'the lost' or 'the unclean'; he wilfully loves the loveless, and seeks out those whom everyone else has given up on. In all of these healing encounters, the remarkable thing about Jesus' ministry is that it discriminates – *for* the unknown, the lost, the marginalized and the victimized. And almost nobody else.

Jesus was interested not just in healing, but how people had been classed as 'ill' in the first place, and what or who kept them there. He was, I suppose, in modern idiom, tough on illness, and tough on the causes of illness. And that is why the Samaritans are sent back to the priests – just like the demoniac in Gadarene. So that the excluders can be confronted by the excluded. Imagine the scene as ten leprous Samaritans return to their village. Imagine the scenes of jubilation. You can't. Because at the first sight of them, folk would have locked the doors and shut the curtains; lights on, but no one home. These lepers were 'lost', and lost they should remain. That just makes sense.

We might also need to remember that when Jesus heals the leper, he makes himself unclean by touching a source of impurity. The radical demand of Jesus is that the Church is required to assume the pain and impurity of the excluded, the demonized and the (allegedly) impure. That is why there are prison chaplains; that is why the Church works *for* and *with* asylum seekers; that is why the Church questions common sense, social control and prevailing political powers. It is just carrying on the job of Jesus, namely looking for the lost, rejected, marginalized and fallen, and trying to, with the love of God, bring them back into the fold of society and the arms of God.

But the trouble with Christians is that we only regard ourselves as honorary sinners, and the Church as a haven for the saved and secure. Yet it is for the lost and loveless. So, here are three lessons to learn about Jesus and his healing of the lepers, and countless others like them.

First, each of the healings seems to indict witnesses, crowds and others who appear to have colluded with the categories of sin and sickness which have demonized individuals and groups. Jesus' healing ministry is decisive in that it questions these categories ('Who told you this person is unclean?' 'He who is without sin may cast the first stone'). Jesus appears here to be a barrier breaker, eschewing the normal categories that dumped people in 'sin bins', or constructions of reality where they are deemed to be less than whole or suitable. In effect, he turns the tables on his audience on almost every occasion, and asks in whose interests is this person being categorized as ill or evil? This is why he is crucified in the end; Jesus breaks down the barriers between clean and unclean; he reorders society; the old rules no longer work.

Second, and correspondingly, Jesus often insists that a person returns to the centre of the community from where they were originally excluded (Mark 5.1–13). One of the best examples of this is the mentally ill man who has been chained up in a graveyard, and who nobody visits, recorded in Luke's Gospel. Jesus' healing of the person is extraordinary, precisely because he insists on returning this person to the community that expelled him from their midst in the first place. Even in the passage from Luke (17.11–19), Jesus sends the healed lepers back to the very people who would have cast them out of the community for his leprosy and uncleanness – and soon everyone knows that the lepers are back.

Third, touching is also a real feature of Jesus' healing ministry: he is willing and able to take on the associated stain, stigmas and taboos of his society by getting his own body and soul 'dirty'. Social anthropologists like Mary Douglas have had much to say about this and point out, quite rightly, that categories such as 'pollution' and 'cleanliness' surface particularly in relation to our bodies, which she identifies, of course, as a matter of politics. Correspondingly, what flows into and out of bodies, or what is deemed to be 'unclean' (such as leprosy), assumes a special character in nearly all societies. Jesus has no fear of healing lepers and embracing people whose bodies are leaking sin and pollution, for which they are excluded from society. He inculcates their stain and suffering, rendering them whole by embracing their exclusion.

The Church's task – its mission – is to look out for today's lepers. To look out for the excluded, the 'impure', the demonized. This is where Jesus will be. He reached out, and he touched. Or perhaps, like our erstwhile St Bernard dog, he searches for lost causes. And he comes with warmth and a drink. And some of those he finds – maybe not many – are truly thankful. That's good. But the love of God is also free to those who don't say 'thanks', and seem not to deserve it. As the *Daily Mail* would say, 'tut tut!' But Jesus doesn't seem to mind this. Neither should we.

62

Receive, Believe, Become

SAM WELLS

Bible passage: Acts 10.44–48

It is sometimes said there are two kinds of people: those who believe there are two kinds of people and those who don't. There may, nonetheless, be two kinds of Christians: those who hear the words 'Holy Spirit' and think 'Praise the Lord, at last someone's talking about the power of God' and those who hear the Holy Spirit and think 'Help – I'm going to be expected to make strange noises or speak in tongues or sing music that doesn't have four-part harmonies or go to services that last over two hours.'

After the four Gospels we have in our Bibles a book called the Acts of the Apostles. In some ways it might be a little easier to understand if the four Gospels were renamed the Acts of Jesus and the Acts of the Apostles were renamed the Acts of the Holy Spirit. Because the Holy Spirit is principally about one thing and that thing is making Jesus present. The Holy Spirit makes present the Jesus of the past and the Jesus of the future. The Jesus of the past is the Jesus who was born, baptized, was tempted, called disciples, taught, healed and confronted those who oppressed the people of God, who was arrested, tried, tortured and crucified, who was raised, appeared to many, and was taken up to heaven. The Jesus of the future is the Jesus who will come again, who will unite heaven and earth in a new realm of joy and perfect freedom, in an unending relationship with God the Trinity, in which all creation will worship God, be his friends and share his banquet. And the Holy Spirit makes the Jesus of yesterday and the Jesus of for ever present today in regular and surprising ways. The regular ways are in the sacraments of baptism and Eucharist, in the practice and experience of personal and corporate prayer, in the reading of scripture and in gestures of mercy and kindness. The surprising ways are in the wise words of a stranger, in the apparent disaster that turns out for the best, and in the way God seems to work through the most surprising people.

Because a lot of Christians are rather scared of the Holy Spirit, I want to set out three key words that express how the Holy Spirit works in the Church, and particularly how that work relates to baptism and confirmation.

The first key word is *receive*. This is a word that makes it absolutely clear that God is not our poodle. The Holy Spirit comes according to its own calendar, not ours. The Holy Spirit is not a puppy that we can train to walk or sit or lie down when we shout the right command. A former colleague of mine spent some time serving a church in Ghana. Like North Carolina, Ghana gets very hot in the summer, but unlike North Carolina there's not much in the way of air conditioning. It so happened that the church didn't have enough money to put any glass in the windows. This had the advantage that it let in a bit of air. The only problem was that there was also quite a strong breeze, so they found that when they brought papers into the church the papers blew all over the place. Eventually they decided that having the wind blowing through the church was intolerable so they got together enough money to put glass in all the windows. The result was simple. The wind blew the roof off.

The lesson is that you can't dictate how the Holy Spirit will act in the Church. The Holy Spirit is to be received, not grasped. It sets its own agenda. A number of years ago I was the pastor of a small congregation in a socially disadvantaged part of eastern England. A visitor came to the church one Sunday, and since we had only 15 or so adults, we were quick to spot a visitor. But this visitor had a rather fixed notion of what it meant to be a church, and he found our service very confusing. My sermon followed the scripture passage very closely, but we had candles on the altar. We sang simple choruses led by a guitar, but I wore traditional vestments. The visitor stayed afterwards and asked me, with a frown on his face, 'What kind of church *are* you?' I thought the best thing to do was to ask Huggy.

Huggy had been part of the church for several years. He was of mixed race, had held a number of jobs and known a good bit of unemployment, and was universally recognized, partly because he weighed over 250 pounds. I said, 'Hey, Huggy, our visitor wants to know what kind of church we are.' Huggy paused to think, and then said, 'Open to God'.

Open to God. That's what it means to receive the Holy Spirit. Huggy's church didn't have preconceived ideas about what God could or couldn't do. The Acts of the Apostles takes us through a series of encounters with people who challenge what the Holy Spirit can or can't do. First there's the Ethiopian eunuch, a Gentile man mutilated but in the wrong way. He comes into the Kingdom. Then there is Saul, a Pharasaic persecutor of Christians. He comes into the Kingdom. Then there's Cornelius, a Roman commander who was both a Gentile and a member of an army that kept the Jews from restoring God's promise. Cornelius too enters the Kingdom. The only issue is whether the believers can keep up with the wildfire work of the Holy Spirit.

This is the scary ministry of the Holy Spirit – dramatic, sudden, surprising. Something we can only receive. But there's another kind of ministry of the Holy Spirit, for which I use the word *become*. Once there was a rich man. He met and fell in love with a young maiden. She was lovely in form, and lovelier still in character. He rejoiced when he saw her. Yet he grieved also. For he knew that he was not like her. His face was hideous and his heart was cruel. He considered how he could win her hand.

Eventually he hit upon a plan. He went to see a mask-maker. He said, 'Make me a mask that I shall become handsome. Then, perhaps, I may win the love of this noble young woman.' The mask-maker did as he was bid. The man was transformed into a handsome figure. He tried hard to summon a character to match. It was sufficient to win the heart and hand of the fair maiden, and they were married. Ten years of increasing happiness followed. But the man knew he was carrying a secret. He sensed that true love could not be founded on deceit. He had to know if his wife really loved him, if she loved the man behind the mask. So one day, with a heavy heart and trembling hand, he knocked a second time on the mask-maker's door. 'It is time to remove the mask,' he said. He walked slowly and anxiously back to his home. He greeted his wife.

To his astonishment, she made no comment, nor showed any untoward reaction. There was no scream, no horror, no revulsion. He searched for a mirror. He looked – and saw no ugliness but a face as handsome as the mask, a face so different from his original face. He was amazed and over-joyed – but bewildered and confused. He ran back to the mask-maker to find some kind of explanation. The mask-maker said, 'You have changed. You loved a beautiful person. You have become beautiful too. You have become beautiful through loving her. You become like the face of the one whom you love.'

The Acts of the Apostles is not just a story of the sudden, spontaneous acts of the Holy Spirit. It is also the story of how people who love Jesus become like Jesus, the story of the slow formation of a community of Jew and Gentile, slave and free, men and women, oppressor and oppressed, of the slow becoming of the body of Christ out of a people who had known so many dividing walls of hostility. The Holy Spirit is about receiving, but also about becoming.

And in the tradition of churches that practise infant baptism, we call the receiving part baptism and the becoming part confirmation. Of course baptism is a sacrament the parents think about long and hard, but tell that to the baby. The baby feels the full force of the sudden action of the Holy Spirit – splash. Young people being confirmed didn't decide to be baptized. Baptism was something they simply received. But they did decide to be confirmed. Confirmation names the Christian's consent to a long process, already begun, and not yet finished, by which the Holy Spirit enfolds them into the body of Christ – in which they wear the mask of Christ's beauty, but have not yet fully become like the face of the one they love. Baptism and confirmation belong together because they reflect the two contrasting aspects of the work of the Holy Spirit – the sudden and the gradual, the part God does alone and the part in which we have a significant role to play, the kind we simply receive and the kind we slowly become.

But I have missed something out. I have missed out the bit between the sudden and the gradual, between receive and become. It is a bit of both. It has the 'be' of become and the 'eive' of receive. Believe. *Believe* in Jesus Christ, crucified and risen, incarnate on earth and ascended into heaven, Son of God and Son of Man. If receive means being tossed a set of football clothes, believe means putting them on and become means running out with the team onto the pitch to play. The Holy Spirit, remember, is always and only about one thing – making Jesus present. Whether it is dramatic, like the roof blowing off in Ghana, or gradual, like the man's face changing under the mask, it is always about Jesus. And that means it is always about faith. Faith is a gift, coming from outside us – we can't make it happen. That is the receive bit. But faith is also something we grow into, by being surrounded by people whose lives show us what God can do.

That's the become bit. Receive, believe, become.

The Acts of the Apostles teaches us not to get too hung up about the order. Sometimes the receive bit comes first, as on the day of Pentecost. Sometimes the believe bit comes first, as in the story about Cornelius' household. Sometimes the become bit comes first, and people seem to be living like Christians when they have neither been baptized nor had a dramatic experience. Don't worry about the order. Too much angst has been spilt over the order. There is no definitive order.

But do ask yourself, which one of these do I find most uncomfortable? Do I find the receive part the difficult bit, because I like to be in control of God and don't like surprises? Or do I find the believe part the hard bit, because I like drama and I sense I'm growing into a community of passion and transformation, but I do find the details about Jesus elusive? Or do I rather find I stumble over the become part, because I like what Jesus has done for me, but I struggle to turn that into participation in a community of discipleship?

Whichever part you find uncomfortable, have the grace to thank God for the gift of the Holy Spirit he *has* given you, and for the fruits that the Spirit has borne in your life. And don't be too shy to ask for those gifts that the Spirit still has in store for you.

63

Prodigal

MARTYN PERCY

Bible passage: Luke 15.11–32

The parable, for Jesus, was a window. The common realities of a harvest of grapes, dinner parties, mustard growing in a field, a woman baking bread; these are all things through which one can see life in an entirely new light. Jesus' parables and allegories are doors opening on to an alternative construction of reality. Parable is genesis. Parable is creation.

Consider the parable of the prodigal son: the very reading of the story involves us in some risk. The younger son leaves home in order to come home. He is unable to appreciate his patrimony until he has forsaken and squandered it. He cannot know his father as parent until he turns his back on home. The son cannot know the joys of return until he has suffered a departure. These are powerful symbolic plots in a single story. The parable is stronger and more durable than stories that consist only of arrivals. There can be no homecoming without a leave-taking.

The prodigal mirrors the journey of Jesus. It has autobiographical overtones. Jesus was at risk when he told the parable: he ventured to risk leave-taking in order to comprehend the bliss of homecoming. Similarly, the father empties himself of dignity and status, not only in giving away his portion of the inheritance, but also in the manner in which he receives the prodigal son.

Of course, the father is insulted by both sons: the younger son for the squandering of the inheritance, and the older for refusing to come and feast. A key part of the parable is the father's initiative in running to the son. Middle Eastern custom would have had the younger son met on the borders of the village by an elder, and a pot broken over the penitent's head as a sign of the irreparable damage that had been done to the village and to family honour. But the father, in running to greet his son – an intemperate and rash gesture for one who embodies dignity – exposes his legs and makes haste. This is an undignified custom on the part of the father, as elders do not run. They walk slowly as a sign of their dignity. It is for slaves, women and children to run; but not for elders.

The Greek text also teases us a little with the potential for conflict at the end of the parable. As the father runs to the son, the text tells us, 'he fell upon the [son's] neck'. Interesting, the neck: vulnerable, breakable, exposed; but also sensitive, intimate and erogenous. Until he is embraced, the son cannot know if he is to be kissed or throttled. This is a parable that is full of passions – extreme ones.

But Jesus, as he so often does in parables, plays more deeply with us than merely toying with our passions. He challenges us on our sense of fairness. Suppose your son or daughter 'borrowed' your credit card and ran up huge debts? To add to the fun, he or she had a wild party lasting several days while you were away looking after needy relatives. You come home with your husband, wife or partner only to find the place trashed, with many things sold or damaged. Your prodigy is nowhere to be seen, and you suspect that your son or daughter has decided not to sit their A levels, after all, but has instead bunked off to the Far East for an early taste of a gap year – or two. When your credit card bill arrives, you discover they have run up bills in tens and thousands of pounds. You have to pay the bill – all of it. The bills keep arriving, month by month. Your calls and texts go unanswered. But you can see from Facebook that they are OK – living it up, indeed. Then one day, silence. No more postings on Facebook. Calls and texts still go unanswered. And you have no money left in your current account anyway.

But lo, some two years later, your son or daughter rings up from the airport, and says 'Hi, Mum, Dad – I'm home …' What do you do? Do you:

(a) say, 'Get the coach home – we'll talk later'
(b) offer a repayment plan spread over several years, and give them a severe dressing down
(c) say, 'We'll pick you up – so glad to have you back that we're organizing a lavish party at short notice'.

Not (c), I think. The neighbours would, for a start, whisper that you were nothing more than a weak, bad, liberal and indulgent parent. Or that you were mad.

But the justice of God is different. The parable of the prodigal plays with our sense of justice. And the older son hates it. Because the message of the parable is this: the love of God is so complete as to be almost unjust – and certainly unfair. Indeed, the love of God might be a bit mad. You see, God loves people who don't deserve it. Not just the goodie-goodies. He loves the lost, the hopeless, the squanderers and the reckless. God's love is mad, in human terms, at least.

Why is the parable like this? Well, the lost son parable builds upon the lost coin and lost sheep stories considerably, by playing off alienable goods against inalienable goods in a subtle, pointed way. (I am most grateful here to my colleague Dr Michael Lakey for his insights.) First, the son values the property of the estate above his father, his place in the family and his honour; all of which ought to have been inalienable. In effect he gives up something not-for-exchange (ergo, priceless) for something that has an exchange value.

Second, in doing this, the son so dishonours his father that an apt response would be to regard him as socially 'dead'. Indeed, the father is being literal when he talks of his own son as 'dead'. This is because the undeniable commodity of honour is so significant to the filial relationship that to lose this honour is to abandon the social basis of interchange in the family. The father's dilemma is to lose the son or to lose that which constitutes him as father.

Third, the response of the father at the return of the son indicates that he values the son over the undeniable commodity of honour, which is itself worth more than alienable property. In effect he gives up an *inalienable* good (his fatherhood) so that he can regain something that has become devoid of value (his son). This is a far more radical move than the coin or sheep parable. As I say, God's love is a bit mad.

Fourth, that the father has become diminished socially by this move is clear from the emboldened response of the elder son, who is free to engage in open challenge and disobedience. This is exacerbated even more by the gentle, almost pleading, nature of the father's final response, in which he reminds the elder son not that he (the father) is lord of the property, but that the elder son will eventually inherit it all.

So there is ultimately a lowliness about the father's behaviour in regard to his sons that seems to embody a willingness to lose face for their sake. At the level of value, ancient readers would think this father had a curious and counter-intuitive set of priorities. Or that he was a bit senile, perhaps? Or again, just mad with love?

But that's the point. Indeed, the word 'prodigal' is interesting here. Martin Luther once said that if the Bible only consisted of the parable of the prodigal son, it would be enough. 'Prodigal', of course, means 'recklessly wasteful' or 'extravagant', but also 'lavish in giving or yielding'. The word 'prodigal' comes from three Latin words: *prodigālis* (wasteful), *prodigus* (lavish) and *prodigere* (squander).

Like so many parables, this one has been misnamed in Christian tradition, and even in Bible translations, where subheadings have been added. We know this parable as 'the prodigal son'. But the true prodigal in the story is the father: profligate, mad and extravagant love. The elder son bears the antonym: the opposite of 'prodigal' is 'cautious'. One thing that God is not cautious with is his love and mercy. This is the parable of the prodigal father. The father cannot bear alienation – either from his younger son or elder, or indeed between the sons. The father will forfeit anything – his dignity and identity, and his whole self – to avoid alienation. As the mystics say, if God has one weakness it is his heart: it is too soft.

So this is not an easy parable for listeners intent on being as generous as God, because the burden of the father's prodigal generosity falls on the faithful brother and his household. The father is now effectively giving away his older son's inheritance – which explains the bitterness of the stay-at-home son. The fatted calf and the feast are really the elder son's. The father's magnanimous generosity comes at a price, paid by others. The parable asks a difficult question of us as Christians. How do you feel when God's riches are poured out – but at *your* expense?

So the parable might be better known as 'the prodigal father'. He lavishes his love on his selfish son; he squanders his status on his wayward son; he wastes his fathering love on a son who wastes his sonship. But such is God's love, is it not? And what might God be asking our lives and ministries to be full of, if not this? To love the loveless. To love the unloved. To serve those who squander us. To hope for those who are hopeless. To be prodigal people in a wasteful world.

This excess is exuberance to the point of extravagance. Indeed, many of the parables that Jesus tells are about things that are thrown away, used up or finished with. Whether it be a banquet that is eaten, seed that is thrown around, or salt that is dug into soil. Jesus' subjects, like Jesus himself, are used and then disposed of.

So why does the parable end with the elder son? And why might he deserve more than a footnote, as the epitome of the failed faithful, filial and forbearing son? Perhaps this is why the elder son is re-addressed so closely at the end, by the father. Again, the Greek text holds some important clues as to the point of the parable. The father calls the older son 'baby' – either as a term of endearment, or perhaps as a form of chastisement. But the younger brother is called 'son'. It is as though the parable asks us all: do you want to sulk about the sinners I celebrate with? Or do you want to join in God's all-inclusive feast? We are all invited, even the ones who in our eyes don't deserve to be. God is mad with love for us all.

64

The Bad Neighbour

MARTYN PERCY

Bible passage: Luke 10.25–37

This parable is another misnamed story: the story of the good Samaritan would be better known as parable of the bad neighbour. Let me explain. The art of listening to parables, as opposed to the art of telling them, is the art of placing oneself in the story world they create. It is this connection between our world and the world of the parable that makes them such a powerful means of communication. Parables invite us in, as the host invites us to the party, but when we enter we do not always find ourselves in the position we might expect.

In their many writings on parables, Dominic Crossan and Marcus Borg point out that the role of the father in the prodigal corresponds to the role of the Samaritan in the parable of the good Samaritan. Just as the Samaritan would not have been expected to come to the aid of the Judaean in the ditch, so the father is not expected to respond to the younger son as he does. Christians are quite willing to understand the father in the story as God and the older son as the Pharisee, but the Church did not want to understand itself literally as the younger son.

As Marcus Borg has often remarked, Christians only really regard themselves as 'honorary sinners'. The parable of the good Samaritan makes some comparable points. Jesus steadily privileged those marginalized in society (the diseased, the infirm, women, children, tax collectors, Gentiles) – and perhaps even Samaritans – precisely because they were regarded as the enemy, the outsider, the victim. Christians would agree with Bernard of Clairvaux: there are four kinds of love. First, the love of self; second, the love of love of God for what he might do for us; third, the love of God for who God is; and fourth, the most difficult, to love our neighbour as God would love them, and as we might love ourselves. This fourth love, says Bernard, is the hardest to achieve this side of heaven.

Perhaps that is why the Samaritan as helper was an implausible role in the everyday world of Jesus; and that is what makes the Samaritan plausible as a helper in a story told by Jesus. The parable, however, is not only about an implausible Samaritan helper. It is about victims. No one elects to be beaten, robbed and left for dead. Yet in this story the way to get help is to be discovered helpless. The parable as a metaphor is permission for the listener to understand himself or herself in just that way. There were many in Jesus' society who could identify with that possibility without strain. Others could not imagine themselves being helped by a Samaritan. That is where the difference lies: how his listeners understand themselves. In the parable, only victims need apply for help.

Crossan and Borg say that we can now reduce the proposition in the parable to these statements: in God's domain, help comes only to those who have no right to expect it; and you cannot resist it when it is offered. Or, help always comes from the quarter that one does not or cannot expect. Or, we might reduce this statement more simply to this: in God's domain, help is perpetually a surprise.

The appearance of the priest and then the Levite would have caused the audience to divide over the issue of the clergy: some would have protested, others would have smiled, depending on whether they were pro or anti clergy. Jesus introduced this preliminary tension within the story in order to heighten the real tension still to come. With Jesus' audience divided on what will eventually prove to be a secondary issue, the Samaritan, an enemy of all parties, intrudes.

Who in the audience wanted to let themselves be helped by a Samaritan? This is the primary challenge, because the appearance of the Samaritan makes no other sense. Had the victim in the ditch been a Samaritan and the hero an ordinary Judaean, then the question would have been reversed. Who would the Judaean audience want to play the role of hero? Clearly, listeners would have found it more congenial to adopt the role of the helper rather than to accept the status of victim – yet this parable is about being a victim.

Among Jesus' listeners, those who would have responded positively to this story were those who had nothing to lose by doing so. Note that the victim in the ditch has nothing to do and nothing to say. The victim's inability to resist the Samaritan's ministrations is a weak form of consent, but it plays an essential role in the story: God's domain is open to outcasts, to the undeserving, to those who do not merit inclusion. The despised half-breed then becomes the instrument of compassion and grace – good and articulate Judaeans would have choked on that irony.

The Samaritan is made to behave in a way that runs utterly counter to expectations. The parable greatly exaggerates his willingness to help. Exaggeration and atypicality add an element of fantasy to the story: listeners can no longer believe their ears – their normal sense of reality is now called into question. The expectation that the real helper might be a Judaean – a possible candidate for the third person walking along the road – is dashed. At the very mention of the Samaritan, Judaean listeners would have bristled, rejected the plot and quit the story. Jesus narrates an offensive scenario. The real message of the parable of the good Samaritan is not just 'love your enemies'. It is, rather, 'let your enemies love you'.

Ouch. Let my enemies love me? Let them touch me? Let them help me? Well, yes. Jesus is again testing us. He is inviting us to see that there can be many agents of the love of God; many conduits through which his mercy pours. And our feeble tribal boundaries, our sure sense of pure and impure, will not last. The walls we build between us on earth do not reach to heaven. So the Samaritan is a hero – but from a Judaean point of view this is highly offensive.

A Radio 4 'Thought for the Day' broadcast got to the heart of this parable in the most surprising way. Broadcast at the height of the Soweto riots and the last days of the apartheid regime, the parable ran to form. An ordinary black man is travelling home from his church one Sunday evening – he shouldn't be out at night, and he knows it's a dangerous journey on the way home. Sure enough, he's set upon and mugged, beaten up very badly and left for dead.

At the first light of day, a community worker sees the body lying in the ditch – a common sight – 'He's probably drunk', reasons the community worker. 'Men of his kind are always in drinking dens, and they give us all a bad name.' Next, a clergyman passes by. He too cannot help and is powerfully aware that bodies lying by the side of the road are sometimes tricks or ambushes – he walks on briskly. Third, two white policemen in a patrol car drive past. The driver stops, gets out of the car and sees the man is already half-dead. He picks him up and puts him on the back seat, and drives him back to the police station. And no, they don't beat him up again and finish the job – the policeman binds his wounds, calls round to the man's family to tell his wife and children that their father and husband is badly hurt but will make a good recovery. That is the parable of the good Samaritan – the enemy is the redeemer. You are the victim, and God in his graciousness and mercy surprises us by sending his love through the last person on earth that we would expect to be of help at all.

We remember, finally, that the parable of the good Samaritan arose in response to a question: what shall I do to inherit eternal life? Jesus answers: love God, and love your neighbour. But the questioner asks, who is my neighbour? And the answer is this: the person you thought was your enemy – but God has set apart to bless you and widen your horizons.

65

David, Goliath and Jesus

ROWAN WILLIAMS

Bible passages: 1 Samuel 17.38–50; Romans 12.9–21

Some people are inclined to think that the Bible is rather short of humour. Most people don't pick up the Bible if they are looking for a good laugh. But those who know it perhaps a bit better may be able to point you to the bits that really are rather funny. For example, there's the picture of David, the shepherd boy, getting ready to go out and fight Goliath. The King offers him his own armour. Now, if you're going out to fight a nine-foot giant, heavily armed and in a very bad temper, you might be quite grateful to have some extra protection. The problem is that we've already been told earlier in the Bible that King Saul is one of the biggest men in Israel, and David is about 15 and doesn't sound terribly robust. So we have this wonderful picture of the King loading David down with armour that doesn't fit him, with a helmet that comes right down over his eyes and a breastplate that hangs down to his knees. And David, it says, 'tried to walk and failed'.

So that's the picture: somebody who wants to protect themselves, but, when they try to, they can't move. They can't do a thing. Quite apart from all the other interesting lessons we learn from the story of David and Goliath that particular detail is really worth thinking about. Sometimes we spend so much energy trying to keep ourselves safe that we cannot do anything – we cannot actually move. We're so concerned with fencing ourselves around, defending ourselves from any risks and any problems, that we end up not really 'living' at all. We have bolted all the doors, we have shuttered all the windows, and we are like David with a helmet coming down to his nose, with a breastplate coming down to his knees. We can't do a thing.

But what is the alternative? We all want to be secure. We would like to be safe; we don't like taking risks. The answer is not to load ourselves down with lots of things that are stopping us living. We don't deal with the problem by piling up things so madly, so obsessively, that we are surrounded with stuff and we cannot move. We need to find another way of reacting when there is a big challenge coming, when things are difficult, when we have got to find new ways of living.

So what does David do? The Bible tells us that what he did was what he knew he was good at. He was not much good at fighting in overgrown suits of armour, but he was quite good with stones and slings, with a little Bronze Age catapult. That turned out to be what he needed. He thought about what he was good at; he thought about the skills God had given him; not what God had given somebody else. God had given King Saul the great grace, no doubt, of being enormous and strong and fierce and the sort of bloke who could walk around in armour like that. But he had given David some different gifts. David thought, 'Well, the only way I can really deal with this challenge – this problem, or crisis – is by remembering what God's given me, what I'm gifted with, what I'm good at.'

That is perhaps the second thing to think about from that story. How are we going to manage when things are difficult, when there are challenges and crises we had never imagined – when things are harder, more surprising, more stretching than we had ever expected? Part of the answer is 'look at yourself'. What am I good at, what are the gifts I have been given, what is it that makes me me? God has given me special things, very different 'special things' from my neighbour, but they are the things that will help me when life is tough and the challenges and crises are fresh and difficult.

That means that if we are going to cope with the challenges and the crises of our lives (and they keep coming whatever our age) we need to know ourselves. What am I really like, what am I good at, what do I love, what do I hope for? And it is really very important, as we grow up, to spend some *time* getting to know ourselves. We spend time with each other, getting to know one another as friends; we spend time exploring what other people are like. But sometimes we need to spend just as much time – maybe even more time – getting to know ourselves, looking inwards, thinking, 'What am I really like, what really matters to me, and what are the gifts and the strengths that I actually have?' Because having faith in God is really a matter of being confident that God has given me, somewhere in myself, the resources I need to respond to a new problem, a new situation, and to make my response, like David, with a bit of courage and a bit of imagination.

So, we get to know ourselves. We spend a bit of time being quiet enough with ourselves to look inside. And there is really no alternative to this – to grow up and to know ourselves we do need a bit of time in peace and quiet. But the last thing to bear in mind in all this is that sometimes it is rather hard work getting to know ourselves. And sometimes when we do look at ourselves, we do not like what we see very much. We look at ourselves and think, 'That's not really very impressive; it's not as impressive as the person next to me. Maybe I ought to be better; maybe I really ought not to know this at all; maybe I ought to blot out what I know about myself and just barge on regardless.' So really to know ourselves, and to know not only what we are good at but what we are bad at as well, to know our weaknesses, our temptations, we need quiet and space for that. But more than anything else, we need to know that somebody loves us so deeply that even the weaknesses we see in ourselves do not matter – something can be done with them too.

And that is where God comes in. God, who tells us that he loves us so much, he can even do things with our weaknesses. Of course God can do things with our strengths, that is obvious, but one of the things the Bible tells us too is that God can do things with our weaknesses. Often it is when we admit we are not brilliant at everything, that we cannot do absolutely everything, when we admit that we need help from one another, that is the moment when, mysteriously, God is able to help us do more than we could ever imagine. Getting to know ourselves is not just a matter of knowing our strengths, it is also knowing what we need – what we need from each other, what we need from our friends and our families. St Paul talks about the importance of living at peace with one another, giving and receiving with one another in the family of God and being able to go to someone else and ask for help. So that bizarre picture that we started with, of David loaded down with somebody else's armour, is a key to some of the things we might need as we move and grow and develop as human beings and as Christians, or whatever faith we profess.

We learn, first of all, that it is no good pretending. It is no good borrowing somebody else's armour and defending ourselves so successfully that we cannot move. We need to look inside. We need, like David, to remember what we are good at and to trust that God has given us the skills we need to face a crisis and a challenge and to keep going when life is difficult. As we learn to know ourselves, and to look inside in moments of peace and quiet, we need also to recognize that we are not good at everything and we are always going to need each other, to help each other along. It is at that moment – when we admit we cannot do everything – that, mysteriously, God comes in and makes a big difference.

The secret is God does not ask each one of us for 100 per cent success in everything all the time. But God does ask us for 100 per cent honesty, not for succeeding all the time but for being open to the truth and admitting who we are, what we are like, what we are good at, what we are bad at, what we need from each other and what we can give to each other. So much in the New Testament is about that pattern of being honest – honest about what we have to give, honest about what we need from each other – and the whole thing made possible by belief in a God who does not give up on us when we admit our failures.

Jesus, in his ministry in the Gospels, is always coming across people who are willing to say to him 'this is what I need'. That is where real wisdom, real grown-up-ness, always begins – not 'I can succeed at everything, I can do anything', but 'this is what I need'. When we are honest about that, then miracles really do happen. I think that what we ought to be praying is that we are delivered from the temptation to load ourselves down with stuff, with protections and securities, to such an extent that we can never move out, never reach out a hand to make a friend. Never, like David, simply bend down at the side of the brook and pick up those little stones that are going to give him the victory.

Look inside. Let us give ourselves the time to look at ourselves, remembering in that quiet time how God looks at us with love and patience and hope – the God who looks at us when we try to be honest and truthful, who works with our honesty and with our weakness as well as our strength, to make us grow up to be more and more like him and like his Son Jesus Christ.

66

Eternal Life

ROWAN WILLIAMS

Bible passages: Job 19.23–26; Matthew 22.23–33

Readers of a certain generation may remember a wonderful film made of Noel Coward's play *Blithe Spirit,* in which the great Margaret Rutherford played a slightly mad spiritualist medium. The theme of that play, in a nutshell, was a man haunted by the ghosts of both his previous wives. It is that kind of sitcom situation that the Sadducees place before Jesus at the beginning of the Gospel passage (Matthew 22.23–33). They are trying to make the idea of eternal life look stupid. 'Imagine', they say, 'all the problems that would arise if the unfinished business of this world were simply projected into the next.' The tangles that would have to be sorted out, the unacceptable choices that would need to be made, the dramas, the comedies and the embarrassments – surely belief in eternal life is absurd.

And Jesus' response, in effect, says, 'Yes, indeed.' Eternal life understood like that is nonsense because eternal life as more of the same, as an unfolding for all eternity, of the crises, the choices and the embarrassments of this life, is a nonsense. Coming at eternal life in that way suggests that the promise and hope of eternal life is really about us, whereas in fact it is about God. Moses speaks of the Lord as the God of Abraham, the God of Isaac and the God of Jacob. He is God not of the dead but of the living, for to him all of them are alive.

Eternal life is being alive to God here and hereafter. God says to Moses in the story that Jesus refers to that he is the God of Abraham – meaning he is the God not only who used to love Abraham when Abraham was alive, but the God who loves Abraham now, who engages with Abraham now, who calls Abraham now. The relationship God has begun with Abraham is a relationship without end because God is without end. To him, they are all alive.

And that is the heart of our own faith in eternal life. As we seek to share the good news with the society we are in, we are not trying to persuade them that there is an endless sitcom to be evolved after death, that eternal life means we go on for ever and ever pretty much like this. What we are trying to persuade people of is that the God we believe in is a God who never lets go of those he has made. It is the God to whom all are alive because he has breathed life into them, and, once he has laid his hands on their lives and left his imprint and breathed his breath, that relationship will never disappear.

So, our hope of eternal life rests on what we believe about God: that God in creating us breathes life into us, something of his own life, and that God, once he has breathed his life into us, will always regard us as alive and hold us in his love. In that sense, Abraham, Isaac and Jacob live before him. And so do all those who have left us the legacy of faith. They *lived* because they were alive to God; because they were alive to God, they kindled the flames of faith in us. In kindling that flame of faith, they passed on that hope of eternal life.

Our good news for the world is in living lives that look as if they are in touch with God, that look as if God truly has breathed into us something of his own nature, something of his own passion for forgiveness and reconciliation, something of his own unqualified reckless generosity, something of his own readiness to stand with the suffering, the forgotten, the poor. That is what the life of God looks like, the life that we see lived out in Jesus in his death and resurrection. And when our lives show that, they show eternal life because, quite simply, they show who God is. The life of God that will never die. When we are alive in relationship to God, and when we show it in those ways, then we show what the hope of eternal life means much more effectively than by getting into the sort of arguments that Jesus' opponents want him to get into.

We live because he lives, a phrase that we come across in different forms in the New Testament. That mysterious passage from Job (19.23–26), 'I know that my redeemer lives', seems to say much the same thing. What is the hope that Job has? Not that things will get better, or that things will go on for ever, but just the hope that comes from the knowledge that there is one who is alive who will never take his eyes from him and never drop him out of his hand. A belief not about us but about God. So to be on fire with the life of the Holy Spirit, to be given and devoted to the task of sharing that kindling flame with a chilly world, we are to live in such a way that our relation with the life of God is clear.

Week by week, for many people day by day, we renew our relation with that life at the Lord's table. Because *there* is life and fire. *There* is the reality of Jesus Christ, the humanity in which God's life was most fully lived, offered as food for our humanity. *There* is eternal life. And when we receive the bread and the wine of Holy Communion it is to deepen, to recreate in us, the relationship we have with the life God has breathed into us. It is to have the seed of Christ sown in us, the passion in every sense of Christ planted in our hearts and our wills and our hopes. It is to anticipate the life of heaven – which is why, for so many Christians, to take part in Holy Communion is seen as the beginnings of heaven. For, heaven is sharing in the life God breathes into us and sharing it with those others for whom we are making it real and who are making it real to us.

At the holy Eucharist, as one hymn says, 'Alpha and Omega to whom shall bow all nations at the doom is with us now.' This, wonderfully and gloriously, this at the Lord's table, this is the end of the world. This is the beginning of the new creation. This is where life begins again and again; God's life, eternal life, that life of reconciliation, of generosity, of selfless identification with those in need, those on the edge of things, those who feel they have no value. And as we go from this table, it is that life we carry in us and that life we wonder at and delight in and reverence in one another.

As we pray for the peace of the nations, we remember those who have been the victims of the conflict, the ravages of sin and violence in our world over the last century. We are conscious, painfully, raw-ly conscious, of those who day by day in our armed forces elsewhere in the world face the risk of death. Conscious of the societies in which they are serving, shadowed day by day by death and horror. That is the world we are in, that is the chilly world that needs the fire of God's love. It is that world in which we seek to show what eternal life is, now, beginning today. To God, all of them are alive. To God, past, present and future, all is alive. And for us, to communicate what God is and who God is, we need to be alive with that life in word and in work.

I have been greatly privileged to see something of what it is for God's servants and God's children in this family of Christ to be alive to God. I have seen that aliveness to God in work with young offenders and people at the end of their lives in a hospice, and in a centre for the homeless. People who are alive to God and are making others alive because their relationship to God shapes who they are, what they do and what they give. And in their aliveness, others come alive too. Eternal life is not a set of abstract speculations about the future; certainly not the grimly comical picture that the Sadducees sketch out so as to trip Jesus up. Eternal life is visible and tangible. Here and now we can see what heaven will be like, what heaven *is* like, because it is where God is and so it is where we are now. We hold gratefully, joyfully, to that faith and if we do so and seek to be brought alive to God, day by day, then the fire of the Spirit is set free once more. The face of the earth will be transfigured.

67

Seeing Salvation

MARTYN PERCY

Bible passages: John 9.1–9; Acts 9.1–22

I don't see too well. I have a rare eye condition called keratoconus, which describes the elongation and corrugation of the cornea. Both my eyes have it. Unchecked, your eyes grow outwards – a bit like cartoon characters with their eyes on stalks. And of course, with the angle of refraction, with light falling on corrugated corneas, you can't make out shapes, letters or faces. Everything blurs and becomes distorted. I was diagnosed with this exactly 25 years ago this week, and as I worked in publishing at the time, it was a bit of a blow. It also accounted for my somewhat quirky proofreading – correcting mistakes that weren't there, and missing ones that were. There is no cure, but the condition can be managed. Hard gas-permeable contact lenses do the trick. To medics, people with my condition are known as 'cones'. Possibly because it rhymes with 'drones' – because people with keratoconus can go on a bit!

The disease is only mildly progressive, and most people cope with it fine. But where does it come from? No one knows. It is not genetic, but spontaneous. It is not related to asthma or hay fever, as people once believed. Nor is it the result of too much reading. Like shit, it just happens. But it does excite interest among high street ophthalmologists, who rarely get to see cases, and when they do, close the shop and invite their colleagues in to gaze deep into your eyes, and offer to make you tea, and ask how long you have.

I recall going to see an optician in Durham when I was training for ministry, because my eyes had become infected. He invited his colleagues in; and, after an hour, announced I had to go to a local eye infirmary for further tests – and straight away. So I trogged off there, and waited. And after several examinations, the eye doctor popped the question: what did I do for a living? I replied that I was training to be a priest. There was a pause. And then he asked, strangely, if I could tell him something of my sexual history. Not unreasonably, I said that it was rather uncomplicated. And besides, had he not heard my answer to the previous question – *I was training to be a priest*! The pause was much longer this time. Before he said, 'Well, you might have herpes, so I just wondered, because, well, you know what seminaries can be like …' Well, I didn't. And subsequent tests revealed a slight tear in both corneas, and a very simple infection. But I have often mused on the encounter, because, I suppose, we all want to know not only what we have, but why, and from whence it came; as did the eye doctor.

Around the same time, I was doing some of my early doctoral work on fundamentalism and revivalism. I was attending healing meetings as an observer, observing participant, participant observer, and sometimes just participant. I kept notes. I was absorbed by the dynamics of the gatherings, and the claims. My purpose was never to ask if the claims to be healed were true or false; theologians can't know such things. Rather, the question was, what do these healing encounters and stories mean to those who are gathered?

I would listen to eloquent sermons and testimonies from healers, who would tell you Jesus could heal anyone and anything. And I would then watch them take off their spectacles, put them carefully in their top pocket, and invite people to the front for ministry. I would puzzle over how illnesses were described and addressed. Some of the things I saw and heard were profoundly moving. Some were troubling and disturbing. Others risible, or just plain odd.

But I suppose if I am honest, what made me struggle was the refusal of most speakers and preachers to really acknowledge the relationship between cause and effect, unless it could be tied to something personal and moral. Yet according to the World Health Organisation, well over 90 per cent of the illnesses and diseases on this planet have a single cause: poverty. We lose 5 million children a year, under the age of two, to perfectly preventable malaria-related fever. Clean the nearby water supply, and you eradicate the breeding grounds for the mosquitos that spread the disease. I sat through many healing meetings that described many individuals recovering miraculously from a fever. But inside protested all the while that, even if true, it was pointless when the causes of fever were not addressed.

In our own country, obesity is now one of our biggest threats to health, and one of our biggest killers. It is not a disease of the rich, but the poor.

To be frank, you can look at maps of the United Kingdom that spell out the demographics of obesity plainly. The concentrations of obesity lie in our poorest and most disadvantaged communities. And the related consequences – cancers, heart conditions and diabetes – follow in their wake. I have been to many healing meetings that have been beautiful, pastoral and powerful. But never to one in which anyone has gone home ten stone lighter. The dieting industry would be ruined if this happened.

I simply raise the cause and effect equation because it is there in the Gospels. Jesus, why is this man blind? Is it his sin? Or his parents? Who or what is to blame? One of the most interesting things about the Gospels and the New Testament is the way in which they play with our sense of perspective. They make us see ourselves differently – and others, and the wider world. We are asked to look deeper, and see relations, cause and effect, consequences and the like, differently, more wisely, and with deeper compassion. So Jesus – as he often does – evades the question about the blind man and who or what caused the blindness. It does not interest him. In the mission of the Kingdom of God, which Jesus ushers in, we all stand before God in need. We are met as we are, and, with mercy, grace, tenderness and compassion, find that our encounter leads to something altogether deeper. It may be a physical healing. But it may be new insight, a spiritual healing, or an earth-shattering heaven-sent epiphany that turns our world upside down, rather as Saul found to his cost, and eventual gain, on the road to Damascus. His blindness – temporary – led to an entirely new insight. Losing sight led to seeing salvation.

The distinctiveness of this gospel story is marked by the earthiness of spit, mud and touching. This is a very physical healing. The man is touched intimately and strongly by Jesus. But all Pharisees do is carry on with their seminar and the theological inquest. Seeing and touching is contrasted sharply by John to cerebral aloofness and intellectual remoteness. Touch, then, not merely sight, becomes the dominant theme of this encounter. And it reminds us that touch can carry so much more weight than words or sight. That what is seen and heard is sometimes not enough – for we ache for embrace: to be held and to hold. Interestingly, so much of our ministry is about holding and touching. Even for clergy, and perhaps especially in the first few years of priesthood, one becomes aware of just how crucial touching and holding can be: cradling a child at baptism; joining hands at a wedding; holding the dying and comforting the bereaved; the breaking of the bread; the anointing with oil. These are all 'touching places' where words are not enough. Here we need holy hands touching the wholly ordinary. To 'see', we need to feel.

My own journey through healing has led me to a different view of my sight, and more insights. When I look at the Gospels, I see that Jesus mostly healed the marginalized and dispossessed; those without means or status; the excluded and the castigated; the despised and rejected. Liberation theology has taught me to see the world, and healing, differently. Not to judge about whether or not healing happens, but rather to be mindful of the places of poverty and neglect where the cause and effects of disease and illness are all too apparent. These are the places where Christ loves and loves to be at work, through you and me, and his Church, his body.

At the Eucharist, Jesus stands before us, and for us. He sees our needs. He sees our sins. He sees our pain. He sees our bodies. He sees the secrets of our heart. He sees our goodness. He sees our inner beauty. He sees our gifts. In seeing all that, he says 'come'. Come and eat with me. Come and eat of me. And come and be touched.

We come to the Eucharist in need, not with assumptions, but with hope. To be met by nothing less than Christ's grace – that unmerited, unstoppable and unpredictable gentle, loving force by which Christ holds us all. Who can say where that will lead? My prayer is that as with every healing encounter, we will not try and judge why someone might have needs, where fault or blame may lie, or whether or not the healing happened. John's Gospel invites us into a much deeper life of prayer: to see more clearly; to love more dearly; to follow more nearly.

68

Diaconal Service

MARTYN PERCY

Bible passage: John 13.1–16

I recently came across a story about the first Bishop of Minnesota, Benjamin Whipple, who tells of an incident in his autobiography, *Lights and Shadows of a Long Episcopate*, of the Dakota Indians under the Presidency of Abraham Lincoln. After being driven from their land, the Dakota tribe revolted and a large number of white settlers were killed in several days of massacre – mostly led by younger Indians, anxious to prove themselves.

The Dakota Indians were rounded up indiscriminately from their lands, and 438 condemned to death by hanging. The Indians appealed to Lincoln for clemency, saying that most of the incarcerated men were innocent, and indeed many of them had risked their lives by hiding white settlers from the marauding bands of young braves. Bishop Whipple tried to intervene for the innocent men, and Lincoln duly commuted 400 of the death sentences: only 38 Indians would die.

But which ones? The elders of the tribe – the oldest men – stepped forward. We have seen our children and our children's children, they argued. We have few winters left. We shall die in place of the young, who, even though they committed the raids and the massacres, have their children to raise. The press reported the hangings, and the newspapers in Washington said that the Indians went to their deaths 'singing their heathen death chants on the gallows'. But Bishop Whipple, who stood by the accused, records it differently. The ones executed were, you see, Christians – Indian converts to Christian faith. And as Whipple tells us in his autobiography, they went to their death at Fort Mankato chanting Psalm 19 in English: 'Many and great are your works, O God.'

This simple story tells us something profound about the nature of service that Jesus alludes to when he girds himself with a towel, stoops and washes the feet of his disciples. It is an act of lowliness, but also an act of deep service that hints at his death. Jesus' gesture of foot-washing – like so many of his acts – is a deeply diaconal act. It is the act of someone, who, in teaching about friendship, service and solidarity, takes on the mantle of a slave and performs an act that only the lowest of the low would perform.

Behold, he will say, I am among you as a servant. But I call you my friends. In taking on the mantle of a servant, he is stripping himself of power and dignity, and hinting at the ministry of the first deacon in the future – that of Stephen, or any other martyr. He is saying something about his and our expendability, and something profound about what he asks from each of us as we serve God in the Church. That we should not strive for power – but for love and service. It is as Brother Roger of Taizé once said, 'He does not ask for too much; but he does ask for everything.' This is discipleship.

To see Jesus' foot-washing at the Last Supper in this light is to get near to the centre of his gesture. He washes the feet of the disciples at this point – so close to his death – because the events of his whole life in ministry ultimately strip him of power, status and authority. So he becomes the servant at table to remind us that true authority lies in our service to one another. How we care for those who are poorest and neediest. What we lay aside of ourselves to enable others to be free and flourish. And yes, sometimes that laying aside even includes our own lives.

It is costly. This is something of what it means to be a deacon; something of what it means to be a disciple; something of what it means to be a priest, who follows the Priest. And as we contemplate the ministry to which he calls us all, we see Jesus not standing before us, but stooping and kneeling at our feet.

69

Peter at Caesarea Philippi

MARTYN PERCY

Bible passages: Isaiah 51.1–6; Romans 11.33–36; Matthew 16.13–20

For the first-time visitor to America, one of the most perplexing things one faces is something that most will take for granted: choices. I recall coming to Boston some 12 years ago and attempting to order a sandwich, something I supposed to be a simple matter. But it was far from that. The sandwich bar was heaving with lunchtime custom, and everybody seemed to be speaking rapidly, throwing menus, options and alternatives at you. When my turn in the queue finally came, I was stumped, as I knew I would be.

'I'd like a cheese and ham sandwich, please, with salad and mayo,' I said, confidently. So far, so good. But it was not to last. 'What kind of bread, sir?' 'Er ...' 'We have rye-wheat-wholegrain-pumpernickel-foccacia-German-crusty-white-softwhite-cheese-herb-tomato-and-basil ...' 'Er ... white ...', I stuttered. (I note, by the way, how the choices virtually all slur into one word. The repertoire is produced in a single exhalation.) 'Now, what kind of cheese ...?' And so we ploughed on through the options on salads, dressings, types of ham, manner of wrapping, cutting and so forth. Ordering a sandwich in America can be an exhausting experience.

Now, when Jesus came to Caesarea Philippi, he too seems to have been one for choices and options. 'Who do you say that I am?' The reply of the disciples is circumspect. Is this a trick question? Is Jesus trying to catch us out? So the disciples do not really answer. They repeat what they have heard, but they do not say what they think. They give opinions, but they do make a commitment. The encounter is a seminal one, for it is at this point in the Gospel of Matthew that choices have to be made. Opinions are all very fine, but they are not what is wanted here. Jesus is looking for a real commitment from the disciples; people to share the next stage of his journey.

But having seen what they have seen, and heard Jesus, what do they think? They are reticent, at first. And this reticence is part of the lesson from the passage in Matthew (16.13–20). Simply put, it invites us to contemplate the difference between knowing *about* God and knowing God. Of course the two are not mutually exclusive, but they are different. Nearly everyone had an opinion about Jesus – as nearly everyone does today. But the question 'Who do you say that I am?' is really another way of asking you, 'If that's what you think, what are you going to do about it? What difference will it make to you?' The question at Caesarea Philippi exposes the potential gap between rhetoric and reality, between knowledge and faith.

Churches know all about such gaps. You will doubtless be familiar with the old aphorism, uttered by a celebrity who seldom went to church: 'I cannot be considered a pillar of the church, for I hardly ever go. But I am a buttress, in so far as I support it from the outside.' And so we have knowledge of God, but not faith in God. Or, as a prominent scholar puts it, many developed nations have now cultivated people who 'believe without belonging'. They know that Jesus is significant – perhaps John the Baptist, Elijah or Jeremiah – but they do little about it.

This takes us to a slightly different understanding of Jesus' question: it is a *demanding* question. In asking it, Jesus is not tendering for opinions. He is, rather, looking for a life-changing commitment. And to offer any sort of answer to this question would require risk; sticking your neck out, risking ridicule, or worse. But it is just this that Simon Peter does. He gives an answer that is going to cost him, for the moment the words are uttered there can be no going back. You can no longer follow Jesus as one might follow a favourite TV programme or sports team. This following will require the total reordering of life itself.

And because of that, Jesus cannot respond to Simon Peter and say 'well done, correct' and to the others 'wrong, you are the weakest link, goodbye'. The response to Simon Peter immediately assumes the character of a charge and a vocation. Getting the answer right was not the point. This was never a multiple-choice questionnaire. No, in answering as he does, Simon Peter has simply uttered one word: 'Yes.' This is a 'yes' to God, a letting go of life, and the embracing of a new future. But it is one that is fraught with paradox and uncertainty.

In answering Simon Peter, Jesus tells him that he is 'the rock' on which the Church will be built. Rocks are not glamorous things. Peter is to be a foundation: that unseen, hard, supporting material for a great edifice. Remember, nobody goes round a great gothic cathedral and says, 'lovely pillars, narthex, nave, sanctuary and stained glass – but what really did it for me was the foundations'. Such a statement would be risible. But this is to be Simon Peter's role.

Actually, the rock metaphor is the key to the passage, and also provides an important link with the passage from Isaiah (51.1–6). In Isaiah we read that we are to 'look to the rock from which you were hewn, and to the quarry from which you were dug'. It is God's reminder to his people that salvation has been founded as of old: it is there, in the depths, as Paul reminds us in Romans. But Isaiah also shows how salvation is part of our story. From Abraham to Sarah and from Eden to the dawn of time, God's salvation has already 'gone forth'.

But here is the catch. Peter, in being adopted into God's story – he is now

Jesus' rock – finds that the language Jesus uses is part of the new story of God's redemption. In that, Peter is a foundation, but he will also be part of that new, transient community of believers, the Church, which will have no lasting foundations, but will look for the city that is to come. Peter will be a rock, but he cannot stand still, for the disciples are called not only to stand firm, but also to be flexible and open. It is this new language that reminds us all of just how costly the vocation to recognize Jesus will be. Knowing God in Christ will mean learning to live with paradox. There will be times to be a rock, and times to be fluid; times to be a foundation, and times to wander in the desert with nothing but a tent. Peter is given the keys to the Kingdom, but later he will not be able to get himself out of jail. The gatekeeper becomes the incarcerated. In other words, nothing is settled for Peter; he is still, primarily, a follower.

Such is the lot of the disciple. But remember, this is God's story of salvation and we are simply actors in the production. And the story itself is, as Paul says, as inscrutable as God. Which is why the gospel is such a puzzle. Who do you say Jesus is? The answer is never an easy one, for to say with Simon Peter that 'you are the Christ, the Son of the living God' is to express more than mere opinion. It is to make a commitment to an uncertain future. It is to become part of God's story, to move from being a spectator to an actor, and to be caught up in the drama of Christ's salvific work.

In discipleship, our lives are woven together with God, and God's story and ours become intertwined. What name, I wonder, would God give to you? Would you be a rock or a stream, an unseen foundation stone or a highly visible pillar, salt or light, a stained-glass window or a door, a tiny unseen hinge, or a supporting beam that holds up the roof? All these material things are comparable metaphors for what God may call us to be. Whatever you identify with, you can be sure that Jesus will build with you, just as he has with Peter.

70

Zacchaeus Reconsidered

MARTYN PERCY

Bible passage: Luke 19

I ought to begin by saying that, at a little over five foot seven, I identify with Zacchaeus. Too small to see the main event, he climbs to get a better view. He may be small, but he's smart. He's my kind of man. Yet the story that Luke tells is not really about the height of a tax-collector.

Luke 19 is full of crowds and numbers – first a crowd in Jericho where Jesus meets Zacchaeus. Then a parable about the ten minas (or talents) – a story of honest fiscal stewardship, and of kingly power. Then of the crowds at the next port of call, which marks the triumphal entry of Jesus into Jerusalem. Before finally ending up in the Temple, where the issue is once again money. Throughout the chapter, Jesus is feted and celebrated by the crowds, who cut down palms from the trees, and lay their clothes across the road as he rides through on his donkey. The Gospels record the event, telling us that the crowds lining the street to see the famous Galilean prophet and healer cried 'Hosanna in highest! Blessed is he who comes in the name of the Lord.' The event must have made quite an impact, and would not have gone unnoticed by the authorities. And yet crowds can be fickle, can they not? The same people who cry 'Blessed is the King' on Palm Sunday need only a few days to change their verdict to crying 'Crucify him!'

The narrative involving Zacchaeus is therefore at the centre of this chapter. It is only here that the crowds and the money come together. And how Luke loves to tell his story. Zacchaeus is a small man. Small people, on the whole, get pushed to the *front* of the crowd, so that they can see what is going on. But Zacchaeus, though small, is shunted to the *back*. He is not supposed to see Jesus – that is the point. Crowds can be cruel. But to overcome this, Zacchaeus is forced to climb – which is why we find him in the sycamore tree. The function and behaviour of the crowd is therefore an important key to understanding this story.

There is another dimension to the crowds that Jesus knew, however, that ought to catch our attention as well. In the midst of great throngs, who were often pressing hard on him, and presumably jostling him too, Jesus was always strangely alert to other things. But alert to what, exactly? We already know that Jesus healed nobodies, the Gospels in most cases not even bothering to name the afflicted individuals. We know that the people Jesus reached out towards were excluded from the mainstream of society and the mainstream of faith.

The people Jesus healed were mostly outsiders, whose stories were 'unpublished', which is the literal meaning of the word 'anecdote'. It is the small, unpublished stories that Jesus constantly turns to. The small man who cannot see, he sees; the small voice in the crowd, he hears; the untouched body in the pressing throng, he feels. The incarnate body is richly sensate to the 'unpublished'. Luke tells us that Zacchaeus was rich, but that he could not see Jesus on account of 'his small stature'. So, he climbs a tree for a better look. Yet it is from that position that Jesus calls to him (there must have been dozens of people who had climbed trees or buildings to get a better look). Jesus invites himself to Zacchaeus' house, and a new story unfolds. One of dangerous, prophetic inclusiveness.

In Christian memory and tradition, Zacchaeus is consistently portrayed as either fraudulent or as a collaborator with the occupying Roman army. In fact, I cannot recall reading a Bible commentary or hearing a sermon when this was not explicitly restated. The reaction of the crowd bears this out. They all 'murmured' that 'he [Jesus] has gone to be the guest of a sinner'. Zacchaeus, meanwhile, has decided that his response to Jesus' visit is to 'give half of my goods to the poor'. And then comes the hidden sting in the story, for Zacchaeus adds 'if I have defrauded anyone of anything, I will restore it fourfold'. 'If.' That 'if' must be one of the most important two-letter words in the Gospels. That Zacchaeus is despised by the crowd is not in doubt. But nowhere does the Gospel say he is dishonest. Zacchaeus is simply hated for what he does and what he represents; but in truth, he almost certainly does this with great honesty and integrity.

So what does Jesus' action signify? Only this. That in the midst of a crowd bestowing their adulation, Jesus refuses to side with their base prejudices. Zacchaeus is affirmed for who he is. He does not repent, contrary to how this story is read – he has no need to. Rather, a person who is despised is allowed to flourish and is now seen as a figure of generosity – he has, after all, given away half of what he has.

Consistently, Jesus sides with the ostracized, the despised, the unclean and the (alleged) sinner. He refuses to allow Zacchaeus to be caricatured. He sides with someone unpopular, but who one suspects has never been understood – and perhaps has never been allowed a fair hearing. So Jesus is no crowd-pleaser; he is, rather, their confounder. Even before the palms are ripped from the trees, and the cries of 'Blessed!' heard, it is obvious that Jesus is a disturber of crowds. He does not want their praise. He wants their commitment. And they make him pay for this – his failure to deliver what they promised themselves.

The power of the gesture that Jesus performs in this story should never be underestimated. Let me illustrate this with reference to a story from South

Africa, and from the dark days of apartheid. Father Trevor Huddleston, an Anglican priest, and member of the Community of the Resurrection, was for a while Vicar of Sophiatown – a rundown area of Johannesburg, but one of the few suburbs where black and coloured people could buy property. To appreciate this story, you need to picture Huddleston in your mind – a very tall, white Englishman, with a chiselled face and a rather gaunt expression. He was seldom seen without a cassock (which often appeared to be too short) and, as an Anglo-Catholic, he would also have sported a biretta.

Morning and evening prayer are said daily, so Huddleston would have made the short walk from his community house up the hot dusty road to the church, passing dozens of people on the way going about their business. Being a polite Englishman, he always raised his biretta to passers-by. And as someone who made no distinction between black, white or coloured, he raised his biretta to every adult he met. His walk always took him past one particularly squalid house, where a black washer-woman laundered clothes each day – to make a living – in her tiny, cramped backyard. Huddleston would greet her and raise his biretta, while a young 11-year-old boy played in the yard.

The boy puzzled over this gesture as the months went by. Who was this white Englishman who raised his hat to a poor black woman? What kind of white man would show such courtesy and kindness? It is a simple gesture, and one that Huddleston, I expect, gave no thought to. But the boy did. It awakened his curiosity. It sparked a thought: that all men might be equal, and that not all white men thought themselves superior. That his mother could be respected as any white woman might be. And that this priest was, in his tiny gesture, showing a new way. The name of that boy in the back-yard at Sophiatown is, as it turns out, known to us all: the boy was called Desmond. Desmond Tutu.

So we now might understand something of the power of Jesus' gesture. Through hospitality and communion, barriers are broken down. The demonized turn out to be not so terrible after all. Indeed, they get preferential treatment from Jesus. They become his friends. The black woman and her son; the betrayers and diseased in the camp; and the tax-collector in an occupied country – Jesus is with them all. It is more than mere gesture; it is radical, incorporative communion.

Christians, it is often said, only regard themselves as honorary sinners: the rest of the world are the real ones. But the Gospels faithfully preach against this nonsense. It is the self-righteous who have to rethink, and whom Jesus' sermons and parables are really directed at. Which is why Zacchaeus having tea with Jesus is such a profound moment in the Gospels. The ultimate crowd-pleaser deciding to have a meal with the man the crowds love to hate. This is where we find Jesus today. Not with those we so easily love; but with those whom we often so easily hate and lazily despise. It is as though Jesus says to each of us, 'See – he is not so bad after all. Behind the role and task he does that you detest, behold, is a generous and forgiven human being. I am going to eat with him, and get to know him better.' He hardly needs to add, 'Go. Do likewise.'

71

The Challenge of Holiness

ROWAN WILLIAMS

Bible passage: Hebrews 12.18–24

This passage gives us two very different pictures of what holiness might mean. First of all there is holiness as something strange, terrifying and deeply dangerous: God descends to speak to his people on the top of Mount Sinai; there is thunder and lightning, and nobody must go near, and there is the sound of the trumpet so terrifying that the people of Israel want it to stop: this is holiness as something alien and something deeply scary. And then, says the writer to the Hebrews, there is holiness as we are experiencing it now: we, as God's people in the present, encountering the holy in a quite different way. You have not come into the middle of the cloud and the darkness, the thunder and the lightning and the terrifying sound of the trumpet, he says. You have come into a fellowship, you have come into an abundant, overflowing environment with more people than you can count, living and departed, angels and humans and anybody else who might want to join in. You have come into the harmony of the whole universe: abundant variety around you, the variety of unique voices all blending together in one act of praise. Instead of holiness as something strange and threatening, this is holiness as something excessive, overflowing and overwhelming in its variety and its joyfulness. This is holiness in the context of the fellowship of all creation. And, says the writer of the letter, it is into this kind of holiness that you step when you step into the family of Christ.

So to come to a holy place is not first and foremost to come to somewhere strange and scary (though for some people, that's what it feels like). It should be centrally and most importantly to come into the harmony of all creation, into a vast diversity of voices acknowledging glory, speaking of joy. But, as I hinted, that can be frightening.

Most people when they come into church these days – most people, that is, who do not normally come to church, which in this country unfortunately is most people – feel rather afraid. Will they be spotted as a stranger? Will people be looking round and scrutinizing them and saying, 'They obviously don't belong here; they don't know what to do'? Here are all these people (us) apparently doing strange things without giving it a second thought. We know the moves, we know the rules, and they do not. It is rather like going into a club whose rules you do not know, or a school whose habits you do not know (if you are a child): so the Church feels to many. It is bizarre, it is eccentric, and it is frightening.

So, we all of us have some good news to share with people who might feel frightened in that way. And the good news is really this: in the infinite variety of voices singing praise in God's universe, your voice – trained or untrained – is as welcome as anybody else's. And the language you speak is a language we all need to hear. Because to be part of that overwhelming, overflowing abundant fellowship is to recognize that no part of it is complete or alive without the others. It is interesting that in another place in the letter to the Hebrews, the writer speaks of all the great heroes of Israel's past, and then says, 'Without you, these people would not be made perfect.' All the great giants of biblical history – Abraham and Moses, Joshua, Gideon and Samson – they are all waiting for you to join them, because without you their joy and their fulfilment are not complete. It is as if when you turn up in the fellowship of God's people, Abraham comes across to you beaming all over his face, asking where you have been all his life! The great heroes, the great saints, the people we think we have very little in common with – they want our company too, because God wants our company and God wants each one of us to grow into maturity, fulfilment and love in that fellowship. So Abraham may have been a man of exemplary, outstanding, unimaginable holiness, courage and devotion, and yet he still needs me and you to make him completely Abraham.

As we think back across the centuries that many of our churches have existed, and the witness that's gone on in them, we might think of all those people who, in these places, have served God with exemplary devotion, courage and sanctity, all looking at us and saying, 'Where have you been all my life? I need your voice, your friendship and your fellowship to be myself.'

Out of that deeply unlikely exchange, the holy fellowship is born: everyone, happily and gratefully, in need of everyone else; each one of us waiting expectantly and joyfully for what the neighbour can give; not only the neighbour in every act of worship, but our neighbours through history and our Christian neighbours in the future. This is not an easy idea to get your mind around, and yet we are also the people that future Christians will need, and we will need them. That is the nature of the fellowship into which we are drawn, and that is holiness, the not being without one another. It is the relationship that makes us who we are, because ultimately the holy God we serve and love, the holy God who comes among us in sacrifice and gift and glory, is a God of relation, Father, Son and Holy Spirit: God pours out to God the life of God and receives God from God in the joy of God for all eternity. And we, in a very distant way, reflect something of that, and as we grow in faith we are drawn more deeply into that relationship.

And so it is that when Jesus Christ comes to the holiest place of his faith, to the Temple in Jerusalem (Matthew 21.12–16), the challenge that he puts to the Temple is not a challenge to the idea of a holy place as such: it is a challenge to a model of the holy that is essentially about the alien and the threatening. Why are the money-changers and the sellers of animals in the Temple? Well, you have to have special money to go into the Temple courts and then you have to stock up with sacrificial animals so that you need not be afraid of God, because you have given him enough presents. Jesus' word and action cuts through that and says, 'No: this is a place of abundance, a house of prayer, this is an image of the restored creation'. Indeed, that is what the Jews of Jesus' day believed: the Temple was an image of God's whole creation. 'Come into the Temple with thanksgiving and enter his courts with praise', and be prepared there to find an overwhelming, overflowing fellowship into which you are drawn. Because this (as many of the texts say) is a 'house of prayer for all peoples'. So we should not then be surprised when we are told in the Gospel that the blind and the lame came to him in the Temple: the people on the outside, in the margins; the people incapable of seriously and faithfully discharging their responsibilities (in the eyes of some) are drawn in to be welcomed, because the abundance of fellowship is for the weak as well as the strong, because the strong need the weak as we all need one another for our joy, our life and our fulfilment.

Celebrating a holy place, giving thanks for a great and wonderful history, is celebrating holiness as abundance, holiness as overflowing, and I use the word well aware of the overflowing that goes on in our midst. What a perfect image that is for the holiness that we are trying to live our way into. We celebrate the fellowship of the universe into which we are summoned. We celebrate the fact that we are now drawn into a relationship so strong, so deep, so anchored in God's own nature that it can transform everything that we are. When Jesus dies on the cross and the curtain of the Temple is torn in two, the sanctuary of God is laid open; the depths of God's being are made accessible to us. 'We may enter', says the writer to the Hebrews, 'through a new and living way into the holy place.' Because through the life, death and resurrection of Jesus, abundance, fullness, has burst out among us: that is our holiness and our hope.

When people do approach the Church with nervousness, with fear and anxiety about whether they will be acceptable, whether they can indeed be part of this fellowship, we have the task of communicating to them that it is not so. But it is worth remembering that for each one of us the fear may still be there: 'Do I really matter? Is my voice really worth hearing?' Or, 'In order to make myself acceptable, do I have to be silent?' Many anxieties may flood in, and not the least of those anxieties is the knowledge that if I am really to be part of a universal fellowship, the harmony of all creation, I am going to have to let go of some of my ways and habits and some of those things I cling to, some of those things I use to protect myself. And when I see that, I realize that there is still something quite properly frightening about the holy, because overwhelming unconditional love is terrifying, showing up as it does our own selfishness and idleness. The holy as abundance, as overflowing fellowship, is still a holiness that is terrible, that summons us to repentance as well as to rejoicing.

So now, our primary task is rejoicing: rejoicing for the holiness that Jesus' life and death and resurrection have made real for us; rejoicing in a holiness that binds us into the universal voice of praise and thanksgiving; a holiness made real as we pray in and with Christ at his table, sharing in the fruits of his self-giving at the holy Eucharist. In the liturgy of the Eastern Church, when people are summoned to share in Holy Communion, it is with the words, 'Holy things for those who are holy': 'The gifts of God for the people of God', as we have it in our own liturgy. That invitation is not a way of saying, 'If you're holy enough, then these holy things are for you'; it's a way of saying, 'These are the gifts that make you holy because they unite you with the fellowship of praise, with the harmony of creation, gathered into one in Jesus Christ, the eternal Son, eternally grounded in, related to the eternal Father and the eternal Spirit, the holy threefold God in whose name and power and life we gather with all those heroes and saints of faith who have gone before us, who without us will not be perfect, with all those we do not see now who are part of our fellowship on the other side of the world, with those who will be worshipping, praying, hoping and loving, here and elsewhere in decades and centuries to come. Together with them and the saints, the angels, the company of the faithful we say, 'Holy, holy, holy Lord: the whole earth is full of your glory.'

72

The Treasure of Education

MARTYN PERCY

Bible passages: Matthew 5.33–end; 1 Corinthians 4.1–5

There is no denying that the Church of England is good at patchwork, and also good at decanting the old wine into new wineskins. The Church being the Church, you can't stop people innovating and adding: pimping the praxis; accessorizing the articles of faith; tampering and tinkering with the tradition.

The discussion that Jesus is having with the Pharisees and teachers of the law is basically about this apparent problem. Who, ask the Pharisees, is this Jesus to improvise with the law and the praxis of the tradition? You don't see the disciples of John the Baptist messing with the law. So why is Jesus sitting so light to the tradition? The answer Jesus gives requires us to pay great attention to the nature of theological and spiritual formation. Superficially, you could read the Gospel as if the old is done with, and now here is the new. But the practice of Jesus is patently not that at all. It is continuing with the old with some significant additions and modifications; but, crucially, in a completely new way. So, not just a new style – a riff on rabbinic rubrics, as it were – but a radically different *approach* to law.

Put more sharply, in Jesus, the law is here to serve humanity and the people of God. It is the apotheosis that is gone: the law is not God. So in proclaiming the new (grace), the old (law) is not redundant: it is fulfilled. So Jesus is saying, be careful how you mix things. Be careful what you put with what, and how. Not every improvisation will work for old and new alike. Sometimes the two need to be held apart, even when ultimately both, being of God, belong together. The covenant from Jesus is that there are no bad foods, only bad diets. Humanity will not now be judged by what it ingests but by how the digesting of law and grace manifests itself in our Christian lives and character.

Old and new together? Patchwork, or mix and match? This is why the old joke about Anglicanism still works. How many Anglicans does it take to change a light bulb? Five: one to put in the new and four to admire the old one. Because Anglicans do admire the past, even if it seems spent. The debate about old and new is always alive and well in the Church, and it continues to press questions about the character of our Christian formation.

Think of what 'new wine' looked like in 1662. Arguably, when we had just the Book of Common Prayer and everyone used the same book, we were able to safeguard against the now familiar problem of most local churches shaping their worship around the character, tastes and dispositions of those who attend it. But should decisions about the practice of worship be made on this basis? In a consumerist Church searching earnestly – some would say desperately – for connections and customers, some may feel inclined to reply that those who have continued to worship according to the Prayer Book are also choosy.

But there is an argument, even if it is deeply unfashionable, that might say that in keeping the Book of Common Prayer, one has not *chosen* one's liturgy according to a pre-existing taste or preference. It chooses you. The liturgy was a given, provided by the Church, and not supposed to be subject to the whims of either incumbents or congregations. It was not a matter of worshippers forming a liturgy, but of liturgy forming worshippers. It was precisely to counter the fashion for experimental liturgies and for locally decided alternatives that Common Prayer was needful and desirable in 1662. So even today, it is not obvious to me that a church that continues to use the Book of Common Prayer is thereby less 'local' than one that seeks to create a special parish liturgy by the 'practice of inculturation'.

One pastor in the Vineyard tradition, but with a great fondness for all things Anglican, writes:

> There is a danger in forming (individual) ecclesiologies, or churches for one. The private God-space can become a therapeutic location in which I am trapped trying to make sense of my Christian spirituality. Gone is the abandonment of myself in worship and service in response to who Jesus is and what he has done. The basis of (individualistic religious) reality is a play-list spirituality, downloaded on demand ... We must consider how we can ever hope to construct a faith that forms us as Christians, with so many ways of doing church that have more in common with ways of forming us as isolated consumers. (Clark, 2011, pp. 54–5)

And yet, commonality always faces and engages with diversity; the Book of Common Prayer, in its day, catered for many tastes by drawing on many traditions. Old and new? We might do well to remember that the Book of Common Prayer is, in reality, a patchwork of traditions. It is a montage of prayers and spiritual practices that owes its life to the many hands and many centuries of authorship, before it became *1662 and All That*. The new was always in the old. Part of its commonality lay in its diversity. Because it is through this gradual patchwork, perhaps surprisingly, that God rather likes to speak to us. As Emily Dickinson reminds us:

Tell all the Truth but tell it slant –
Success in Circuit lies
Too bright for our infirm Delight
The Truth's superb surprise

As Lightning to the Children eased
With explanation kind
The Truth must dazzle gradually
    Or every man be blind.

Our prayer for the Church today is that we will all become discerning disciples of the Kingdom. That we will revel in the old and new treasures God
gives, and share them with the world that Christ has asked us to serve.
Stewards, indeed, of God's mysteries, bearers of his gifts, and ambassadors
for his Kingdom.

Note

J. Clark, in S. McKnight, K. Corcoran and J. Clark (eds), *Church in the Present
Tense: A Candid Look at What's Emerging*, Ada, MI: Baker, 2011.

73

Sound in Spirit, Soul and Body

ROWAN WILLIAMS

Bible passage: 1 Thessalonians 5.22–24

> May God himself, the God of peace, make you holy through and through, and keep you sound in spirit, soul and body, free of any fault when our Lord Jesus Christ comes. He who calls you keeps faith: he will do it. (1 Thessalonians 5.22–24)

'God keep you sound in spirit, soul and body'. The purpose of the consecrated life is, of course, the soundness, the health, of the whole Church. It is undertaken in the conviction, unlikely as it may seem to secular minds, that health is as contagious as its opposite. And the soundness of the whole Body of Christ? 'Sound', says St Paul, 'in spirit, soul and body'. So what might that health be about – the health of spirit, soul and body – for a religious community, and especially for a Benedictine community?

Sound in spirit, sound in the air we breathe, sound in our lungs, you might say. And the air that we breathe, if St Benedict is to be believed, is an air that carries the atmosphere, the ethos, of humility and trust. Famously, St Benedict has more to say about humility than almost anything else in the Rule. He spells it out in relentless detail, but it is not simply something whose characteristics are listed and left; it is something pervading the whole of the Rule. It is something very clearly connected with that very remarkable and very distinctive feature of Benedict's Rule which impresses upon communities the need for mutual listening and the need for attention to those you think least likely to be of use to you, especially, in Benedict's context, the juniors. So the healthy spirit is the listening spirit. The healthy spirit is a community environment in which a great deal of listening goes on, especially to the unlikely, especially to the marginal, in and out of the community. There needs to be a spirit of listening to the young not in a fashionable focus group kind of way, but a willingness to be taught by those who haven't learned the wrong lessons of experience. Listening in attention to those who do not usually get listened to, in and out of community, where the expectation is always that the other carries to you a word of Christ – indeed the Word that is Christ, so that the spirit of listening, the spirit of that sort of humility, becomes the particular way in which the Spirit of Jesus of Christ is alive in you.

And what about soundness of soul? I am going to take that definition of 'soul' which says it is what gives form, what gives shape to the body. Soundness of soul is having a robust and durable shape, a sense and a rhythm to the common life. And that sense and rhythm of the common life – of monastic life overall, but very especially of Benedictine life – has to do with the shape that the psalms give to the day, the shape the psalms give to the human voice and the human imagination. Health of soul is a healthy inhabiting of the world of the psalms. And that is the world of praise, the world of lament, the world of bafflement, sometimes of protest and anger, a world of the naked. The soul that is the psalms of David is a pattern of speaking with one another to God that allows all the areas of our human life and experience to be inhabited by God the Holy Spirit, that allows the voice of protest and anger and that carries the voice of praise and thanksgiving.

When St Augustine wrote about the psalms, as he did so extensively and so unforgettably, he reminds us of the varied tones and voices of the psalms: of anger as well as praise, of protest as well as gratitude, those voices are all, so to speak, taken up into the one voice of Christ who has taken into himself the voices of all humanity so that they may be woven together in an offering to God the Father. Health of soul is to inhabit the voice of Christ in the psalms, to let that voice be ours, that is, to know and recognize it in ourselves: those tensions and darknesses which drive human beings to anger, protest and outcry, and to recognize in ourselves also those areas of the human heart that uncontrollably surge up in praise and thanksgiving, sometimes almost incoherent praise and thanksgiving, the great, chaotic outpourings of the psalms of praise.

And soundness of body? Well it does no harm to be absolutely prosaic and pragmatic about that and suggest that religious communities ought to be places where people are healthy. The question for any community, any community at all, is: is this a healthy life? That is to say, is its physical and material balance a great coherent, settled one, or has that spirit of rush and anxiety that controls most of our civilization penetrated our community? 'Surely not!' I hear you cry.

This morning some of the newspapers carried as their lead story the publication of a letter from a number of experts on childhood telling us what I think we might well know already: that the experience of children in our society is more and more catastrophic. More and more, children are being denied childhood by being denied space, air, freedom, patience. They are being corralled into tests and hoops to jump through, they are being confined physically in where they can play, and they are being pressured into the consumer culture.

But, dare I say, that the health of a religious community is rather like the health that we are seeking for a good childhood. We are seeking to say to the world around us something about health of body, a something that is quite different from the obsessive cult of health that turns one more screw in the ratchet of anxiety. We are saying something that has to do with the balance of work and leisure, which itself has something to do with connectedness to the ordinary physical rhythms of the world. We are saying something, in fact, that in the Rule of Benedict has always been associated with the invitation to work and prayer, by which I do not imagine that Benedict or anyone else meant simply that you should be constantly muttering devout invocations as you go about your business. But your work should be part of a sound life, a life with shape, with substance, a life that is not consumed by anxiety, over-excessive care, that knows about Sabbath rhythms that the Bible will endorse.

This is the soundness – the health that is about listening, inhabiting Christ in the psalms, the Sabbath rhythm of work and recreation, the breathing in and out without which nobody lives sanely.

74

Gideon's Angel

MARTYN PERCY

Bible passages: Judges 6.11–23; 1 Corinthians 1.20–31

The encounter that Gideon has with an angel is one of the best-loved stories of the Old Testament. But it might not be familiar to you, so let me paraphrase. Gideon belongs to the tribe of Israel – but one of the weakest clans. Moreover, for the last seven years, the Israelites have been oppressed by the Midianites. Actually, more than oppressed. They have been economically savaged. And the Midianites take everything – crops, sheep, goats, cattle and all the food the Israelites grow. The Israelites are reduced to growing crops in secret. The Midianites feed off the Israelites, says the Bible, *like locusts*.

There are some parallels with the 1998 Pixar film, *A Bug's Life*. In the film, you may recall, a bunch of grasshoppers come every year to the anthill and eat what the ants have gathered for themselves. The 'offering', as the ants call the ritual, is a part of their fate. Flik – the lead bug, so to speak – sets off to find bugs that are willing to fight the grasshoppers; nobody expects him to succeed, by the way. And due to a misunderstanding, Flik returns with a circus crew who are announced as the agents of redemption that everybody longs for. It is about as absurd as Gideon taking on the Midianites with his friends.

The film *A Bug's Life* is of course a retelling of Aesop's fable *The Ant and the Grasshopper*, and Akira Kurosawa's 1954 film *Seven Samurai*, in which seven masterless Samurai save villagers from rampant exploitation at the hands of marauding bandits. A later Americanized version of this film appeared as *The Magnificent Seven*, with exploited Mexican peasants now playing the role of economically ravaged Japanese villagers. That the Israelites are 'ant-like' should not surprise us. The book of Judges goes out of its way to stress Gideon's utter resourcefulness. He is even threshing wheat in a winepress; hard, secretive work that he has to do for his people, as well as serve his oppressors.

Marauding bandits, it seems, are the same the world over. You just need one small ant to save the day. Or a small guy called Gideon, who, somewhat laughably, is referred to as a 'mighty warrior' by the angel. Gideon is no fool, though. And he is not easily flattered, either. So when the angel tells Gideon that they are going to fight the Midianites and win, Gideon is understandably sceptical. His reasoned reply to God can be summarized as follows: 'When it comes to fighting I'm pretty crap (but I can cook a decent stew). And we are in a crap situation with crap resources, living in a crap time. But you say we are on the point of victory. That must be more crap, God. But no offence meant.'

None taken, it would seem. The angel knows that the scepticism of Gideon would be deep and rational, and it is well founded. It would be like someone saying Scotland are about to win the World Cup. We should not underestimate the absurdity of the promise to Gideon. So, not unreasonably, he asks for signs from God. The reason being, I think, that he does not want to raise false hopes. The signs he asks for are not about his lack of faith – though I expect he was sceptical to the core – but rather his responsibility and fidelity to his desperate people.

The Old Testament is not only full of people demanding signs; it is also full of the strange signs by which God speaks to us. The irony should not be lost on us. A burning bush, a rock that flows with water, a pillar of flame, or even Balaam's ass – God can speak through all these things. But the actual sign is often not the point. A religion that regularly gathered around the hind quarters of a beast of burden, hoping to hear the Oracles of God, would be a very odd faith. So would cooking a stew and expecting a message from God in the ensuing instant flambé; or one of Gideon's fleeces to say a word or two.

In a book by Larry Keefauver, the author writes that 'God sent an angel to tell a nobody that he was indeed somebody in God's sight'. God does that. God uses those who are small in their own eyes to do great things. Keefauver also writes that the story can encourage anyone to derive their confidence from 'choosing to see themselves as God sees them': Gideon saw himself as weak and helpless. But the angel declared God's perspective on Gideon: 'O mighty man of valour' (Judges 6). So, we are challenged to see ourselves as God sees us. The invitation is to simply let go of those insecurities that often keep us from enjoying the fullness of God's hopes for our lives. God sometimes commands his angels to lift us up: to propel us above poor self-imagery or other circumstances that conspire to grip and shape our thinking.

And that's the connection with the passage in 1 Corinthians 1.20–31. Jews demand signs; Greeks wisdom. But no sign shall be given, except the sign of the cross – foolishness to the Greeks, and a stumbling block to us all. The love of God, says one hymn-writer, is broader than the measure of our mind. So it is with wisdom, which is why God uses simple things to shame the intelligent, and the foolish to confound the wise. God's messages often come through unexpected sources. He even chose to reveal the word made flesh through a baby – who could not speak, at least to begin with. God's wisdom is not like ours; it surprises, undermines and confounds. It does not confirm; it often disturbs.

One of the reasons why the stories of the Old Testament are so likeable is that the characters are all quite flawed: the good, the bad and the ugly are all mixed up. And frequently, the resolution and salvation for individuals is to let go and let God. Think of Jonah on his sulky journey to Nineveh. Or any of the other prophets who come and go. Even Gideon is pretty hopeless.

But what of Gideon's angel? Well, sometimes the messenger is the message. We don't have a physical description of the angel, but what we do know is that the angel was prepared to be tested by Gideon. And tested until Gideon could be reasonably sure that the near suicide mission he was being asked to embark upon might have a sliver of a chance of succeeding. Gideon was being invited to pitch his pathetic compatriots against the combined forces of the Amorites, Midianites and Amelekites. He wanted to be sure that the angel was truly a messenger from God, and not simply a hopeless optimist. The angel obliges Gideon on each of his tests – the so-called 'fleece test' being the last. But Gideon still has to commit his puny forces against the might of his enemies. And at the risk of a cliché, to do this, he has to set aside his fear and step out in faith. The message and messenger all say the same: you can haggle with God, but you can't hide. The angel is God's negotiator, closing the deal.

Yet it is only when Gideon lets go of the negotiations and stops testing God with signs that he begins to experience the blessing of God. But a blessing can be a shocking revelation. Indeed, it can turn your world upside down.

When we are lifted out of the darkness, we find that God has something else for us. You can see the point of Gideon's angel. The angel comes in Israel's darkest hour with a message of deliverance. But the angel confounds our wisdom at the same time. Gideon, who thought he was just a weakling, is now to be called 'mighty one'. Perhaps just like the angel that spoke to a peasant girl called Mary 2,000 years ago, and called her 'favoured one', when she clearly wasn't, on one level. Exactly how is a pregnancy outside marriage 'favoured', at a time and in a culture when it is in fact a matter of disgrace and taboo? Both Gideon and Mary, however, have to respond to God's invitation – no matter how unwise this might look if you start to rationalize it – to become a mighty warrior or a favoured peasant girl. The angels all seem to say the same thing in the midst of our darkest hour: 'I have something quite extraordinary for you to do; but don't be afraid, for the Lord is with you.'

75

Prayer and Persistence

MARTYN PERCY

Bible passage: Luke 18.1–13

According to the American writer Anne Lamott, the prayer of the daily offices can be simply summarized. Morning Prayer, she suggests, can be condensed into a single word: 'whatever'. And Evening Prayer needs only two words: 'ah, well ...' Lamott says elsewhere there are only three other prayers, really: 'Help', 'Thanks' and 'Wow!' We perhaps spend too much time asking, she suggests – pleading, really – and not enough thanking. And very little time just saying of and to God, 'Wow'. Lamott would also agree with Woody Allen: 'If you want to make God laugh, tell him your future plans.'

Prayer, I suppose, is one of those activities that Christians (indeed, people of all faiths) engage in, but seldom pause to consider what it is they are doing. The habitual, impromptu and mysterious nature of prayer is part of its fascination. Here we have the language of faith, of desire, of hope, of healing – and even occasionally of justification and commination. And occasionally the quirky: 'Hail, Mary, full of grace, help me find a parking space': a prayer that not only rhymes, but also seems to work – for some.

Several years ago I was an honorary chaplain to a professional rugby club. I performed all the usual duties. Perhaps inevitably, in all the fracas and fury of a game, the name of God would often be invoked by the supporters. And after a crucial-but-missed kick, my neighbour might turn to me and say, 'I don't think your boss is helping us much today.' The retort from me: 'Sorry. But I'm more sales and marketing, not production ...'

In rugby, the wages of sin are a penalty. When there was a kick for goal, a prayerful hush would descend on the ground. Invariably, my fellow fan might turn to me again and exhort me to pray ('Say one for us, Padre ...' – the classic request, so beloved of our vernacular spirituality). If the kick went over, I would be thanked for my successful prayers. If it missed, I'd be asked why God no longer favours the home side! And this is the heart of the matter. Every passionate sports fan *prays*. But does God intervene to answer prayers?

If the ball goes through the posts, has my prayer been answered, or is it just coincidence? If it does not, has God declared his support for the other team? Or is it just that God doesn't care, being generally indifferent about rugby, and perhaps preferring chess, or maybe netball? So how does God act in the world? Can God affect the outcome of a rugby game? If that is possible, then should God actually do that sort of thing? Clearly, in the interests of fairness, the answer is 'no'. But that does not stop us praying for victory. So what happens when we pray? And, as Luke asks, how should we pray?

Prayer is supposed to be a process whereby the petitioner is transformed, as they express their hopes and fears. In being and waiting before God, we slowly become conformed to the will and image of God. So, we do not pray for victory, but a rightful outcome. We do not pray for the kick to go over, but for the kicker to do his best. But we also remember to remind God that we will be utterly desolate and miserable if we lose. God understands that. Not all of Jesus' prayers were answered; he, too, tasted the bitter chalice of defeat.

And how does God return our prayerful petitions? Here are three very preliminary thoughts. First, any intervention from beyond, and by God, is often subtle and ambiguous, seldom conclusive or coercive. Second, the petitioner can never have the impossible: there is a final whistle, a result, death and disappointment. It is no good praying that your team has won, when the result was announced five minutes ago. Prayer has to cope with realities, not side-step them. Anyway, sometimes there is victory. Third, the answer to our prayers is sometimes 'no'. In expressing our hopes in prayer, God may refuse us. Not because God is fickle, or supports the other team, but because there is wisdom and maturity to pursue – God does not satisfy all our desires, no matter how weighty or worthy they may seem to us.

This is why some of the great prayers we have in the English language are actually *about* prayer. They teach us to pray, as Jesus does. One thinks of Cranmer's majestic Collect for Purity: 'Almighty God, unto whom all hearts are open, all desires known, and from whom no secrets are hidden, cleanse the thoughts of our hearts ...' In other words, sift and sanctify our desires and dreams. Do not give us what we want, but do give us what we need, and what is good for us.

Similarly, George Herbert comprehends the mystery of prayer – as a journey of the senses and soul, as it were – when he writes:

Prayer – the church's banquet, angel's age,
God's breath in man returning to his birth,
The soul in paraphrase, heart in pilgrimage ...
... A kind of tune, which all things hear and fear;
Softness, and peace, and joy, and love, and bliss,
Exalted manna, gladness of the best,
Heaven in ordinary, man well drest,
The milky way, the bird of Paradise,
Church-bells beyond the stars heard, the soul's blood,
The land of spices; something understood.

Jesus, in teaching his disciples to pray, keeps the matter simple. God will answer your prayers. He listens to persistence. But please note, sometimes the answer is 'no'. We are to hallow the name of God; seek the coming of his Kingdom; name our needs (but note, *not* desires – God can *always* see what we *want* – 'no secrets are hidden', as Cranmer says); ask forgiveness for our wrongdoings; forgive others; and pray for deliverance. In his Gospel (18.1–13), Luke illuminates this with some additional comments.

First, God will listen to what is absorbing and consuming us. Some of these may be obvious needs – the real hunger for food, justice, mercy and deliverance – be it ours, or that of others. And sometimes, the prayer requests may be a mix of desire and need – the kind of prayers where 'the thoughts of hearts' will need cleansing even as we petition. Yet Luke seems to be saying that God is attentive to our petitions, even when they are flawed. But even Luke has the wisdom to tell us that the prayer is answered, with God giving the widow justice because of her persistence.

Indeed, Luke seems intent on encouraging us to pray persistently: to ask, knock, seek. Yet this advice is more gnomic than it at first appears. We are not told that God will answer our prayers directly, or according to our (flawed and sinful) petitions and agendas. Rather, Luke suggests that God is consistent in his attentiveness, and will always answer in love. No one who wants bread will get a stone; no one who wants a fish will get a scorpion. Remember what the mystics say: God does not know how to be absent. He does not know how to forget you or overlook you. He sees every sparrow that falls. He numbers the hairs of your head.

God can only give good things. He can only bless; he does not curse. As the rabbis say, God rules by blessing. But we need the wisdom to see what he is giving as he blesses us. Prayer, then, is attuning the soul to God's heart and mind; our wisdom finding something of an echo with the wisdom that comes from above. Mature prayer is not a shopping list to place before God. It is the self placed before God, through which the needs and desires of the world and the individual can be set before the true light that cleanses 'the thoughts of our hearts', so that we can love and worship more perfectly.

As John Macmurray reminds us in his wonderful book *Persons in Relation* (1970), it is important to distinguish between genuine and deceptive religion. The philosophy of deceptive religion runs something like this: 'fear not; trust in God and he will see that none of the things you dread will ever happen to you'. But, says Macmurray, genuine faith and mature religion have a quite different starting point: 'fear not – the things you are most frightened of may well happen to you, but they are nothing to be afraid of'.

In the same vein, Harold Kushner, in his best-selling *When Bad Things Happen to Good People* (1978), reminds us that God is not fickle. Kushner is a rabbi who dedicated his book to the memory of his young son, Aaron, who died at the age of 14 of an incurable genetic disease. So the book is written by someone who prayed hard, but whose son still died. And here are reasons people give (but Kushner rejects) for why you might not get what you pray for: you didn't deserve it; you didn't pray hard enough; someone more worthy was praying for the opposite result; God doesn't hear prayers. Kushner also reminds his readers that there are improper prayers, at least according to the Talmud: God won't change what already exists (e.g. the earlier result from that football game, or the sex of a baby); he won't change the laws of nature (e.g. Origen – you cannot pray for the cool of winter in the heat of summer); someone else can't be harmed; we can't ask God to do something within our power, so that we don't have to do it – like pass my law exams for me.

So what's left to pray for? Well, for deep strength and Christian character, so that we can deal with adversity and reality. This seems to me to be partly what Jesus is driving at in this passage from Luke. God may not bring us success or what we desire, but he does offer justice. He will reward faithfulness:

> [P]eople who pray for courage, for strength to bear the unbearable, for the grace to remember what they have, instead of what they have lost, very often find their prayers answered ... God ... doesn't send us the problem; He gives us the strength to cope with it. (Kushner, 2001, pp. 125–7)

It was Bonhoeffer who, many years ago, said God loved us enough to see Christ pushed out of the world and on to the cross. God usually meets us in weakness, compassion and love; not in absolute power. Most people know the so-called 'Serenity Prayer', or at least the first part of it. Very few, however, know that the original was written by Reinhold Niebuhr in the darkest days of the Second World War. The prayer goes like this:

> God, grant me grace to accept with serenity the things that cannot be changed; courage to change the things which should be changed; and the wisdom to know the difference ... Living one day at a time, enjoying one moment at a time, accepting hardship as a pathway to peace; and taking, as Jesus did, this sinful world as it is. Not as I would have it, but trusting that you will make all things right, if I but surrender to your will. So that I may be reasonably happy in this life; and supremely happy with you forever in the next. Amen.

May almighty God give us all the faith, hope and love we need for our frail petitions. He always listens, he always loves – so let us always pray.

Note

H. Kushner, *When Bad Things Happen to Good People*, New York: Random House, new edn, 2001.

PART FOUR

High Days and Holy Days

76

Sonnet for St Mark

MALCOLM GUITE

Mark

A winged lion, swift, immediate,
Mark is the Gospel of the sudden shift
From first to last, from grand to intimate,
From strength to weakness, and from debt to gift,
From a wide desert's haunted emptiness
To a close city's fervid atmosphere,
From a voice crying in the wilderness
To angels in an empty sepulchre.
And Christ makes the most sudden shift of all;
From swift action as a strong Messiah,
Casting the very demons back to hell,
To slow pain, and death as a pariah.
We see our Saviour's life and death unmade
And flee his tomb dumbfounded and afraid.

77

Sermon for International Nurses' Day

MARTYN PERCY

Bible passages: Zephaniah 3.14–20; Matthew 28.1–10, 16–20

Spending much of my life, as I often do, reading student essays, I am continually struck by the declining standards in English language. But don't worry, this is not going to be a rant about how things used to be or could be. I am simply opening up in this way to make a point about how vital it is to pay attention to details, particularly in texts. And also to say something about the value of learning to read between the lines.

In her best-selling book *Eats, Shoots and Leaves* (2003), Lynne Truss draws our attention to how the sense of sentences can be altered by tiny and apparently inconsequential omissions. For example, if you omit the hyphen from extra-marital sex, you get a rather different cadence of what might be on offer later this evening. Equally, she adds, it is only with the introduction of a hyphen that the pickled-herring merchant can hold his head high. But what has this to do with us?

Well, strictly speaking, the Bible could claim to be a rather disorganized text. When the parts of the Bible that we now know as the New Testament were first written, they contained no punctuation. The texts were written in capital letters, with no distinction between upper and lower case. There were no chapter or verse numbers. No paragraphs. No subheadings. And that's just the Greek. The Old Testament uses Hebrew that has to be read from right to left, and often omits vowels when referring to the Almighty.

I mention this all for one simple reason. We often read texts – sacred and secular – through the sieves or lenses that others have bequeathed to us. We rarely stop to question whether the text, read freshly and without the overlaid interpretations and modifications of others, can mean something other than what everyone else once assumed it to mean. Such problems don't merely occur in religious traditions. You can find plenty of examples in various professions, or in the complex business of statecraft. When a simple word like 'invest' is used, it does not necessarily mean that there will be extra gravy, and with no economies. You can stretch a word like 'invest' to mean almost anything: 'investing more' can mean extra staff and resources.

But it can also refer more generally to time, energy, attention, and even to rationalization and savings. Streamlining can be a form of investing.

Similarly the plain meaning of a text is far from plain. For example, many people regard the end of Matthew's Gospel, chapter 28, as 'the Great Commission'. The words that Jesus is said to have uttered have been framed by a phrase he never used – 'great' and 'commission'. Moreover, the writer of Matthew's Gospel, as I have already said, did not provide his readers with subheadings. This particular one was added in many English translations of the Bible during the nineteenth century, to complement the burgeoning missionary activity of the Victorians throughout the Empire.

But in truth, whatever we might want to say about the text, it is not necessarily 'a', and certainly not 'the' Great Commission. Other words from Jesus might just as easily make a claim to be the Great Commission. What about 'love your neighbour as yourself'? Or 'turn the other cheek'? Or 'whatever you do for the least of these, you do also for me'? To put this more personally, and to put it to you, what is *your* Great Commission? What sends you out into the world, with hope and joy, and a mission to transform it?

The Christian life contains a number of competitive theories as to what its main priorities should be. But there is a common thread that runs through them all, and it is this. Out of the ashes of Good Friday, of failure, defeat and tragedy, hope and new life are born. And the disciples are to be the ambassadors of the new hope and transformation that is wrought in the person of Jesus. And this role is one that is primarily predicated on developing a dynamic sense of vocation. The resurrection, in other words, is something that does not draw disciples so much into a new sect, as it does send them out into the world, with joy, conviction and a desire to serve the world and the needs of others in the name of the living Christ.

Many of us who work in service-led and caring professions – whether in education, medicine, nursing, social work or the Church – are faced, daily, with a simple dilemma. How do we begin to complete and apply the task that our forebears bequeathed us? How do we bring resurrection and transformation to the base materials, situations and people that we are here to serve? How do we heal the sick, comfort the lost, illuminate the confused; bring hope, joy, peace and wisdom to those who are searching for or needing health and completeness?

Invariably, the things that inspire us – and here I choose my words carefully – are not the formal rules, regulations and codes that often govern our professions and institutions. I, for example, do not get especially excited by reading canon law, the Ordinal, or the Bishop's latest *ad clerum*. What motivates and inspires me in my life is the example of others. What is set out and lived in the life of others is what can transform us and make us into better people ourselves. One saint, in his own charge to his community, says: 'Go and preach the gospel throughout all the world. If absolutely necessary, use words.'

So what, then, of nursing, and its life as a career and vocation? In a world that is increasingly driven by codes of conduct, reviews, statements, numbers – our world is almost overly data-rich – we need to remember that many of the costliest and most worthwhile roles in society are about being and doing, and not about saying. The English word 'nurse', as I am sure you know, comes from an old middle English term – *nurcie* – which referred to the process of an infant suckling. The words 'nourish' and 'nurse' come from the same etymological stem. To 'nurse' was to feed and give life, to teach and to care, to protect and cherish. I am not, here, as I hope you will appreciate, trying to re-feminize nursing; nor am I trying to say that its significant professional and technological advances are somehow a betrayal of its soul. That would not be fair. But equally, however, it is always to pay deep attention to our original text. What makes us a profession is our vocation, and our roots.

In our own fragmented society we badly need a new ethic of nourishing and service in which all citizens participate, but in which others take a lead. Service cannot just be something we sell, procure or receive. To treat it like this would be tantamount to saying that what was once a role and a way of life is now only a collection of tasks.

I recall an incident during my own ordination training some 15 years ago. On placement in a parish, I found myself leading a Bible study on this Gospel passage (Matthew 28.1–10, 16–20). I invited the people in the group to reflect on an incident in their lives when they had humbled themselves. The stories were very moving. One spoke of costly service and support in the midst of demanding leadership. Another spoke of taking a lead in serving and performing very menial tasks while others enjoyed themselves. But when it came to the Vicar's turn to speak, he was stumped. Eventually he told a story about how he had once been humiliated and had not sought redress. The room fell silent. Then a woman spoke: 'There is a difference, you know, between being humiliated and being humble. They are related, but we want to know how you have humbled yourself.' He couldn't think of any time at all; the fear of losing his position, and of keeping his status, had stalked him all his life. He could not give an inch of the tiny ground he stood on.

In his seminal *After Virtue* (1981), Alasdair MacIntyre tells us that our society no longer speaks a shared moral language and has no sense of what the 'common good' might be. When we speak of goodness or service today, all we are doing is handling the fragments of an old system of thought, but without understanding that they are *fragments*: the vessel is broken. What society now needs, he says, is not a programme or a prescription, but rather persons who will help us to recover new forms of community and service that will endure through the new Dark Ages 'that are already upon us'. MacIntyre hopes for a new 'and no doubt very different St Benedict' who will achieve this.

For many, of course, Florence Nightingale did this in the nineteenth century. Moving among the sick and wounded, carrying a lamp, she brought care, skill and hope to those who were in the darkest situations. It is no accident that the motto of the Royal College of Nursing is an oblique but religiously resonant phrase: 'tradimus lampada' – 'we pass on the lamp'. One of the pre-eminent forms of care and service in modern times also has its own form of Great Commission. To make sure that the original flame burns brightly in all that we do, all that we stand for and all whom we seek to serve.

So I put it to you that the Great Commission for nursing is to continue paying attention to its roots. To truly connect with its call to pass on the lamp is simply this: to nourish the sick, and to do this in many and varied ways. Nourishing through the simple offering of our company, with kindness and care, with tenderness and time, with skill and compassion, with excellence and diligence, with imagination and vocation. In other words, for all of us who are engaged in the work of care and service, we need continually to think about how our profession and vocations were originally *punctuated*, as much as we need to pay attention to how they are now laid out in codes, texts and guidelines. Very often, it is the original charge or commission that continues to give life to the very purposes we have. Whatever subheadings our work now has, or whatever titles we may now possess, the cadence of our calling remains remarkably clear. We are to bring light. And with light comes hope, and the possibility of transformation through lives that are dedicated to the lives of others.

78

Time to Go: Ascension

SAM WELLS

Bible passages: Acts 1.1–11; Luke 24.44–53

One of the most helpful lessons I've learned about management is called the Four Stages of Work. Stage one is called Unconscious Incompetence – you don't know what you don't know.

We all know what that means – it means coming into a new environment and trying desperately hard not to embarrass yourself or show your ignorance or lack of appropriate skills. It means looking back and cringing at some of the things you said and did on your first day at work. The second stage is called Conscious Incompetence – you know what you don't know. This is what people call a fast learning curve – you realize there's a whole history, vocabulary, set of relationships and approach to the job you've got to master, and you have a sense of the scope of what those are but you know you're a way off having them just yet. The third stage is Conscious Competence – you know what you know. This is when you are thriving in your work and on top of every aspect of it. The task of the manager is to get you to this point as quickly as possible and keep you there as long as possible. But there is a fourth stage, called Unconscious Competence – where you've forgotten what you know. We all reach this stage sooner or later, and when we do it's time to stop or do something else. Those who like to say 'Son, I've forgotten more than you'll ever know' aren't doing themselves many favours, because the point is, they've forgotten it, so it's useless to them or anyone else. The people you want around are people nearing the end of stage two – and if you think you're turning into a stage four person it's time to look for another place where you can become a stage two or three person.

The trouble is, it's hard to retire. Even if the truth is that we've been at stage four for years, we create a fantasy that we can stay at stage three and remain consciously competent indefinitely. The fantasy may blend a number of layers of self-deception. We may say to ourselves, 'I don't think they could cope without me.' Or we could pretend, 'I want to get this organization to such a level that my successor can't ruin it.' Or we could think, 'I've given a lot to this place, the least I can ask in return is that I get to serve out my last few years without the same level of expectation on me.' Or we might have been humiliated by having been shown, perhaps repeatedly, how dispensable our services were and so be determined to hang on to a post so at last we would be the one to decide, rather than simply be told, when to leave. But in all these stories we may be hiding the truth, which may be more like this: 'If I don't come to work I don't know who I am – all I have left is the unresolved issues in my home, the mirror of my own mortality, and rather less money coming in to make either more palatable.'

Retirement is a relatively new phenomenon in human experience. It arises from increasing longevity, which means most of us live longer than our span of paid employment, and increasing affluence, which means more than a tiny minority can afford to spend their later days without a full weekly salary. It offers an opportunity that previous generations didn't have.

I want to suggest that the story and doctrine of Jesus' ascension to heaven may speak to the stories we tell ourselves about retirement. The doctrine of the ascension is pieced together from the different New Testament accounts. Mark and John tell us nothing about it. Matthew records a final conversation with the disciples on the mountain in Galilee but doesn't tell us what happened next. Luke seems to record all his Easter stories, including the one we read today of Jesus being carried up to heaven, as happening on one day. Paul assumes that Jesus who died and was raised is now at the right hand of the Father. Only the book of Acts gives us the time frame that shapes the Church's year, placing Ascension forty days after Easter and Pentecost ten days after that.

Ascension tends to be neglected in the Church's imagination. Those who get stuck on the physics of it find it hard to see past ancient paintings where Jesus' feet are glimpsed disappearing out of the top of the picture. Those for whom faith is largely a matter of personal piety concentrate on letting Jesus reign as king of their hearts. But both of these perspectives miss the key theological issues involved in Jesus' ascension, of which I suggest there are four, each of which I propose has something to say about retirement.

The first thing the ascension tells us is that Jesus stopped because he'd finished. He really had done everything he needed to do. He really had given us everything we needed to receive. This claim is at the heart of Christian theology, and the peg on which it hangs is called the doctrine of the ascension. But it is always unfashionable because Christians tend to be less thrilled with what God has done than they are bewildered by what God hasn't done. Given us life, given us creation, given us a covenant friendship, restored that friendship over and over, given us Jesus, given us forgiveness, given us eternal life, yeah yeah yeah blah blah blah. We take that part for granted. But what about hunger, what about disasters, what about AIDS, what about war? It is as if we are so mesmerized by the market economy that we see even our relationship with God as a market transaction and we feel the contents of salvation aren't what it said on the side of the tin, so we want our money back. All we can think of is what God hasn't given us.

And into this litany of what's wrong with God comes the doctrine of the ascension. Jesus went back where he came from because he'd finished. He'd finished. He didn't hang around to work on a few odd jobs around the edges of salvation – there was *no more to do*. A lot of us rebel against this – surely there's plenty left unredeemed in the world. How can Jesus have finished? Well, he had taken the poison out of the sting of sin, he had shown us the heart of God, and he had broken through the wall of death. In other words, he had done what only God could do, what matters most – and he had left the rest to us. This seems a good deal to me. Salvation remains today what it was on Ascension Day. Not a life without disappointment, a life without discomfort, a life without disillusionment; but a life with a faith to look back on, a hope to look forward to, and a love to live.

I am not holding up Jesus as a comprehensive model for retirement. I am not saying we should all go at 33 having achieved salvation for the world. But I do want you to notice the logic of what it means to say Jesus stopped when he had finished. It means none of us is indispensable. Jesus is indispensable – he did what no one else could or can. But you and I are not indispensable. If we live our lives thinking we are the only one who can save the world, we are not just insulting our colleagues, wearing out our family members and heading for burnout ourselves – we are denying that Jesus has already saved the world. Of course there are crisis moments when it may be we can bring something important or even unique to a situation: but to create a world in which every moment is one of those crisis moments is to make up a story in which we take the place of God. It is a lot easier to retire when you recall that Jesus has already done the real work.

I said there were four lessons from Jesus' ascension – so here's the second one. Wherever Jesus went on the day of his ascension – whether he really went up or just went up 'in a very real sense' – either way, he went some-where. Where did the bodily Jesus go? The point about the doctrine of the ascension is not so much that Jesus went up as that he went somewhere – and that that somewhere is at least as real as here. I say 'at least as real' because it may be more real. This life is passing, everything in this existence is relative, this world will one day pass away: but where Jesus is, at the right hand of the Father, is for keeps. What we call 'heaven' is the company of God – the presence of God where all are gathered as God's companions. Imagine that for a moment. There is another world, more real than this one.

What that means for retirement is that you don't have to get it all right this time round. People love to say 'life isn't a rehearsal'. Well it is, actu-ally. You don't have to get it all done, you don't have to leave it all tidy, you don't have to ensure it for ever remains just the way it is now. Jesus has gone to the place where all is as it should be, and the promise of the coming Kingdom is that God's heaven will someday come to God's earth, so that all is finally as it should be. Not because you and I got it right, but because God said, 'It is finished.' People do sometimes get depressed when they retire. It is a very serious matter. But we don't want to collude with the notion that when you finish work you have nothing to look forward to. You have everything to look forward to. You are a step away from thinking the world depends on you, and a step closer to discovering how everything depends on God. You are closer to the *real* real world.

And the third lesson from the doctrine of Jesus' ascension is that Jesus was fully human. That means he can only be in one place at a time. Ascension means that Jesus is no longer on earth – he is in heaven. Being divine didn't make Jesus any less human – it made him more human. It made him more alive, more aware of the wonder of creation, more bursting with joy and compassion and laughter and reflection, all those uniquely human attributes. But Jesus' being human, as we always reflect on at Christmas, means he also entered fully into the more mundane aspects of human life. And this brings us back to retirement. Because retirement is in many ways coming to terms with the more mundane aspects of human life. You haven't got a mask to put on each day to protect yourself from your fragile reflection in the mirror. But you are as fully alive as you ever were, as fully human as a young graduate starting out on a career.

And that brings us to the final lesson from the doctrine of the ascension. We find it in the words of the two men in white robes who speak to the disciples after a cloud has taken Jesus from their sight: 'Why do you stand looking upward towards heaven?' In other words, Jesus may have finished, but this could mean a whole new beginning for you. If retirement is just about looking back, is just about leaving, is just about wistfully pondering the past in nostalgia or regret, then it is bound to be distressing. But it must also be about the future. We may retire from work, but we don't retire from being a disciple. And while we may experience a vocation to a walk of life such as business, teaching, healthcare or even ordained ministry, that professional vocation never exhausts what it means for us to be a disciple. Retirement can be a time when we make new and transforming discoveries in understanding scripture, making friendships, enriching service, befriending children, sharing faith and building up the Church. The words 'Why do you stand looking up to heaven?' are a challenge to us to remember that God still has good things in store, that the best is yet to come, that the future is always bigger than the past.

Not everyone reading this may have thought much about retirement, but sooner or later it is an issue for almost all of us. Jesus' ascension shows us some significant things. It shows us he had finished, and thus that salvation doesn't depend on us, but on him. It shows us that there is another place more real than this one, and thus that we don't have to hold out in this life till we have everything just right. It shows us that Jesus was fully human, and thus not to be fearful or ashamed of our own human needs and frailties. And it shows us that there is no use lamenting what is gone because there are still fresh discoveries in discipleship to be made. And if we still face the reality of our retirement, sooner or later, with bewilderment, Jesus has the same transforming words for us as he had for the disciples that first ascensiontide. Whether you are on the threshold of retirement, or of any other of life's great transitions, think about these closing words: 'Stay in the city, and you will be clothed with power from on high.'

79

Up, Up and Away ...? Ascension

HELEN-ANN HARTLEY

Bible passage: John 17.6–19

For me, Ascension Day carries a number of important memories: it is the day on which I was confirmed; it is the feast day I chose to sit my driving test on, and passed, so it must have worked! But in my previous home city of Oxford, Ascension Day was the day local churches got 'out and about' and undertook a great tradition known as the 'beating of the bounds'. Picture the scene if you will, of appropriately robed clergy and choristers followed by groups of keen parishioners wielding long sticks making their way round a city centre marking out the boundaries of the parish. Never mind the fact that one of the parish boundary markers is now located in the lingerie department of a large store, never mind that, the gospel knows no boundaries quite like that! Beating of the bounds on Ascension Day was and still is an important reclaiming of church territory, an assertion that the connection between faith and land and property still matter, and indeed between faith and commerce, our city streets. On such a day, the deeper meaning of the Church being that which is 'called out' becomes important. We are not so much about the gathered as we are about being engaged with those round about us, those in our midst.

But even if it is just for ten days, all this talk of Jesus going away, how can we make sense of that?

In John 17.6–19, Jesus delivers one of his farewell discourses. John peppers his narrative with deep clues as to Jesus' identity, hints that Jesus is far more than he appears, in his humanity there is woven the profundity of divinity. We glimpse Christ, we see God, we see one another as the face of Christ, we become the presence of God in the midst of our peoples and communities. That Christianity had and has a strong commitment to ethical behaviour is a vital part of acknowledging that our faith is not just about words, it is about actions too. John offers us a window through which we can wonder about how it is that the resurrected Christ is not here and yet is here; is of this world and yet is not of this world.

I can almost hear my brain cells trying to engage.

Jesus here speaks the words in an extended prayer to God, like the depiction of the ascension narrative in Luke-Acts, Jesus looks upwards to heaven and addresses God as God himself of course. It is an example of what many call a 'thin place', where the barrier between things earthly and heavenly seems so thin you can reach out and touch beyond. Perhaps you can picture yourself in a location where you have felt close to God and have experienced a deeper sense of the mystery of the one who calls us into being and surrounds and enfolds us as we journey on.

Jesus looks up to heaven and talks to God. Jesus has made known God to those around him through his life and ministry; he has through his incarnation rooted himself in context. This of course is not a process without risk, and the typically Johannine language of love and hate pierces the beauty of this narrative discourse.

Love is a verb; it is a doing word. What Jesus is doing here is reminding his hearers (for we have to assume that his disciples are listening in to this conversation) that the implication of their having faith in him will meet with a hard response, as much as love impels us to reach out to one another, so in hatred, the world can turn against and reject, in ways that are violent and perverse. Faith just isn't meant to be neat and tidy.

Ascension Day isn't about Jesus saying 'beam me up, Scotty', it is something that makes it possible for the Church to come into being. This time between the ascension and Pentecost is a space in which we can wonder about how it is we came to be here, to reconnect with a sense of what Church is and what Church might be at this time. If we are to proclaim Christ as risen, ascended and glorified, then how are we to express this in ways that are helpful, meaningful and inspiring?

The answer to all of that isn't that hard, because for all the talk of 'fresh expressions' and trying to find new and jazzy ways of making faith appeal, we forget that we are actually the Body of Christ in the world. In sharing our gifts with one another, in service, in music, even in making the coffee, we are sharing in Christ's presence in our midst. It is not about the scientific impossibilities of ascending, that is not what the narrative asks us to consider, it is beyond that to a working out of how the Church, called out (that being the literal meaning of the word for church in Greek, *ecclesia*), welcomes others to gather, recognizing and celebrating the diversity of our community.

And it is so true that sometimes we simply don't know the effect that our lives will have on others, often in the most unexpected of ways and in the most unlikeliest of circumstances. But as this prayer of Teresa of Avila reminds us, ministry is indeed about incarnationally walking the walk and talking the talk because of Christ having done the very same thing in his earthly ministry.

Christ has no body now on earth but yours,
no hands but yours, no feet but yours;
yours are the eyes through which he is to look
with compassion on the world;
yours are the feet with which he is to go about doing good;
and yours are the hands with which he is to bless us now.

80

Pentecost

MARTYN PERCY

Bible passage: Luke 24.50–53

Pentecost commemorates a number of events. Principally, it marks the coming of the Holy Spirit after the resurrection and ascension of Jesus. A frightened group of bereft disciples are suddenly empowered by the Spirit, resulting in the birth of the Church. Luke, the writer of the book of Acts, begins his work by describing the phenomena, the Spirit settling on disciples like 'tongues of fire'. The disciples become apostles, sealed by the Spirit.

The use of the word 'tongue' is important here, for what follows in the book of Acts provides a narrative link. From tongues of fire, we move to speaking in tongues. According to Luke, the disciples are able to stand before a vast and cosmopolitan crowd and address each person in their own language. Suddenly, the apostles become multi-lingual, with the gospel being preached in Latin, Greek and the like.

Like me, you may have questions about the story, as well as the general phenomenon of speaking in tongues. And you are not alone. Although Pentecostalism and Revivalism claim to practise the art, the origin, use and interpretation of speaking in tongues requires more careful explication.

A preliminary observation to note here is that the account in the book of Acts can be read analogically. In the Old Testament (Genesis 11), the story of the Tower at Shinar tells of how all the different languages in the world came to be. Once upon a time, all nations spoke with one voice. But then people got ideas above their station, and decided to build a tower to heaven, in order to get on God's level. God, who liked his privacy and primacy, sowed dissension among the ranks of builders by inventing new languages that hampered the construction. Shinar became Babel, from which we derive the English word 'babble'. Not for the last time, an ambitious building project is scuppered through poor communication.

The account in Acts is probably an attempt to redeem and reconfigure this fable. The message is this. In the Church – a construction of the Spirit – all languages are recognized and spoken. The Spirit is universal, not local: the gospel is for all people. So, the first act of the Spirit is to reverse the tragedy of Babel: God now speaks to everyone, and the Church becomes a global *lingua*. The language is that of the Spirit.

It is important not to take the account in Acts too literally. When early Pentecostal missionaries thought they had received the gift of tongues at the turn of the century, they often assumed they were beginning to speak a new language that would enable them to preach the gospel in some far-flung corner of the globe. At the end of the century, more sober scholarship and reflection has drawn back from this.

On the matter of complete languages being spoken by people who have never learned them, most Pentecostal scholars now agree that there is no hard evidence of anyone miraculously receiving Arabic, French or Spanish directly from the Spirit, as the book of Acts implies. Academics in the field of consciousness studies also point out that you could not confidently speak a language you had never learned. Otherwise, how would you know you were saying 'Jesus is Lord' instead of 'Haddock and chips, please'?

I don't mean to mock. The more common tradition of speaking in tongues is that which Paul describes as 'sighs and sounds too deep for words'. But most linguists and psychologists agree that whatever these 'tongues' are, they do not add up to a language. It is more like an ecstatic utterance, a kind of 'sound salad' that is full of feeling and meaning, but with no vocabulary, grammar or anything else that could enable it to be translated. It is the articulation of the unutterable.

A teacher of mine who specialized in primal religion, and spoke the languages of the people he studied, would sometimes spend his sabbaticals visiting charismatic churches. When the time came to prophesy, he would often chip in, and speak one of the primal languages he knew so well. Congregations were invariably impressed and, without fail, his words were usually interpreted by someone 'led by the Spirit' – as a prophecy for the church, or a word of encouragement. But in actual fact he was simply repeating a recipe for a type of corn porridge made out of goat stock. This seems a bit cruel now, in retrospect. But the point he was making was a sincere one: tongues, whatever they are, are not languages in the way that we conventionally understand them. Tongues are, rather, sighs and groans too deep for words. They are modes of communication that defy translation.

But in interpreting tongues for our own time, what are we to say about deep and mystical experiences that seem to defy description – let alone clarification or understanding? I speak from personal experience, as one who found myself experiencing an intense spiritual epiphany at the shrine of St Frideswyde quite recently.

Granted, I can make some sense of that experience. I was baptized at one of the very few churches dedicated to her shortly before my first birthday. The graphic spiritual experience seemed to centre on the relationship between the water of baptism and the healing water she once drew from a well. But I cannot, I'm afraid, communicate in words anything of the intense, compelling and deep nature of what I felt on that afternoon that reduced me to my knees and rooted me to the spot. It just happened: it was undeniable.

So, what might tongues and Pentecost mean for us? I would like to make two brief observations. First, and as I have already implied, I do not consider the gift of tongues to be a 'language', but rather a kind of 'overflow' of praise; a release of the heart and mind when words will no longer do. As the French sociologist Danielle Hervieu-Leger puts it:

> One could ask whether the search for ... non-verbal forms of emotive communication does not also express a protest against the stereotype nature of approved religious language, something about the diminished quality of articulate religious quality in modern culture. The place taken in these groups by the gift of tongues raises the questions directly ... tongues, defined by scholars as 'phonologically structured human expression without meaning, which the speaker takes to be a real language but which in fact bears no resemblance to any language, living or dead', is not a vehicle for communication but for *expression*. The content is of little importance: tongues find [their] meaning not in what is said but in the very fact of speaking and responding, in this form, to an immediate experience of great emotional intensity. In the emotive response there is a general sensation of the presence of the divine, profound joy, and inward well-being which finds the means of expressing itself. (2000, p. 59)

And as one modern poet (Miller, 2007) puts it:

> ... years later a friend tells me
> tongues is nothing but gibberish – the deluded
> pulling words out of the dust. I want to ask him
> what is language but a sound we christen?
> I would invite him to a tent where women
> are tearing their stockings, are on the ground
> pulling up fresh words to offer as doves to Jehovah.
> I would ask him if he sees no meaning here
> and if he never had the urge to grunt
> an entirely new sound ...

Second, the gift of tongues reminds us that God – who was and is incarnate in Christ – remains radically available in our contexts and language: we hear the gospel in a tongue we can understand. This is important, for we can appreciate how easy it is to exclude all kinds of 'minority interests' in the Church. Black, lesbian, gay, feminist and other kinds of theology or Christian expression, for example, can be narrated as substandard or even offensive 'dialects', marginalizing them as 'bad language' over and against the suspect claim that the Church has one true language. Moreover (and perhaps tellingly for the Anglican Communion), the biblical text suggests that although the apostles spoke to their international audience 'each in their own tongue', it doesn't follow that the apostles necessarily under-stood one another at the same time. In fact, the message of Pentecost is that there are many tongues of fire. And because much is lost in translation, the hermeneutical task of the Church – what one theologian memorably describes as 'reaching across distances' – becomes even more urgent. The Caribbean theologian Kortright Davis expresses it simply enough:

> Western theologians are [now] attempting to educate themselves about the new theological surges emanating from the Third World. They have finally realized that there is no universal theology; that theological norms arise out of the context in which one is called to live out one's faith; that theology is therefore not culture free; that the foundations on which theological structures are built are actually not transferable from one con-text to another. Thus, although the gospel remains the same from place to place, the means by which the gospel is understood and articulated will differ considerably through circumstances no less valid and no less authentic. (1990, p. 70)

Quite so. Put another way, we might say that the lesson from Pentecost is that theology (or Christianity) is always spoken in tongues, so that each can understand in their own language (but, by the way, not necessarily one another). There is no Christianity that lacks a local accent; there is no one, singular 'pure' version. Theology and faith is always contextual, but that does not suggest an ultimate capitulation to eventual relativism.

On the contrary, the Pentecost experience can set the soul alight, so that the tongues produced themselves become mystical vehicles that produce harmony, unity and creativity. But we have to work on translation and interpretation in the meantime. In short, tongues of fire, flickering in the Babel of modernity (making sounds of significance in a world where mere words are losing their power) point us forward.

These are the signs and groans that are too deep for words. This is God's jazz: composition and improvisation blended together in dynamic spirit-ual overflow and praise. Text, music and tradition combine as the Spirit blows where it wills. We wait for the birth of an age to come: where all shall eventually see, speak and understand – face to face, each in their own tongue.

Notes

K. Davies, *Emancipation Still Comin': Explorations in Caribbean Emancipatory Theology*, New York: Orbis Books, 1990.

D. Hervieu-Leger, *Religion as a Chain of Memory*, Cambridge: Polity Press, 2000.

K. Miller, 'Speaking in Tongues', in *There is an Anger that Moves*, London: Carcanet Press, 2007.

81

Trinity Sunday

MARTYN PERCY

We only seem to be able to imagine the Trinity visually, as relations, persons in communion, iconically. But suppose, for a moment, we shut our eyes, and imagine that we don't have a visual imagination, we can only hear. What then? Polyphony, music, harmony, unity, diversity, purpose, rhythm, voices and silence suddenly become possibilities. The many tongues of Pentecost speaking of the Three in One and One in Three.

But before we get there, I want to say something about the Trinity today. I am not thinking of Don McLean's American Pie song – 'the three men I admire the most, the Father, Son and Holy Ghost'. I am more intrigued by films such as *The Matrix Reloaded*. Hollywood, that most ardent purveyor of secular discourse, seems to have found religion (again).

In *The Matrix Reloaded*, viewers are exposed to a full-frontal exposé of our spiritually saturated (yet opaque) postmodern world, in which we encounter characters called Trinity (a she, by the way) and Neo (a sort of Messiah) in their quest for Zion. And we discover a plot in which a computer-generated virtual reality Dark Age is battled against by the forces of light. Angels (who dress in cool black leather, shades, etc.) are pitched against demons (more cool – Armani suits, shades, etc.) for the soul of the true world. The film is yet another long Hollywood homily that extols the virtues of America's favourite myth: the power of redemptive violence.

But for most *Matrix* fans, the religious resonance will be mostly lost. This is a pity, as the scriptwriters have obviously gone to some trouble to offer a tale that could easily be interpreted as a kind of postmodern religious pastiche. In particular, it is surprising to see a character named 'Trinity'. Why? Because few Christians would really know what the word meant, even though it appears in the creeds and most of our collects.

Yet it is a fact that the word 'Trinity' does not appear in the Bible. Leaving aside the widely discredited reference in 1 John 5.7, there is nothing in scripture that explicitly links together the Father, Son and Holy Spirit doctrinally. The Christian doctrine of the Trinity was arrived at slowly and painfully over a 400-year period. Like many doctrines, it is a testimony to the partiality of truth as we know and experience it. It is partly a social consensus bound by time, and partly a political settlement that attempted to bind up arguments and paradoxes in order to capture the essence of a mystery – something that was glimpsed in a mirror, but only dimly.

The partiality of the witness of scripture is an important key in coming to terms with the Trinity. For the true Christian response to the mystery of the Trinity is not theology or philosophy, but worship. The complexity of the doctrinal formulae points beyond itself. God cannot be seen; his nature is hidden; truth is only dimly perceived.

Thirty years ago, two theologians, Daniel Hardy and David Ford, suggested that it might be fertile to think of the Trinity as music – and most especially as jazz. Their analogy offers an insight into the trinitarian nature of God: the composer–performer–listener linkage can resonate with the Father, Son and Holy Spirit. Music is also created in time, and yet creates its own time. It also involves law and freedom, and its practice always reveals 'more than there is'.

Music changes us too, by wooing us into participation. Music is 'a harmonic language' that is attentive to mood: sadness, celebration, reflection and dynamism are 'caught' in music. Moreover, music is a gift, and as we learn to read, understand and use it, we learn more about the God who has given it. Gifts express the giver.

In thinking about the Trinity analogously as jazz music, one becomes mindful of its combinations: its formal dimensions married to its innovative nature, and its capacity to cover a spectrum of needs from celebration to commiseration. Moreover, there are the many *different* sounds that make up *one* sound. Divine music is simultaneously scripted yet improvised, formal yet free. When the Church corresponds to the Trinity in worship and appreciation, it becomes an *orchestra* of praise and participation.

Likening the Trinity to jazz is not as strange as it first sounds. Jazz is a genre of music that is normally associated with both freedom of expression and formality, where improvisation and composition meet. It is both transforming yet traditional, never predictable and yet reliable. Order and freedom coexist, with passive listening turned into participation and communion. From an apparently tense synthesis of composition and improvisation, inspiration, liberation and dance can issue. To worship the Trinity is not to understand each note and sequence, nor is it to deconstruct the score musicologically: it is to listen, learn and participate.

Ultimately, all the doctrine of the Trinity is trying to do is say something about the abundance of God. In one sense, it is another way of speaking about justification by faith: God is there first, with us, on our side. The Trinity says the same: in God there is an excess, an overflow of grace, truth and love abounding – and it is near you. All our theology is nought but intellectual fumbling for truth and reality – a matrix that eludes us. But each insight on the Trinity represents a signpost along the way; something that says that the journey of faith is worthwhile. Yet it is in worshipping the Trinity, not understanding it, that you begin to enter the divine matrix.

So, as much as we might stare in wonder at our beautiful icons, and imagine how the Trinity looks, we do well to remember that these are simply aids to reflection. Artefacts that help us look deep inside and way beyond ourselves for the truth of the Trinity. And it is, in the end, not about theology, but worship, God known to us in mystery. If we close our eyes we can imagine the sounds of God, resonating in our lives and world, the Spirit with Christ drawing all things to the Father.

82

Sermon for John the Baptist

MARTYN PERCY

Bible passages: Isaiah 40.1–11; Luke 1.56–67, 80

According to a psychologist from the University of Hertfordshire who has studied humour, the world's funniest joke goes like this:

> Two hunters are out in the woods when one of them collapses. He doesn't seem to be breathing and his eyes are glazed. The other guy takes out his mobile phone and calls the emergency services.
>
> He gasps, 'My friend is dead! What can I do?' The operator says, 'Calm down, I can help. First, let's make sure he's dead.' There is a silence, followed by the sound of gunshot heard in the background. Back on the phone, the guy says, 'OK, now what?'

Humour depends on making connections that are a bit quirky. Our minds, I suppose, work by making patterns – stories or sayings, for example. But when a familiar connection is disrupted and an unexpected new link is made, laughter occurs as the new connection is made. This theory explains a lot about jokes. For example, why jokes are only funny the first time they are told: once they are told the pattern is already there, so there can be no new connections, and so no laughter. This is why jokes often rely on stereotypes: the use of a stereotype links to familiar expected behaviour, making the pattern easier to disrupt. Thus, 'a nun walks into a bar ... ouch' – just about works, but it is not that funny.

You may well remember from some years ago a TV programme called *Connections*. In the book and TV series, James Burke invited viewers and readers to consider how trivial, apparently incidental discoveries were in fact connected. For example, telecommunications exist because the Normans wore stirrups at the Battle of Hastings – a simple advance that caused a revolution in the increasingly expensive science of warfare. Europe turned its attention to making money to wage wars. As mineshafts were dug deeper, they became flooded, stimulating scientists like Galileo to investigate vacuums, air pressure and other natural laws to mine deeper silver. This led to the discovery of electricity and magnetism. And this relationship led to the development of radio, and deep-space telecommunications that may one day enable contact with galactic civilizations. But all of this is because of the stirrup, which afforded horsemen greater speed and direction. Big patterns are changed by tiny attention to detail.

So, and for example, when Jesus says, 'I am the vine, and you are the branches', he is speaking about some very real connections. He is saying, I suppose, that you and I, the Church, are very real extensions of his body: by tasting the fruit of the vine from the branches, you will know something of the real quality of the true vine. We are connected. We live in a world of deep and intricate connections.

So what has John the Baptist got to do with us? In what way does his life and example connect to what we are about? At the risk of another joke here, he is for ever the man who lost his head at a party, the one for whom death was ultimately brought about by a seductively placed wager. Here is a costly ministry that fought against opulence and vice, among other things – but was then ended at a feast. Yet the Gospels, it seems, cannot quite face this unbearable fate: the prophet killed in the midst of one of the very contexts he spent so much time preaching against.

Sometimes it is uncomfortable to own the connections that bind us to history, and perhaps to one another. Is it true, for example, that there couldn't be Blair without Thatcher? The one prepares the ground for the other. And so it is with John the Baptist: without him, there is no preparation for the Messiah. No John, no Jesus.

This is not as heretical as it may at first sound. After all, the Gospels make a virtue out of utilizing and subtly re-narrating the narrative from the book of Isaiah: 'Prepare ye the way of the Lord ... make way' is how it is expressed to us. Now, there are two senses of 'make way' here, and both are implied. One is clearly proactive, namely make *the* way: clear the path; make the rough places smooth; create the road. But the other is more humbling: 'make way', as in 'get out of the way', because he is coming. Here, we are to step aside, and take all obstacles, including ourselves, out of his path. For we are not the message or the messenger; the One who is to come is not to be obstructed.

Whichever way one reads the use of the passage from Isaiah by the synoptic writers, it is clear that for those who follow John the Baptist, the common denominator in the vocation is the ministry of preparation. For those of us who follow him, we are the seed, not the fruit; the cause, not the result; the start, not the finish; the beginning, not the end. We are those who prepare the way.

So, arguably, there cannot be a more apposite saint for Christians. For here the ministry of preparation is life-giving, one in which, behold, we are God's midwives, bringing new life into the world. The progeny he has begun and will continue. The fruit of the Spirit is planted in Mary; but it needs an Elizabeth and a John to help this all come to full term. John's role is to prepare the ground; to make a way in the desert. On this, Jesus can come.

I imagine in some small way that Jesus' words in the Gospel of John give us a vital connection to the ministry of John the Baptist and to that of Jesus. Significantly, Mark, the first and briefest of evangelists, places these words in a context in which the road is wide open. I refer, of course, to the very beginning of the Gospel of Mark, where the prophecies of Isaiah all seem to be coming true. And yet it is already the case that 'unless a grain of wheat falls into the ground and dies, it remains a single grain. But if it dies, it bears much fruit.' We already know how John's story will end, I think.

The connection here is one of paradox. Unless we step aside – die to ourselves – we cannot bear fruit. We must yield ourselves, our power, our identity, our heritage, ourselves, so that what God longs to give birth to will grow and flourish. This is no easy lesson, but it is the only one we have to ponder on as we learn from the example of John the Baptist. For in the end, John the Baptist's example embodies a kind of prayer: one that I think we all wish for every Christian, namely, to have a good death. I don't mean by that one of peace, surrounded by friends – because that is not always granted to us. By a good death, I mean one that brings life-bearing possibilities to others, that in letting go, finally, we make way for life.

I sometimes think that in my role at a theological college, and for the community more generally, the only ministry we have is that of John the Baptist, the ministry of preparation. It is to be a nurturing womb, a context and community that prepares and feeds but is ultimately supposed to let go. It is, I guess, a kind of mothering. And that is why we might celebrate Elizabeth today as much as we remember John. For she too has her ministry of preparation, of yielding, of letting go, of bringing to life, but then stepping aside, of bringing into being and preparing the ground – but all the while knowing that she is not the central actor in God's drama. Like all Christians, we are part of the supporting cast.

This is one reason why Elijah figures so prominently in Jesus' teaching, and in early Christian writing. Elijah finds the God of Abraham outside Israel. Like Moses, to whom Jesus also looked, God is also encountered in the wilderness, and beyond tribal boundaries and national borders. And like Elijah, John the Baptist cared enough about society, and his enemies, to protest against the abuses of power and inequality. He loved individuals and society enough to summon the words – in sermons and speeches – that spoke against the forces of evil abuse. Like Elijah with Ahab, John the Baptist loved his enemies; prayed for those who persecuted him. Like other prophets before him, and since, his passion and love meant he paid with his life. His ministry could not have been more costly.

John the Baptist's day is, then, a bitter-sweet feast. For we remember and celebrate a life that was cruelly cut short: 'the grass withers and the flower fades', as Isaiah puts it rather gently. But God is coming, and John's ministry was to make way – to prepare the ground for the coming of the Messiah. Unless this grain of wheat had fallen into the ground, there could be no fruit.

It is John's willingness to both make way and give way that is so remarkable – his ministry of preparation, a life of extraordinary sacrifice, in which the connection between repentance and hope is now fully realized. And John the Baptist prays one of the few short prayers that we as followers of Christ ever need: 'He must increase – and I must decrease.'

83

Sonnet for John the Baptist

MALCOLM GUITE

Love's hidden thread has drawn us to the font,
A wide womb floating on the breath of God,
Feathered with seraph wings, lit with the swift
Lightening of praise, with thunder over-spread,
And under-girded with an unheard song,
Calling through water, fire, darkness, pain,
Calling us to the life for which we long,
Yearning to bring us to our birth again.
Again the breath of God is on the waters
In whose reflecting face our candles shine,
Again he draws from death the sons and daughters
For whom he bid the elements combine.
As living stones around a font today,
Rejoice with those who roll the stone away.

84

Sonnet for St Peter

MALCOLM GUITE

Impulsive master of misunderstanding,
You comfort me with all your big mistakes;
Jumping the ship before you make the landing,
Placing the bet before you know the stakes.
I love the way you step out without knowing,
The way you sometimes speak before you think,
The way your broken faith is always growing,
The way he holds you even when you sink.
Born to a world that always tried to shame you,
Your shaky ego vulnerable to shame,
I love the way that Jesus chose to name you,
Before you knew how to deserve that name.
And in the end your Saviour let you prove
That each denial is undone by love.

85

Sonnet for St Thomas the Apostle

MALCOLM GUITE

'We do not know ... how can we know the way?'
Courageous master of the awkward question,
You spoke the words the others dared not say
And cut through their evasion and abstraction.
O doubting Thomas, father of my faith,
You put your finger on the nub of things:
We cannot love some disembodied wrath,
But flesh and blood must be our king of kings.
Your teaching is to touch, embrace, anoint,
Feel after him and find him in the flesh.
Because he loved your awkward counterpoint,
The Word has heard and granted you your wish.
O place my hands with yours, help me divine
The wounded God whose wounds are healing mine.

86

Sonnet for St Mary Magdalene

MALCOLM GUITE

Men called you light so as to load you down,
And burden you with their own weight of sin,
A woman forced to cover and contain
Those seven devils sent by Everyman.
But one man set you free and took your part,
One man knew and loved you to the core.
The broken alabaster of your heart
Revealed to him alone a hidden door,
Into the garden where the fountain sealed,
Could flow at last for him in healing tears,
Till, in another garden, he revealed
The perfect love that cast out all your fears,
And quickened you with love's own sway and swing,
As light and lovely as the news you bring.

87

Sermon for a Festival of Celebrating Gifts of the Spirit

MARTYN PERCY

Bible passages: Galatians 5.22–26; Luke 4.14–30

Kate Fox, in her book *Watching the English*, uses an interesting word to capture our national fondness for moderation and complaining. 'Eeyeorishness' is her word for mild moaning and an unerring capacity for understatement. 'Mustn't grumble', 'OK, I suppose', 'could do worse', 'curates' egg', 'all things in moderation' are part of the national canon of our most cherished casual phrases. It is as though passion and excess were some kind of nasty continental disease that you might get on holiday – a rash, as it were, to be treated with cream.

Anglicanism, as you probably realize, rather plays up to this. It is a relaxed, mild, temperate form of ecclesial polity, not easily given to extremes. Rather like the climate of the nation that gave birth to its national Church, it is often overcast, but also occasionally sunny; mild, with warm spells. We imagine meteorological extremes, but they are, in reality, merely trifles. As Bill Bryson observes in his *Notes from a Small Island*, the world giggles when our newspapers have headlines like 'Phew, what a Scorcher' or, more risibly, 'Britain sizzles in the 70s'. In most parts of the USA and the Continent, that is a cue to fetch the cardigan – not strip off and sit down with an ice cream, plus a flake.

One of my predecessors at Cuddesdon used to describe Anglicanism as a matter of 'passionate coolness'. I rather like this stylistic interpretation of the Anglican mood, since it suggests an actual energy for temperate ecclesial climes. But it has a weakness too, which is that people can often dwell on the comfort that the accommodation and temperance bring. And temperance can be an over-rated virtue if it is allowed to dictate moderation and exclude the excess of passion. If it sets the tempo all the time, then the radical of excess, which drives religion, is inhibited.

One of the characteristics that marked out the early Christian saints is that they understood faith to be passion. Faith, in terms of discipleship, is often not reasoned coolness. It is passion that spills over, the love that is stronger than death. It might be thought through. It may even be willed reason. But it has to be willed with every fibre of your being. I mention this because it is sometimes easy to misunderstand the place of religion in the modern world, and for people of faith to collude – unintentionally, and sometimes naively – with secular reasoning.

For example, excessive, passionate faith is not the same as extreme faith. The former is intemperate and immodest; but it abounds in energy and love because it cannot spring from the liberty of God. It is released as a kind of raw energy, precisely because it breaks the chains of inhibition, and springs forth from spiritual encounters that can border on ecstasy. But this is not, as I say, extremism. It is merely passion resulting from encounter, conversion, conviction, resurrection and transformation.

Or then again, think about how the Enlightenment and the legacy of modernity has made religion into some kind of 'subject' that is essentially apart from 'ordinary' life. It is as though a religious experience was specious, atypical and abnormal. We talk too easily of having a 'religious' or 'spiritual' experience, as though all other kinds of experiences were 'normal'.

But if you turn the phrase around for the moment, you might ask yourself what might it mean to have a 'secular experience'? It would be an odd phrase to use – even in conversation with an atheist. Yet most religious people have accepted the goalposts being moved all too easily. Religions have allowed themselves to be marginalized and particularized, and have even naively participated in the progressive programme of modernity's de-normalization. Religious passion, then, is often narrated as extremism – in most newspapers, TV news reports, and the like. Religious experience is seen as 'specious', when in fact spiritual feelings and intimations of the divine are perfectly normal and very commonplace. But under such prevailing and reigning secular conditionality, spiritual restraint quickly becomes a virtue that services the controlling of religion: 'all things in moderation', as the English say.

But I'd like to suggest that this understanding of temperance is actually an abuse of the term. Temperance is not about control from without. It is, rather, the deep spiritual exercise of restraint for the sake of the self and the other. It is a spiritual discipline and a virtue that can only be exercised in proportion to the energy and passion that wells up from the same source. It is not a dainty refusal to take an extra portion. It is a steely and willed act of moderation or self-control that emerges out of passionate convictions, grace and love. That is why the list of the fruits of the Holy Spirit from Galatians is so important. Love, joy, peace, patience, kindness, self-control, humility, gentleness and faithfulness are all rooted in the passion of Christ – a putting to death of our desires, and seeing them reconfigured through the Holy Spirit into the heart of God. So excess and abundance are of God; extremism, however, is of the flesh.

In terms of Christian discipleship, these observations are important for several reasons. First, spiritual passion is not just about the expulsion of energy. It also has another meaning in religion which is concerned with the absorption of pain, sacrifice and suffering – like the passion of Christ. Here, passion is absolutely for the other; but it is passion that is almost entirely configured in its receptivity. Much like the passion of a parent or a lover, God's passion is sometimes spoken in eloquent silence; in sacrifice and in endurance; in solidarity and in suffering; in patience, kindness, self-control, humility and gentleness.

Second, it is perhaps important to remember that the example of the saints – those people who inspire us in our faith – is often to be found in the delicate combination of passion, practice and reason. You might be surprised at this, but one of the qualities I sometimes look for in ordinands is the inability to contain their passion – for the Church, for Christ and for others. I don't think there are many laurels or crowns being dished out in heaven for being slightly left-of-centre. Discipleship is not about being liberal, conservative or even somewhere in the middle. It is about knowing your place before God and being passionate for the possibility of the Kingdom.

Third, the temperance we seek – which is good and rightful for social ordering and ecclesial polity – should not be allowed to blunt the energy and enthusiasm that flows from living the gospel. To be sure, orderedness and calculation have their place. But if they are allowed to control and marginalize passion, then there is a great danger that temperance can become totalitarian. The excess of energy, at this point, is almost guaranteed to be narrated as extremism. But religion, of course, is about extremes: extreme love, extreme sacrifice and extreme selflessness that go beyond reason. Religion in moderation is, arguably, a contradiction in terms. It should offend, cajole, probe and interrogate. More colloquially, one might say that a faith that does not get up your nose is hardly worth the candle.

So when Jesus stands before his congregation in the synagogue and speaks, we have a proclamation, even though it is misunderstood, about the excess and abundance that God intends for all who suffer and struggle. But it is not about extremism. The work of the fruit of the Spirit is already here. The Kingdom will not be known for moderation, but for liberation. The gospel is a new power; it is foolishness; it is offence. It is, in its purest form, a radical expression of the in-temperate – God's radical risk in Christ; a love that is stronger than death; a passion and zeal for the other that is beyond manners or common sense.

This is why the language of the Bible is sometimes stark. The manna that rains down from heaven does not drizzle – it rains. The Lord appears in a dazzling cloud, and in fire. The message of the New Testament is 'make a choice' for Christ; it is not 'suck it and see'. Our call, then, is to consider the radical nature of commitment, and to call others to this radical discipleship. This is a faith that revels in the excessive, but is not extreme. It is passionate, and yet compassionately held in such a way as to be persuasive rather than repellent. So you may find this strange, but I happen to think that the good old Church of England might just be on to something here. It is easy to despair of its tepid nature and its interminable vacillations.

And yet, I find it strangely full of the fruits of God's Spirit – exactly the kinds of abundance and generosity listed in Galatians. As Paul says of the fruits of the Spirit, there are no laws against such things. So as we celebrate the gift of the Holy Spirit, let us also celebrate this part of Christ's body – the Church of England – into which God has been gracious enough to cultivate an abundance of fruit to savour.

88

Transfiguration

HELEN-ANN HARTLEY

Bible passages: Daniel 7.9–10, 13–14; 2 Peter 1.16–19; Luke 9.28–36

The intrepid detective duo Sherlock Holmes and Dr Watson, in preparation for their adventure, decided to go hiking. At the end of a long day, they pitched their tent under the stars and went to sleep. Sometime in the middle of the night Holmes woke Watson up and said, 'Watson, look up and tell me what you see.' Watson replied, 'I see millions and millions of stars.' Holmes said, 'And what do you deduce from that?' Watson replied, 'Well, if there are millions of stars, and if even a few of those have planets, it's quite likely there are some planets like Earth out there. And if there are a few planets like Earth out there, there might also be life.' And Holmes said in a rather exasperated tone, 'Watson ... it means that somebody stole our tent.'

You may have heard that joke before, or variations thereof, but its point is simple: sometimes we try our best to say what is in front of us but in so doing, maybe by the language that we use or the paths we take to navigate tricky realities, we risk missing the obvious.

Like Dr Watson, the disciples in the passage from Luke (9.28–36), which also features tents, fail to see or indeed to understand what is in front of them.

The transfiguration focuses on Jesus' identity and his place in the purpose of God. In the verses just before this passage, Peter declares Jesus to be the Messiah, but this episode reveals that this disciple does not yet appreciate what this means.

But this event in Jesus' life is much more than an example of the impact of holy washing powder, an advertiser's dream of a substance that can transform any white shirt into a dazzling white glow; it is more than a reflection on how to stay calm when the clouds descend around us and we can't see further than the tip of our nose; we don't all have access, after all, to a holy satellite navigation system that can show us the way to go. At the very least we need to navigate ourselves into a place of figuring out just what transfiguration means. An attempt to Google the word pretty swiftly takes you to a Harry Potter website. Leaving that to one side, consulting a theological dictionary more helpfully (perhaps), tells us that transfiguration is about a change that glorifies or exalts.

While this Gospel story of the transfiguration is about a deepening of identity, it is not just Jesus' identity; it is also about what we see and what we do not see and how we fit into all of that. We can sit and listen to the gospel passage, but, we may well ask, what has that got to do with us, where we are now? The Australian author John Marsden's *Tomorrow* series tells the story of how a group of teenagers respond to the surprise invasion of their country. They head out into the wilderness for a camping trip, and return to discover an altogether changed state of affairs. Told from the perspective of one of the characters in the story, Ellie, the narrative is written in the narrator's present. Near the end of the first book, which is entitled *Tomorrow, When the War Began*, Ellie reflects: 'It's hard to work out where stories begin – I seem to remember saying that at the start of this one. And it's hard to work out where they end, too. Our story hasn't ended yet' (Marsden, 1993, p. 283).

The story is told because of the relationship that the narrator has with her own story and that of her companions, and a desire to impart wisdom to others for the ongoing journeys of their lives through the shared knowledge of what has taken place. In this way the narrative is future-oriented, which is of course reflected in the first word of the book's title: *Tomorrow*. This narrative of past, present and future is very much part of how the Gospel story works, and especially so because this transfiguration story doesn't end with future glory; the glory is right in the middle of the action, half-way through, perhaps where we expect it the least. Although we are located in a particular place at a particular time, we are inevitably linked to the generations of Christians in the past and those that will follow us. The transfiguration is therefore also about the role and purpose of tradition. Great figures from Israel's past, Moses and Elijah, appear in the story, but their role is to allow tradition to help us see things in new ways, in ways that can challenge and surprise us, if we allow them to, ways that perhaps were there all along, only we didn't realize it to be so. Likewise, in its anticipation of the journey to Jerusalem, using the language of the Exodus, that nation-shaping event of Israel's past which also forms part of its present identity, the transfiguration story looks beyond to the resurrection; it challenges our humanity out of complacency towards accountability.

To give Dr Watson his due, back where we started, he was (so he might argue in hindsight) looking beyond the absence of the canvas that had previously provided shelter to engage with the wonder of the night sky. So we mustn't forget that as the transfiguration confronts us with the reality of who Christ is, it also connects our rootedness with eternity, where in Jesus' identity we see God-with-us – Emmanuel, the same yesterday, today and for ever. The poet Seamus Heaney describes, in one of his poems, how some monks were at prayer when:

A ship appeared above them in the air.
The anchor dragged along behind so deep
It hooked itself into the altar rails
And then, as the big hull rocked to a standstill,
A crewman shinned and grappled down the rope
And struggled to release it. But in vain.
'This man can't bear our life here and will drown,'
The abbot said, 'unless we help him.' So
They did, the freed ship sailed, and the man climbed back
Out of the marvellous as he had known it.

(from Heaney's collected poems, *Seeing Things*)

Notes

S. Heaney, from 'Lightenings', in *Seeing Things*, London: Faber & Faber, 1991.
J. Marsden, *Tomorrow, When the War Began*, Sydney: Macmillan, 1993. This book
was released as a film in 2010.

89

Transfiguration

MARTYN PERCY

Bible passage: Luke 9.28–36

There are two occasions in the Christian year when we hear the Gospel describing the transfiguration. The first is on 6 August, the Feast of the Transfiguration. The second is the Sunday before Lent. Both work well. The story looks forward to the very end of Lent, Easter Sunday – the Son of Man glorified and raised, dazzling. But the feast day also shares another anniversary, the Enola Gay over Hiroshima, Japan, 6 August 1945. A cloud, a dazzling light. The transfiguring in a weapon of mass destruction.

When you read the story of the transfiguration, the first thing that might strike you is its strangeness. There is a dazzling light – but yet a cloud. There is revelation; yet things are hidden. There is a voice; yet we do not know what is truly heard. Clouds are common imagery for divine presence, and they serve an ambiguous purpose, to remind us that the revealed remains hidden, that the extraordinary comes to us in the ordinary.

In a mirror image to the gospel account, Elijah puzzles over the presence and absence of God. Surely God will be in the earthquake, or the wind, or the fire? But no; God is in the silence. God does not shout; God whispers. And here we sense the 'thick sound of silence' in God's heart, as he waits for Elijah to be fully attentive.

In today's world we are bombarded with noise. When my sons are ever away, I have noticed how eerily quiet the house can be, as I have worked at home. The most noise I have to cope with in the morning is the melodic wallpaper music of Radio 3, and the occasional well-modulated and gravelly voices of Radio 4. But it is basically quiet.

But there are many kinds of silences. In the Gospel story, Jesus and three disciples break away from the crowds and the hubbub to get some peace, quiet and calm. It is in this context that the transfiguration happens. In a place of solitude and quiet. And it is interesting to note that the transfiguration story ends when Peter speaks; the end of silence breaks the spell.

As there are many kinds of silence, so there are many types of listening. A church cannot be a teaching church unless it is a learning church. A church that speaks cannot truly speak unless it can listen. Now, there is listening and listening, but the listening that God asks of us is a deep listening. In the words of that famous song, we need to learn to listen to 'the sound of silence'. Deep prayer is founded on the discipline of deep listening.

I often wonder how the transfiguration story might have looked if Jesus had taken three different people with him up the mountain. Say, for example, Mary Magdalene, Luke and perhaps another. I wonder, first, if the vision would have been interrupted by any of them, as Peter did. And I wonder if anyone would have suggested a building project. Recall Peter: 'Let us build three booths.' Typical. To every epiphany, mystical experience or revelation, there is someone on hand to turn it into a religion. But this course is rejected by Jesus. Building three booths is pointless. God is not going to be cooped up in a booth with his friends. Peter's response, as on other occasions, shows a remarkable lack of understanding. He should listen and watch; but he talks, and tries to build.

In the middle of this ex-stasis – standing outside oneself – Peter's instinct is to routinize, memorialize and religionize. Let us enshrine the experience. Let us have raiments that are white and glisten; incense for clouds, the apostolic succession of Moses, Elijah and Jesus. Let us make a memorial and a place for the ethereal. Let me speak, let me build. But Peter is only required to do one thing: watch, and say nothing; listen. It is interesting, isn't it, that the moment Peter speaks, 'a cloud overshadowed them'. And that Peter only spoke because he didn't know what to say.

Some years ago I was powerfully reminded of this. I had been in my own fog. I had wondered about my job, my work and my future. I had talked much, and I had waited for a sign. But all I had was the fog; and like Elijah (and like many men), I retreated to my cave – my shed, as it were. Spiritually, I was a little lost – halfway up a foggy mountain, stuck in a cave. Like the disciples.

The story of the transfiguration is about learning to live with the cloud *and* the light, and learning that the voice of God comes in the quiet ways. Our demand for a sign is, more often than not, childish. This is partly what this encounter in the Gospels is all about. There is the bread that we eat, and there is bread … the bread that truly feeds us. God wants us to cultivate a patience and a stillness that can truly discern the depth of his presence, and can truly listen. It is no accident that the transfiguration story ends with these words: 'This is my beloved Son; *listen* to him.' It is what we don't do, so often.

But what is deep listening? Several things come to mind. First, it is about the development of a slow, patient spirituality. In our world of instant food, we expect instant results, instant nourishment and instant answers. But spirituality is a slow business; it is a gentle marathon, not a sprint. Listening comes about by becoming attuned to the silent, subtle voice of God. It is often mellifluous. It is about real bread.

Second, deep listening comes through deep relationships. It is about a depth of attending to the other. It is not a technique, but part of a committed relationship in which there is a willingness to give of yourself, and also receive. It is born of desire – deep desire – to both know and to be known.

Third, it is about restraint. For someone to speak, someone must be silent. And for someone to speak, truly, there must be someone to listen. Being listened to fully is a deep privilege, and although we often presume that God will listen to us in prayer, it is rare, perhaps, for us to expect God to speak to us, and for us to listen. We need to be silent.

In the stillness of this season, we sometimes have the opportunity to pause and reflect more deeply than perhaps we normally do on the space we need to be still. It can be a time when we resolve to say less and listen more – to each other and to God. This is important, because sometimes what seems natural and obvious to us is not what God would have us do. The transfiguration story cuts through our plans, words and activities, and says powerfully, 'listen'. Above all, we are sometimes asked to wait. We cannot hear God in a microsecond; we have to stop so we can engage and hear. It takes time.

Waiting for God can often mean being available to God in silence. In Christian ministry, we can often become absorbed with doing – this is, ultimately, Elijah's problem, and Peter's. They are both activists, and used to seeing the hand of God in works and wonders. But as for hearing God, they have yet to learn of his deep silence – the conduit through which he speaks. So the lesson is to stop doing and take time to listen. The presence of God is in the cloud; the voice and the light are behind it. It is in the sound of silence that we can begin to hear the stirrings of God. It is in waiting that we are directed.

90

Sonnet for St Matthew

MALCOLM GUITE

First of the four, Saint Matthew is the Man;
A Gospel that begins with generation,
Family lines entwine around the Son
Born in Judaea, born for every nation,
Born under Law that all the Law of Moses
Might be fulfilled and flower into Grace;
A hidden thread of words and deeds discloses
Eternal love within a human face.
This is the Gospel of great reversal:
A wayside weed is Solomon in glory,
The smallest sparrow's fall is universal
And Christ is the heart of every human story:
'I will be with you, though you may not see,
And all you do, you do it unto me.'

91

Sonnet for St Michael and All Angels

MALCOLM GUITE

Michaelmas gales assail the waning year,
And Michael's scale is true, his blade is bright.
He strips dead leaves, and leaves the living clear
To flourish in the touch and reach of light.
Archangel bring your balance, help me turn
Upon this turning world with you and dance
In the Great Dance. Draw near, help me discern,
And trace the hidden grace in change and chance.
Angel of fire, love's fierce radiance,
Drive through the deep until the steep waves part;
Undo the dragon's sinuous influence
And pierce the clotted darkness in my heart.
Unchain the child you find there, break the spell
And overthrow the tyrannies of hell.

92

Harvest

MARTYN PERCY

Bible passage: Mark 10.23–27

At this time of year, churches will be awash with tinned food, packets of cereals and various displays of local produce. Improbably large marrows will jostle for position with baskets of fruit; loaves of bread will vie with sheaves of wheat. Brownies, Cubs, Scouts and Guides will parade, and the clergy will try to say something sensible about Harvest Festival, a curiously popular service, despite the fact that people's connection with food is mostly with supermarkets and fast-food restaurants, and hardly ever directly with the land that provides the food.

Although there is a sense in which harvest has always been celebrated (Lammas and Rogationtide come to mind) the modern fondness for harvest is traceable to the Revd Robert Hawker, a Devonian priest, who began the new services we now recognize as 'harvest festival' in 1843, at his parish in Morwenstow in north Cornwall. It was Hawker who, building on earlier Saxon and Celtic Christian customs, began to decorate his church with home-grown produce, a practice that has now become widespread for 150 years. Throughout the Victorian era, the festival was steadily embellished and romanticized, probably to act as a counterweight to the growing influence of the Industrial Revolution and secularization.

R. S. Hawker was a typically interesting clergyman. As an undergraduate at Pembroke, he was told one day that his father could no longer afford the fees. It is said that he instantly rode to Cornwall and proposed to his very wealthy godmother, a woman 21 years his senior called Charlotte Eliza Rawleigh. She rode back with him to Oxford 'pillion style', where he remained as a kept man for the rest of his time as an undergraduate. She died at 81 years of age and at her funeral Hawker wore a bright pink brimless hat, for which he claimed the Eastern Orthodox churches offered sanction. He continued as Vicar of Morwenstow, and married again the following year.

My point here is perhaps obvious. Faced with poverty (if leaving Pembroke early counts as this), Hawker found a solution. So what, then, are we to make of Jesus' rather laissez-faire attitude to wealth and provision? Most of us might not go to the lengths Hawker did to resolve our financial difficulties – but the Gospels rather suggest we shouldn't even bother trying.

The poignancy of Jesus' words is rather haunting, is it not? Can you imagine churchwardens escorting an archdeacon around a church on a quinquennial visitation and saying, 'Well, we could repair the tower, but having read Matthew 6.25–33 we have decided to take Jesus at his word and not worry too much about the state of the buildings. God will provide.' It is important to understand the words of Jesus in context. The Church is always a halfway house. Halfway between heaven and earth, ideology and reality, and being a human work and a divine revelation. It is, in other words, incarnational – divinity and humanity, as the living body of Christ. So, on the one hand, we have few cares, for it is Christ's body. On the other, we have to work like fury to nourish that body, pay due regard to its members and care for it.

So, Jesus is not actually advocating a kind of laissez-faire attitude to the Church, including its buildings and structures. Rather, he is saying that God does provide: that is the good news. The bad news, if you will, is that he will provide through you and me. The reading in Joel puts it well: we are to rejoice at the harvest, the growth and the provision of God – he provides the rain and the sun.

But don't forget to plant the seeds and prune the vines: there will be no bread and no wine if you don't do some of the work yourself. The growth of God's Church is a spiritual partnership, not only with one another, but also with God, who multiplies our gifts.

To be sure, it will be hard going at times. However, growth is often painful in places, for individuals or communities. We will be no different; but we should remember that the opposite of growth is not maintaining the status quo – it is normally imperceptible decline. We want our churches to live and work to the praise and glory of God – it is as simple as that. That requires intensive prayer, working together, imagination, hard work and deep engagement with our communities and our own lives. It requires sacrifice too. We worship a God whose being is centred on love and gift; as we receive, so shall we love and give in return. If we trust God, 'all these things shall be added unto you'.

I want to make three brief points. First, a word from Dennis Potter, the playwright, before he died: 'Religion is not the bandage – it is the wound.' Yes, we turn to Christ and the Church for comfort, hope and healing. But in receiving it, we are marked by the cross, which requires us to expend our own lives sacrificially in offering and gift.

Second, we are a communion of people, one part of the body of Christ. We have a real responsibility to care for that body, and participate with God in its growth in our spiritual lives.

Third, money is not the answer to everything, and it isn't the answer to all our needs or prayers. The most rewarding part of raising money for our buildings is working and praying together, discovering new gifts in ourselves and others that God has already bestowed. Money raised is the by-product of that fellowship.

That is why, with Timothy, we do not simply seek money for its own sake; our security does not rest there. Where it does rest, however, is in 'godliness combined with contentment', to quote Paul's letter to Timothy – which we can only aspire to if we have worked hard and prayed hard.

But if all of this is about the nourishing of our inner life, what then about the fruits of our discipleship for a wider world? At harvest time we think about gift, growth, fruit and nourishment. We reflect on this in a world that is hungry, and in a world that aches and longs for justice and equality.

This is why God speaks to us about the simple things of life, and in so doing invites us to reflect on something much richer. Again, I want to make three small points. First, you cannot guess what will come of the seeds you plant, and the seeds that are planted in you. Some seeds are tiny, and some are huge. But the biggest seeds do not necessarily produce the biggest plants or the most food. Some of the tiniest seeds produce the most. As we reflect on God's provision, we are sometimes asked not to despise the tiny things that can easily be overlooked. They sometimes have the most to offer.

Second, fruit is complicated. Think of an orange. With its unique skin, it can float in water. But if you take the skin off, and thereby make the orange lighter, what happens? It sinks. The skin is, in other words, a kind of lifejacket provided by nature. We peel it off and throw it away, thinking nothing of it. But for the fruit this provides buoyancy and protection, enabling the fruit to travel to new places when it falls.

Third, seeds and fruits have more than one use. One New Year's day a few years ago, I read the following advert in my newspaper, which reminded me of the importance of connections:

Why not buy a tree for Africa as your gift to the world this year. For the same £3 a foot you paid for a Christmas tree, you can buy a tree for Hope for Africa ... which is planting thousands of trees in the [most] fragile areas, providing income and nutrition for local people ... you could buy a *dowadowa* tree, which grows to 45 foot. It is known as 'the tree that is blessed by God', because it provides so much ... its seeds are used to make *soumbala* balls, a local delicacy that women sell. Young roasted pods makes sweets in times of plenty, and are dried in times of famine. Leaves feed the cattle; the twigs make toothpaste; the gum hardens earth floors and can be used to glaze pottery; the flowers treat leprosy; the roots treat epilepsy, and can also be made into strings for musical instruments; the bark is used for tanning, for plastering huts and for embalming – other parts of the tree are used in marriage, childbirth and initiation rituals.

This tree is a kind of parable. It suggests that our lives and our work – offered aright to God – can produce an abundant harvest. But it is all about offering and receiving. It is all about looking to the hand of God to feed us, and, just as we are fed, looking to others who need feeding, and being prepared to receive from the hands of others.

It reminds me of Thornton Wilder's excellent novel, *The Bridge of San Luis Rey* (1927). A Franciscan monk meditates on the pointless death of five individuals who fall from a bridge. What is the point of this, he muses; where is God's purpose in this tragedy? He writes in the introduction that 'some say we shall never know, and that to the gods we are like flies killed on a summer day, and some say, on the contrary, that the very sparrows do not lose a feather that has not been brushed away by the finger of God'. But Wilder ends his novel with an answer to his question, one that affirms what our gospel assures us of, namely God's total care and love, wherever and whoever we are:

> [Eventually] we shall die and all memory of [us] will have left the earth, and we ourselves shall be loved for a while and then forgotten. But the love will have been enough; all those impulses of love return to the love that made them ... There is a land of the living and a land of the dead and the bridge is love; the only survival, the only meaning.

Note

T. Wilder, *The Bridge of San Luis Rey*, New York: Albert & Charles Boni, 1927.

93

Sonnet for St Luke

MALCOLM GUITE

His Gospel is itself a living creature,
A ground and glory round the throne of God,
Where earth and heaven breathe through human nature
And One upon the throne sees it is good.
Luke is the living pillar of our healing,
A lowly ox, the servant of the four,
We turn his page to find his face revealing
The wonder and the welcome of the poor.
He breathes good news to all who bear a burden,
Good news to all who turn and try again,
The meek rejoice and prodigals find pardon,
A lost thief reaches paradise through pain,
The voiceless find their voice in every word
And, with our Lady, magnify our Lord.

94

All Saints

SAM WELLS

Bible passage: Revelation 7.9–17

'I might believe in the Redeemer if his followers looked more Redeemed.' So said the nineteenth-century atheist philosopher Friedrich Nietzsche. And it remains one of the most damaging criticisms of Christianity. Most of us have had moments, seasons or even decades of being so ashamed of what has been done in the name of Christ and the Church that we wonder if we can still truly belong to Christ, and still belong to the Church. Many of us have felt profoundly let down by a person we looked up to or disillusioned by a form of Christian witness or disgusted by the way a movement or culture has turned the faith into an excuse for manipulation, extortion, oppression or exploitation. We know, in our heads, that just because Christians so badly struggle to live the good news, that doesn't mean the good news is not true. We know that the good news is chiefly about our sins not being counted *against* us, rather than our sins being eradicated. But still, it is hard not to be with Nietzsche. The problem with the redeemer is that his followers don't look redeemed.

And it is just as true of ourselves. We may be deeply hurt by the Church or resentful of God, but few of us swagger around thinking we are better than everyone else. More likely, we have a picture of what being a Christian is supposed to be like, and we are profoundly embarrassed that we don't reach anywhere near the mark. In my experience as a pastor, what keeps many people away from the Church isn't laziness or being caught up in the busyness of life or even unbelief. The biggest thing that keeps people away is hurt, and the fear that we can't say these words and sing these songs and still hold back the tears or the anger any longer. And the second biggest thing that keeps people away is shame, and the terror that if we get involved in a community of faith people will really see who we are and they will be appalled. We could say, 'I might believe in the Redeemer if *I* looked more Redeemed.'

One spiritual writer, Léon Bloy, said, 'There's only one sadness: the sadness of not being a saint.' It's true. Half our troubles come to us from others, and if we had grace of heart, and perseverance of spirit, and generosity of nature, those troubles wouldn't get us down the way they do. The other half of our troubles are those we bring on ourselves, and if we had transparent goodness, and lived in unblemished truth, and our souls were ones of inner beauty, then surely those troubles would diminish or disappear. There is indeed only one sadness: the sadness of not being a saint. All other sadnesses are versions of this.

For all of us there are times when we would rather be left alone in our sadness than allow anyone near us who said they wanted to make us happy. But unless we have completely lost the joy, our hope is to fill out the sails of life like a wind blowing a boat to its maximum speed. An early theologian, Irenaeus, said, 'The glory of God is a human being fully alive.' When we reflect on our own shortcomings and resentments, what we're doing is perceiving the ways in which we are not fully alive. In fact there is only one being who is fully alive. Only God is fully alive. God's glory is bringing us to full life. The saints are those in whom we see this full life most clearly.

Look into the mirror of your soul for a moment. Are you fully alive right now? It could be that you are furious with me for even asking the question. For many of us, life is a patched-together quilt of tight-lipped accommodations, suppressed frustration, half-acknowledged guilt, festering bitterness and disappointed hopes, and the person we avoid is the one who is able to hold a mirror up to us and make us face the gaping holes in our garment. There are two kinds of problems. One concerns the limitations of human life – most obviously pain, suffering and death. The other problem is sin. There is no evidence that the saints manage to avoid limitations like pain, suffering and death. But somehow, in the lives of the saints, pain, suffering and death become windows into the glory of God, and not occasions for grief and doubt and sorrow. How?

Historically the Church has had two answers when it comes to the sadness of not being a saint. The first answer is to say, '*It doesn't matter*. You can't ever be fully alive and you can't ever be truly good. But the life that matters is the resurrection life God gives you and the goodness that matters is the holiness God sees in you by the gift of Jesus' life.' This is called justification. Think of what Jesus says to the repentant thief beside him on the cross. 'Today you'll be with me in Paradise.' There is no evidence the thief became a good person, changed his ways, or lived a full life: all he did was turn to Christ in his last breath and say, 'Jesus, remember me when you come into your kingdom.' And Jesus replied, 'Today you will be with me in Paradise.' It seems that if we get to heaven, that thief is going to be the first person we see.

Justification has brought joy and life to countless people. It has led myriads of believers to cease feeling miserable over their limitations and sins and trust in God to make something beautiful out of their broken failures. For many parts of the Church, it is more or less the whole gospel. In fact, some would object to our celebrating All Saints today because talking about saints distracts from the fact that we are all sinners and there is nothing we can do to deserve the grace of God, which we can only receive and never earn.

But it is not hard to see there is a problem with this as the whole gospel. A friend of mine took his family to visit the Dachau concentration camp in Bavaria. Afterwards, in the car, his son kept pressing him with questions. 'Was that a church, Daddy, just outside the walls of the camp?' 'Yes, son.' 'Did the prison guards and commandant go to that church on a Sunday, Daddy?' 'Yes, son, I gather they did.' 'Did they confess their sins and pray to the God of Israel and the God of Jesus Christ?' 'Yes, son, they must have.' 'Did they walk out of the church and, the next day, go back to the camp and kill hundreds of Jews?' 'Yes, son, that's exactly what they did.' 'Did they still call themselves Christians, Daddy?' 'Yes, son, I think they did.' ... 'How does that work, Daddy?' 'I don't know, son. I just don't know.'

The way it works is that if conversion and justification are the whole gospel, then the process doesn't require lives to change. And the church in Dachau is simply an extreme example of that.

So there has to be a second answer to the sadness of not being a saint. This second answer says, 'You *can* become a saint, albeit gradually. You can go on to perfection. You will get there, but you must allow the Holy Spirit to form you. And this means adopting disciplined habits of holiness, and allowing these to become your second nature, so that you become shaped into the likeness of Christ.' This is called sanctification.

Once I had the privilege to see for myself the wonder of sanctification. I went to visit the Protestant village of Le Chambon-sur-Lignon, in the hills of southern France. A man named André Trocmé went to be its pastor in the 1930s. After the fall of France in 1940, Jewish refugees started arriving in the village. Trocmé was a pacifist. He believed in hospitality. His parishioners were wily. They had been shaped over centuries in the arts of cunning resistance to the majority Catholic culture. Together they hid Jews in safe houses, they passed Jews off as labourers, they spirited Jews across the Swiss border. Altogether over five years they saved hundreds of Jews from the death camps. The witness of André Trocmé and his people is one of the most beautiful things I have ever seen. It is what happens when people see Christ in the stranger and don't avert their gaze, when they truly depend on one another, and when they allow the Holy Spirit to do incredible things through them.

One account like this can make up for a dozen stories of sordid shortcomings and tales of tawdry turncoats. Some Christians really do look redeemed. But there is a problem with sanctification too. Striving to be holy can harden our hearts and make us judgemental and ungracious towards others and even ourselves when sin turns out to lurk at the door after all. Sanctification proclaims that every sinner has a future. But justification recalls that every saint has a past. Don't forget that the disciples had three years with Jesus being shaped in the disciplines of holiness. Yet as soon as the soldiers came to arrest him, they bolted. We never stop being sinners, not till the very day we die.

So should we ask to be left alone in our sadness at not being a saint? Revelation seems not to think so. In Revelation 7 we're given a dazzling picture of the ingathering of the nations. Here is 'a great multitude that no one could count'. That's good news, to start with. This isn't an exclusive club. There is every invitation for us to be in it. And the people come 'from every nation, from all tribes and peoples and languages'. Well, that's pretty big news, too. It turns out there isn't a most favoured nation, there isn't a special race – or gender for that matter. There is no one who can't come to the party.

And what are we told about this great multitude? We learn two things. The first thing is that they have come out of the great ordeal. In other words, they have faced the horrors of human life – suffering and pain, and exposure to the cruelty and perversity of the harsh and merciless. And the second thing is that they have washed their robes in the blood of the Lamb. In other words, their own sin has been taken away.

Together these two things dismantle the trials of human life, which we saw earlier were suffering and sin. It is these trials that inhibit us from being fully alive. So what we are seeing in this picture in Revelation is multitudes of people becoming fully alive.

And what does it mean to become fully alive? It means being *in the presence* of God, being sheltered by God, letting the Lamb be your shepherd, being led by the Lamb to the springs of the water of life, and worshipping God day and night. And it means being *united* with God, never being hungry or thirsty again, and not being subject to the hot sun.

There is a word that describes these wonderful ways of being fully alive. And that word is communion. In the Greek of the New Testament, the word is *koinonia*, which means fellowship or solidarity. But in the Latin, the word *communio* conveys an even richer range of meaning. Because it combines our greatest desires. When we love God, we have an overwhelming desire to become one with God, indeed to become God, to be folded into the wonder of full life and true eternal, abiding existence.

That's *union*. But we still want to be ourselves, our particular, distinct, idiosyncratic, personal beings, in the presence of God. That's being *with*, or, in Latin, *com*. Union ... and com ... communion. Communion means *both* being in the presence of God *and* being united with God. Think about it this way. God is Trinity, three persons so with one another that they are united with each other, and yet are still three persons. The Trinity is both union and with. When we are in heaven we are so with God that we are united with God, but are yet still distinct persons. This is communion.

As Christian communities, we practise this communion in two ways: in baptism and in holy communion. Baptism and Eucharist are both forms of communion, in which we are united with God and yet remain in the presence of God, retaining our own identity.

And that's not all. Communion is what justification and sanctification were striving for. Justification is all about us being able to stand in the presence of God, like a child being forgiven by a parent in spite of everything. And sanctification is all about us being made holy and being folded into the character of God, like flour being folded into egg and milk and butter. Justification is the com and sanctification is the union. Communion is the everlasting fulfilment of everything justification and sanctification were all about.

So this is what it means to be fully alive. Not to live without limitations, without pain, suffering or death. Not even to live without sin, either our own or other people's, for it always lurks at the door. But to live in communion, united with and yet still fully present to God, united with and yet still fully present to one another. Communion doesn't take away pain and, in this life, it doesn't take away sin. But it embraces you with the only power that is stronger than both of them, and puts them in their place, until every tear is wiped away from every eye.

Live your life united with and fully in the presence of God. Live your baptism. Live a eucharistic life. Live in communion with God, with one another, and with the created world. That's being fully alive. That's being a saint.

There is one sadness, the sadness of not being a saint. And there is only one gladness. The gladness of communion. The gladness of the communion of saints.

95

We Feebly Struggle, They in Glory Shine?
All Saints

HELEN-ANN HARTLEY

Bible passages: Daniel 7.1–3, 15–18; Ephesians 11.1–23; Luke 6.20–31

The Gospel passage comes from Luke's Sermon on the Plain, which takes its name from the level place on which Jesus stood. In Matthew's Gospel this appears as the Sermon on the Mount and is considerably longer. The context for Luke's presentation of Jesus' teachings is important. Jesus, who has spent the previous night in prayer before choosing his disciples, now addresses them, but in the hearing of a great crowd. The Beatitudes are meant for everyone, not just the chosen few. If we weep and are hated, well we are blessed; if we are rich or full, well that's bad news; if we laugh or if people speak good of us, that won't do either. But is it as stark as this. Surely laughter is a good thing; remember Monty Python's famous parody of the Beatitudes from Matthew's Gospel – *Blessed are the cheesemakers ...*

In fact, Luke's Gospel is rich with the imagery of roles reversed; think about the Magnificat. Luke is keen to suggest that there is something about the gospel message that is deeply unsettling and challenging. He is not saying that difference between rich and poor, happy and sad will be eradicated; he is saying that everyone, whatever their state in life, will find themselves turned upside down by the power of a gospel proclaimed by God who became incarnate, one of us, in the powerlessness of a baby, and who picked as his closest companions a group of ordinary women and men. It just doesn't make sense.

I suspect that part of the unease with saints is that they seem like spiritual superstars, their sheer ordinariness airbrushed away and the full Hollywood treatment applied; it's a world of imagery not far removed from the passage in Daniel. It is disappointing that the lectionary doesn't give us the full details of Daniel's fabulously 'out-of-this-world' vision, including the fourth beast with its iron teeth and ten horns. But speaking as someone whose home country is backed by a saint who famously wrestled with a dragon, it is no wonder that my own sense of saintliness is as fantastical as the apocalyptic visions of Daniel. 'We feebly struggle, they in glory shine', so say the words of the most popular hymn sung on All Saints' Day.

During my secondary school years, I was educated by the Sisters of Mercy at St Anthony's School in Sunderland, in the north-east of England. If anyone ever lost anything, classes would be halted and fervent prayers to St Anthony would be offered, which was quite handy as St Anthony is the patron saint of lost items. Just occasionally we would hide an object, claim it was lost, say a prayer and a miracle would occur, the lost item would be found, and the nuns would be very happy indeed. I am far happier with St Andrew, the patron saint of the land of my birth, Scotland, and the saint who gave his name to the university city where I spent four years as an undergraduate, though now perhaps more synonymous with golf than anything else!

But my own encounter with the sometimes tricky world of sainthood was brought into sharp relief when the builder of the church of which I served my curacy in Oxford was made a saint by Pope Benedict during his visit to the UK in 2010. Cardinal John Henry Newman became Blessed John Henry Newman. Newman built the church of St Mary and St Nicholas in Littlemore, which stands now as it did then in a socially deprived suburb of the city of Oxford in the mid-nineteenth century and he clearly had a passion and a vision for community that continues to this day. Somehow the words of the letter to the Ephesians speak of the real work of saints – saints in fact as ordinary people in the here and now, not people who are given the appellation after death having performed a dodgy miracle or two and whose relics are venerated in a rather macabre way. 'I have heard of your faith in the Lord Jesus and your love towards all the saints, and for this reason I do not cease to give thanks for you as I remember you in my prayers.'

The troubling and terrifying visions of Daniel gain meaning in the promise of a Kingdom that offers an alternative vision of reality. The whole point of apocalyptic literature is to get the message across that whatever God's intentions are, they certainly aren't what we might expect; they will challenge and unsettle, and, most of all, they will require the work of each and every one of us to bring that vision to fruition. The Kingdom of God as it is proclaimed by Jesus in Luke's Gospel is utterly transformative and full of the riches of God's grace, and it is the Church, as Ephesians tells us, that is Christ's body, the fullness of him who fills all in all.

The saints, both those living and those whose light graces another shore, are part of our stories. As we make our own pilgrimages along our life's journeys we become part of the God-shaped narrative that is the heritage and the promise of our faith, a narrative that may take several unexpected twists and turns in life. In the words of Alan Jacobs:

Christians manage even such dramatic swervings by remembering that the way we follow is not, primarily, the way of a pastor or theologian, teacher or bishop, administrator or prayer-warrior. The Way is, simply, that of Christ. It is followed by those who were once children of Adam and are now co-heirs, with Christ, of his Father's kingdom. (Jacobs, 2008, p. 81)

The remarkable poem 'The Bright Field' by R. S. Thomas, from which this book takes its title and which is reproduced on p. xxi, speaks to us of the glimmers of hope that do exist in a world that the media would often portray as deeply troubled, and reminds us too that we dwell with all the saints in the light, hope and peace of eternity, eternity that is beyond our comprehension, mysterious and yet real, present in God's Kingdom in our midst.

Note

A. Jacobs, *Looking Before and After: Testimony and the Christian Life*, Grand Rapids, MI: Eerdmans, 2008.

96

All Souls

SAM WELLS

Bible passage: Luke 22.14–18

We live our lives by two stories. There's the one we present at interview, when we want to impress people; and there's the other one we tell only to a counsellor, a confessor, or the most trusted friend. The Church also lives its life by two stories. There's the story of faith, courage, martyrdom, sacrifice and perfect love. That's the story we call All Saints. And then there's the story of fragility, fear, failure, foolishness and forgiveness. That's the story we call All Souls.

Every Christian makes the same mistake. We all think God wants our posh story, our All Saints' story. But the truth is, God wants the real story, the All Souls' story. Being a Christian means longing to be a saint – but, in the meantime, offering to God the reality of our soul.

The title of Kate Atkinson's 1995 novel, *Behind the Scenes at the Museum*, gives a clue to its theme. The novel is a *museum*, because it is full of memories, mostly about four generations of women in the family of the narrator, Ruby. But it's *behind the scenes* because, one by one, elements are reintroduced into the story that have been forgotten, denied or suppressed. The plot rattles along through post-war British history on a hilarious roller-coaster course, and you are never sure if the intention is simply to evoke rib-tickling laughter. But that leaves you wholly undefended for the moment when suddenly, very near the end, the savage twist clasps you like a stomach cramp and you're gasping for air.

By this time, Ruby is a young adult. Piecing together stray remarks and inexplicable anomalies, she is driven to rummage through the shoebox that contains the family's most precious treasures. In the shoebox Ruby discovers the buried key to her whole existence. She comes upon a birth certificate, and realizes she had a sister, Pearl. Not just a sister – a twin, born on the very same day as she, Ruby. She was born a twin. Ruby and Pearl. And there, to prove it, a locket, with a photo of the two sisters, one on each side. But then, a death certificate, dated four years later. Cause of death: drowning. The precious Pearl had drowned, aged just four.

Ruby seeks out her mother. In dismay she yells, 'You can't just blot some-one out like that … You can't pretend someone never existed, not talk about them, not look at photographs.' Her mother replies, defensively, 'There *were* photographs. And we *did* talk about her. It was *you* who blotted her out, not us.' But Ruby's outburst has unlocked a chamber in her mother's soul. They open up the locket with the photos of the twins and look at it for a long time in silence. Ruby demands to know, 'Which one? Which one is Pearl?' Her mother points to the one on the left, and says, 'My Pearl. My Pearl', and begins to weep.

Think of that locket for a moment. On the right is a picture of Ruby – the story Ruby thinks she knows, the story it is easier for everyone to tell. And on the left is a picture of Pearl – the story full of regret, and guilt, and grief, and loss, and sadness, the story no one really wants to tell. Except Pearl, perhaps. And, deep down, Ruby and her mother, desperately, achingly, wrenchingly – Ruby and her mother, who can't truly tell any kind of story to one another until they have gone back and told a truthful story about Pearl; the fact that she lived, and the way she died.

Think of that locket as the two stories of the Church – on the right All Saints, the story we want to tell, and on the left All Souls, the story of what took place behind the scenes, the story we have suppressed, forgotten, denied – but the story God knows, the story God remembers; and the story we *have* to learn how to tell if we are to stand truthfully before God and be restored in our relationship with one another.

On All Souls' Day we bring to mind the left-hand picture in that locket. We name some of the faces and hear some of the voices our society and our Church has tended to forget, tried to suppress or sought to deny. We are mindful of those memories and experiences in ourselves that, like Ruby, we try hard to bury behind the scenes in the museum of our own imagination.

Why are such voices integral to our worship? Because when we stand before the throne of grace, as a person, a society or a church, we can only ask God to redeem that which we bring with us. If we show God just the right-hand side of the locket, if we try to tell God just an All Saints' story, God will either laugh or cry.

At the Last Supper Jesus took bread and broke it, to represent the breaking of his body. And he said, 'Do this, and remember me.' Do this, he said, and re-member. That is our hope. Not that our lives and memories and lockets aren't broken. We know they are. But that we will be re-membered in God. That is what resurrection is – God putting all our members back together, going behind the scenes and literally re-membering us. And so to open our lives to the suppressed, the forgotten and the denied members of our society and our church is to anticipate heaven, by the same process of re-membering.

The last chapter of *Behind the Scenes at the Museum* is called 'Redemption'. Ruby is talking to her surviving sister, Patricia. Patricia is trying to encourage her sister to move on. She says, 'The past is what you leave behind in life, Ruby.' Ruby is having none of it. 'Nonsense, Patricia,' she retorts. 'The past is *what you take with you.*'

And that is the gospel. We are on the left-hand side of God's locket; but God doesn't suppress us, deny us, forget us, or leave us behind. Broken as we are, God re-members us and embraces us, and says, 'I'm taking you with me.'

Note

K. Atkinson, *Behind the Scenes of the Museum*, London: Doubleday, 1995.

97

Remembrance

ROWAN WILLIAMS

Each year there is so much to remind us that our active remembrance is a legacy of the First World War. On the anniversary of Armistice, it is inevitable that many people should be reflecting on the fact that the generation for whom that was first-hand experience has almost entirely passed away. Does that make a difference? Why should the legacy of that particular conflict still be so significant for us? (I pass over for now the remarkable fact of the revival of public interest, of enthusiasm for the act of remembrance, in the last couple of decades – a striking testimony to the need in our society for common acts of looking beyond our immediate concerns.)

But I want to reflect briefly on what it is about the First World War, and the experience of those who fought in it, that still has something uniquely significant about it for us as we reflect on war and peace, conflict and struggle, in our own generation. Why is it that that conflict remains, in the imagination of so many, a definitive moment?

Two things were central to the experience of those involved in the First World War. The first of these was the bitter awareness of the gulf between the reality of modern war and the rhetoric and metaphor used very often by people comfortably at home. Those returning from the trenches on leave found themselves almost incapable of talking about what they had seen and endured because the language used by politicians and the press in this country, the language of chivalry and swords and knighthoods, bore so little relation to what was actually happening. It was a gap that obliged so many people to think again about what real heroism might be. The almost legendary language of swords and chivalry that was so often used presupposed that glory in war was a wonderful, straightforward, righteous affair.

But those who fought in the trenches understood that glory, real heroism, had a great deal more to do with endurance, loyalty and the daily struggle to retain integrity and humanity in the midst of unspeakably awful conditions. Glory, it seemed, had to be redefined, had to become more prosaic, more to do with that daily giving up of fantasy and illusion for the sake of one another and a common cause.

The second thing that was central to the experience of so many was an understanding of how the nature of war itself had changed. Not only was the First World War the first major war fought with modern technology (so that long-distance destruction could be assured), it was also a war whose effects reached out into almost every household in the land. This was not war as a campaign far away, fought by heroes and knights. This was a war where *everybody* was vulnerable. The very means of long-distance destruction, which came with modern warfare, technological warfare guaranteed that the slaughter would be of unprecedented levels; it guaranteed that traditional levels of protection and defence would not be adequate. Everyone was involved.

And those two discoveries in the trenches shaped so much of the twentieth century's understanding of war, its risks and its challenges. It was that kind of legacy which, when the Second World War began, saved at least some people in this country from making extravagant, self-righteous claims, part of what made them speak in sober terms of reluctantly taking up their duty.

Archbishop William Temple, Archbishop of Canterbury from 1942 to 1944, wrote in November 1939 to a friend of how he was wholly committed to the decision that had been taken to go to war, and yet he said, 'We recognise that this is all to do with the sin in which we're all implicated so that the *best* thing we can do is still a *bad* thing.' That sober recognition of a duty undertaken in the knowledge that it might be the best thing to do in an imperfect world, that refusal of high-pressure, high-temperature rhetoric about heroism and chivalry, was part of what made the experience of the second war so very different from that of the first for many, many people: a duty, a solemn and sober duty; the least bad thing to be done because 'War in itself', said Archbishop Temple, 'never produces a positive good, though it can restrain worse evils.'

And something of that legacy has remained very firmly with us. A very proper, very humble wariness about turning up the temperature, about empty talk, about heroism when set against the realities that people have to endure. And because in the last decade the experience of war has come closer to us yet again, it is important that that legacy is still alive. The memory of what was discovered in the trenches of the First World War about the nature of modern war; the awareness of the gap between rhetoric and reality; the awareness that we are all in some sense involved: that is still important. Those now serving in our armed forces know a great deal about the heroism of trying to preserve humanity, loyalty, generosity and integrity in situations that place them under almost unbearable pressure. And all of us know something about how modern conflict has us all involved, even if it is only through our awareness of the terrorist threat that is part of the shadow that surrounds modern conflict.

We know, in other words, what may be perhaps a more adult approach to violence and conflict than we once did as a culture. We still (on the whole) recognize that there are circumstances where it may be a way of restraining worse evils. We know that people actually serving will be in situations where their integrity and their humanity are under strain, are compromised, confused, an intensely pressurized environment. We know that there is nowhere we can hide from the consequences of conflict.

And perhaps in our awareness of these things we are brought back to two fundamental Christian realizations. The first is to do with glory. From the very beginning of the Christian faith, glory has been redefined. Instead of being a reputation won by aggression and success, glory has been understood as that radiance of truth that can shine out in the middle of suffering and even of failure. Glory has been understood to be bound up with the integrity of God, and God's human creatures, because glory is supremely for the Christian shown in the cross of Jesus Christ where the integrity of unconditional love blazes out in the midst of a situation as horrific as that of the trenches in the First World War. And those who spoke most sense from the Christian point of view about the experience of the trenches were those who understood that somehow in that experience something of the cross was appearing to them and through them.

'The glory of God', said one of the earliest Christian theologians, 'is a human being fully alive', and that is a very different definition of glory from the reputation won by being a successful aggressor or even a successful defender. Glory is life, integrity, humanity and wholeness. And if we are aware of that, then in both peace and in war glory will be something deeper and more complex, but more lasting and more true than some of the definitions of glory that those who love war would like us to cling to.

But also from the very beginnings of Christian faith, believers have been conscious of their interdependence. No one can hide from the consequences of humanity's suffering. No one can protect themselves for ever from the consequences of the lack of peace. We learned in this country, in the most painful, dramatic ways possible during the twentieth century, how war could not be contained somewhere else. We learned through the long-distance slaughter that flattened some of our towns and cities, the slaughter that was inflicted on towns and cities on the continent of Europe. We learned that war could be brought to our doorstep, and that we could not hide.

The Christian would say that that is a way of discovering – a terrible and tragic way of discovering – the truth that the gospel has always insisted on: that is, that the good of one and the good of all are inseparable. In John Donne's words, 'Every man's death diminishes me.' And positively speaking, that means that the vision nurtured and strengthened through the terrible experience of war is bound to be a vision of interdependence and mutual service. It is not an accident that out of both the First and the Second World Wars came renewed and deepened commitment to justice and equality in our own society. People had discovered how profoundly they were bound to one another and how deeply the wounds of others wounded them.

Glory and mutuality, glory as the integrity of compassion; mutuality as the most significant thing human beings will ever experience. These realities are also part of the legacy of what was discovered in those dreadful years in the second decade of the twentieth century, and that so marks our annual commemorations.

As we remember again the anniversary of the Armistice, we should remember also the discoveries of those years in the crucible of the trenches, discoveries that we forget at our peril, discoveries that have to do not only with our understanding, our experience and our attitude to armed conflict, but bear upon the whole sense of our humanity and our human society.

In giving thanks for the courage and the self-giving of so many who have stepped into the breach and risked their lives for the sake of others, for the sake of justice, for the sake of liberty, we remember a world into which we are called by those discoveries: a world where indeed the glory of God is a human being fully alive, so that our duty and our call is to help people come alive to God's glory, in a world where we fully recognize the suffering of one and the sufferings of all cannot be separated.

May God give us the strength and the clarity to work for those things as the best way of honouring those whose sacrifice we commemorate today.

98

Remembrance

MARTYN PERCY

Bible passages: Jonah 3.1–5, 10; Mark 1.14–20

The idea that good may come out of evil, and that self-sacrifice can bring liberation, are two basic paradoxes that lie at the heart of many religions. And one of the stranger things about the month of November is the way in which we are all gathered up into acts of remembrance – All Souls, All Saints – that underline how death can also be the bearer of life, and that light is only truly appreciated when the darkness begins to cover us.

But there is more to remembering than mere recollection. We don't recall events merely to test our memory. The function of memory is much richer. It is something in our processing – our mulling, sifting and discerning of events – that makes memories richer, not vaguer, as we get older. It is easy to recall things. But memories are what hold, value and discern the significance of what we recall. And as we grow in wisdom – hopefully! – we find new, richer meaning in what we recollect.

Of course, we live in an age of cultural amnesia. It is no better in the Church. The fact that the Church lives in difficult times is not the problem, says the Dutch missiologist Herbert Kraemer. The fact that we constantly forget the Church has always lived in difficult times – that is the problem. This is partly why *remembering* is so vital in our time. In an age of rapid consumerism and short-term solutions, we do well to dwell on what it means to remember, and why this might be important not so much for our past as for our present and future. Of course, remembering is at the heart of the gospel: 'Do this in remembrance of me' are among the last words Jesus utters to his disciples. And 'Lord, remember me when you come into your kingdom' are among the last words uttered to Jesus on the cross.

But remembrance is not merely fond or regretful recollection. It is, rather, a deeper mystery in which the past, present and future become bound up together. When we remember, we *re-member*, in the sense that we re-assemble and recall. We bring out of the past and into the present those people whom we have loved and lost; those whom we still love, yet see no longer; those to whom we owe a debt, yet cannot pay – or thank enough. Re-membering, then, is not merely making sure we don't forget. Re-membering is, rather, the opposite of dismembering. To dismember is to take apart; it is a destructive act, pulling apart something that should be held together.

In contrast, re-membering is putting something together that was already a whole, but had come apart. So when the thief says on the cross to Jesus, 'Remember me ...', he is not trying to jog Jesus' mind. He is instead saying 're-make' me; 're-create' the me that should be together – but this time as the whole person God intends.

Remembrance, then, is not an act that simply brings out memories of the past into the present. It is an invitation every year to re-make and re-new the world. By recalling, we are asking God to re-shape our lives; to be re-fashioned, re-made and re-deemed. To be re-membered as individuals, as a society, as a country and as nations. To come together in a simple act of worship, and to pray, be silent and recall, is in a real sense to build on the dedication and self-sacrifice of the past – for the present and for the shaping of our future together, and apart.

Our memories, then, perhaps assume a greater importance at this time of year than at others. For we recall not only acts of heroism and tragedy, but also the unexpected moments that we can't fully explain. Why one lives and another dies; how we managed this or that; what it was like when all seemed to be lost. One of the great services historians have performed for us in recent years is a re-engagement with the ordinary stories of ordinary people, fighting for their lives, colleagues, kinsmen and countries. They are profound in their simplicity.

I think of the British officer caught by a single German officer behind enemy lines on D-Day. But both have to dig a trench together, to avoid the shelling of the British ships off Normandy. They carry on arguing about who will win the war as they dig together, before the British officer is eventually placed into captivity. But by this time, the two have become friends. Or of the young lad who witnessed the murder of 250 civilians in the early days of the purge of Jews from Warsaw – he hid under the corpses of his friends and family, and made his escape at night. Or the British soldier who shot and killed an advancing German at Dunkirk, but then sat there frozen, unable to come to terms with what had happened. He was evacuated by his friends. Or the young American navy doctor at Pearl Harbor, trying to separate a mother from her dead child.

Then there are the numbers. Six million Jews dead; 3 million of them killed not in concentration camps, but in forced marches and massacres. Around 25 million Russians dead, with perhaps more than half killed by their own side. The Blitz visited on London is the equivalent of a 9/11 happening every month for a whole year. Eighty-five per cent of Germany fought against the East; the rest against the West. And many, many more civilians died in our two great wars than those in combat. Millions of people were mere collateral damage, the casualties who were the consequence of war. And where, we wonder, is their memorial?

Forgetfulness is the enemy of justice, and the destroyer of lasting peace; the task that beckons on occasions like Remembrance Sunday is not 'forgive and forget', but 'remember and forgive'. This is true not just of the world wars, but of South Africa, Northern Ireland, Rwanda and other places. For our reconciliation with each other stems from our reconciliation with God. So it is important that we never forget; but equally important that we move and strive to forgive. 'It is only by accepting the past', wrote T. S. Eliot, 'that we can alter its meaning and power.' Yet this is no easy task.

And in the midst of all this, we have stories about journeys. Jonah's journey is one that is all about the numbers. God spares the vast majority of innocent people in Nineveh. The book of Jonah ends with God sparing all the people, and many cattle. And God asking Jonah, 'What is that to you?' But God cares about the falling sparrows, the innocent, the potential collateral damage.

Then Mark has Jesus coming to Galilee, proclaiming the good news – another journey. The breakneck speed at which Jesus calls and gathers his first disciples should not surprise us. Mark's Gospel is the shortest, and to some extent a kind of shorthand account of Jesus' ministry. It is reasonable to assume that Jesus had much more to say to the crowds than 'repent and believe, for the time is at hand – believe the good news' (v.15). One can imagine long, eloquent sermons, parables and lively exchanges, even from the outset.

So Mark, in summarizing the essence of Jesus' early teaching, is trying to say something about the urgency and immediate impact of the preacher from Galilee. Yet what is so intriguing about Jesus is the range of people he chose to share in this work. It included women and men – and not all of great repute – along with fishermen, tax-collectors and others. The ensemble was hardly at the cutting edge of scholarship, leadership and eloquence. Yet this is where the 'Jesus Project' is born. In choosing widely, Jesus gives us a foretaste of what the Kingdom will be like and the Church might become: a place both of diversity and unity, and a true home for all. Though many, one body. Re-membered. This is, perhaps, what we need to remember. And it is also what we give thanks for. Remembrance, though it is sometimes born out of tragedy and pain, is also for thanksgiving: Eucharist.

The philosopher Alain de Botton tells us that thanksgiving is part of the fundamental core of faith and religion. One of the differences between religious and secular lives, he says, is that in the former, one says thank you all the time: when eating, going to bed, waking up, for this day, for life. But why does the secular world tend not to say thank you? It is possibly because to live in a state of gratitude is also to embrace our human vulnerability. As de Botton (2010) says:

To feel grateful is to allow oneself to sense how much one is at the mercy of events. It is to accept that there may come a point when our extraordinary plans for ourselves have run aground, our horizons have narrowed and we have nothing more opulent to wonder at than the sight of a bluebell or a clear evening sky. To say thank you for a glass of wine or a piece of cheese is a kind of preparation for death, for the modesty that our dying days will demand ... That's why, even in a secular life, we should make space for some 'thank yous' to no one in particular. A person who remembers to be grateful is more aware of the role of gifts and luck – and so readier to meet with the tragedies that are awaiting us all down the road.

So, in remembrance and gratitude, we give thanks for God's graciousness. That he numbers the hairs of our head. That he does not forget the fallen sparrow. That God remembers. He cherishes what he knows of us – his creatures, and his creation. Nothing is lost to him.

And so, in our turn, we remember and give thanks too. For all those who have gone before us. For those who gave their lives so we might live. For the costly and sacrificial gifts that have been given; for the yesterdays of others that have enabled our tomorrows. For the souls and saints we cherish; those whom we love yet see no longer.

We remember those who have kept and held us together when we felt we might fall apart. For all those who have re-membered us when we thought we might be dismembered. We do this in remembrance, and with gratitude. In dwelling on the generosity and goodness of God, we remember that we are loved by the God who remembers each and every one of us, and all the hairs of our head. And he looks upon us with gratitude for the love and service we render to one another.

Note

A. de Botton, http://theschooloflife.typepad.com/the_school_of_life/2010/03/alain-de-botton-on-gratitude.html.

99

Christ the King

SAM WELLS

Bible passage: John 18.33–37

The great jazz trumpeter Wynton Marsalis was top of the bill one night at a famous club in New York City. He was playing 'I Don't Stand a Ghost of a Chance with You' and reached a dramatic moment in his conclusion. At that moment a cellphone started ringing in the auditorium. Audience and trumpeter paused in a moment of anxious tension as the embarrassed caller scuttled out into the lobby. Then Marsalis began first to play, then to improvise on the cellphone's ringtone. Over the next few minutes he resolved the improvisation and arrived back at the moment where he had left off, at the closing bars 'with you' (see Jones, 2004, pp. 79–80).

The arrested, insulted and assaulted Jesus stands before Pontius Pilate on the first Good Friday morning, and Pilate asks the question, 'Are you the King of the Jews?' Here we witness the same moment of anxious tension we noted in that New York jazz club. What is Jesus going to say, or do? What he does is what Wynton Marsalis did – he weaves the rude interruption into a much larger canvas that displays the full character of his mission and his rule. 'My kingdom is not from this world.' He doesn't say no, I'm not a king; he doesn't say yes. He says, 'You ... have ... no ... idea.'

It is a cryptic answer, so it may not be surprising that over the centuries the Church has tried to fit it into a couple of simpler agendas. The first one says, 'Jesus isn't king of this world, he's king of the next. He's not king of the physical, he's king of the spiritual. He's not king of earth, he's king of heaven.' Now there's an old joke that traditionally the bride's father tells at an English wedding. He says, 'In my marriage, we have a division of responsibilities between the important decisions and the unimportant decisions. My wife decides the unimportant things, like where we should live, and where the children should go to school, and when we need to buy a new car. I make all the important decisions like which party should be in government and when our country should go to war.'

The joke is based on a similar distinction of the separation between worldly and spiritual arising from Jesus' reply to Pilate. In this view Jesus is too darn heavenly to be any earthly use. We know Jesus is looking after our long-term interests but that tells us next to nothing about the here and now. And if we are pragmatic people, which we mostly are, we will look for the most effective and efficient way of running things in this world, confident that Jesus has the next world buttoned up. There is a harsh way to describe this view of Jesus' spiritual authority, and that is to call it practical atheism. It is practical atheism because, while it is confident in Christ's eternal promises, it is hard to point to a single concrete step it makes differently given that it believes Christ is king. Christianity ends up being the icing on a cake that is really about pragmatism or power politics.

Let's look at the second way the Church has tried to understand the words, 'My kingdom is not from this world.' This view says, 'Jesus is king of heaven and he's taking over the earth too and we're his followers so we get to take over the earth on his behalf.' The logic of this view says, 'Jesus is king; he doesn't seem to be king right now in a number of influential areas; so we must assert his right to be king in those areas by being king there ourselves.' The trouble with this is it ends up as if Jesus had said, 'My kingdom is very much from this world.' The Church's certainty that it has a right to rule is seldom matched by its desire to rule in the spirit of love, joy, peace, patience, kindness and gentleness. Like George Orwell's *Animal Farm*, where the revolutionary animals gradually become more and more like the humans they have displaced, this triumphalist reading of Christianity ends up with the Christians in charge but ruling no differently from their worldly predecessors.

If we are going to celebrate Christ as our king, we can't let ourselves lapse into spiritualization or triumphalism. Spiritualizing Jesus makes him king, but not king over anything that really matters. Triumphalism asserts Jesus as king, but is really more about proclaiming ourselves as king. Remember the tragic words of G. K. Chesterton: 'Christianity has not been tried and found wanting; it has been found difficult and not tried.' If Christ is king, then Christ is king of everything that matters. And we are not.

My parents were two of the worst car drivers I have ever known. The number of car accidents they each had when they were driving with me beside them in the car was only exceeded by the number of accidents they each had when they were driving without me beside them in the car. I am glad to say they never injured anyone but themselves. You can imagine how tempted I was to be a back-seat driver. I sometimes imagine how many hours of worthwhile things I could have done had I come sooner to the conclusion that my vigilance towards the windscreen and wing mirror wasn't going to prevent any of these little surprises. Christ the King is the day when we resolve not to be a back-seat driver in Christ's car. Christ is the king. We are not. And unlike my experience on the back seat growing up, that should come as a relief, not a threat.

Pontius Pilate knows nothing of what it means for Christ to be king. He fears the triumphalist king who will make trouble for him. It is easy to see why he would execute such a person. And he has a vague sense of the spiritual king who is too heavenly minded to be any earthly use, although if we regard Jesus as only a spiritual king we have to find some explanation for why anyone would have thought it necessary to execute him. The trouble is, we understand Pilate's kingdom better than we understand Christ's Kingdom. We are so captivated by Pilate's kingdom that it is not that we try Christianity and find it wanting; instead we never really try it.

Just imagine how different our lives might be if we really believed Christ was king! Just imagine how different Christ's Kingdom is from Pilate's kingdom!

Pilate's kingdom says, 'Life's too short.' You may have caught yourself saying it. 'Life's too short.' It is a way of telling people you're busy, efficient, and not one for wasting time. But if Christ is king, life is plenty long enough for the things that matter, for embodying goodness, for discovering truth, for beholding beauty. Yes, life is too short to cram in visits to every tourist site in the Lonely Planet's top thousand places to see before you die; yes, life is too short to study every subject the university has to offer; yes, life is too short to read every book written or learn every language or play every sport to varsity standard or leave an indelible mark on the world. But aren't those aspirations a sign of anxiety that Christ is not king and that we must substitute for the quality of his rule with the quantity of our endeavours? Are you living your life in a terrific hurry? Are you trying to squeeze in just a few more people, just a few more experiences, just a bit more candy than will really fit? Are you living a breathless existence right now as if life really was too short? Hear the gospel: Christ is king over time and eternity. He reigns over life and eternal life. He made time and he has redeemed time. In him there is always time for everything that really matters.

Pilate's kingdom says, 'Life is unfair.' These are words of despair and resignation in the face of injustice. Or they are words of malevolence and cynicism from the perpetrators of injustice. But if Christ is king, justice will roll like a never-failing stream. When we see terrible injustice and wanton oppression, the kingdom of this world says we must pile in and set things straight, however clumsy and ignorant we may be in doing so, and if we need force to set things straight we must do whatever it takes and make whatever alliances we need to ensure we have the right amount of force at our disposal. But in the Kingdom of Christ God says, 'Vengeance is *mine*, not yours; *I* will repay.' There will indeed be a judgement day, a great day with the righteous marching, and the Lord will wipe away the tears from the sore oppressed and put down the mighty from their seat and exalt the humble and meek. Do you long for a just and free world?

How much of that passion for justice rests on an anxiety that in the end Christ is not just, Christ is not Lord, and Christ is not king? Any justice we make for ourselves is provisional. We can never know all the facts, we can never set everything straight, we can never undo the past, we can never ourselves restore the years the swarming locust has eaten. But if you are lapsing into cynicism or despair, hear the good news: Christ is Lord and king: he brings a justice that we can never find; he shows a mercy that we can only dream of. He is the justice of God.

Pilate's kingdom says, 'Responsibility is the payback you make for privilege.' If you have advantages in life, you take on what used to be called *noblesse oblige*: you're supposed to give something back by running things as selflessly as possible. But if Christ is king, the world is fundamentally run by him, not by us. Our job isn't to be responsible, it is to be faithful. And being faithful means living the kind of life made possible when we believe that Christ is king over time, over injustice, over all rulers and powers and dominions. Being faithful means living a life that makes others wonder where we get this freedom, this joy, this carefree way of just being, this peace that passes all understanding.

We might think it is our job to run the world, but hear the good news: *Christ* is running the world. He has been running it a good while now. Our job is to live a life like his – a life that witnesses to our faith that the world isn't made by us, isn't sustained by us, and can't be finally set right by us, but has been made, is sustained and will finally be set right by one who loves us more than we can imagine, suffers more for us than we will ever know, and shapes his whole life to be in relationship with us. If Christ rules by being born into a homeless family, soon becoming a refugee, living a life of obscurity in an unfashionable small town, spending his time with fishermen, carpenters, lepers and sinners, and being executed alongside thieves and rebels, who are we to say we have better ideas?

Pilate's kingdom says, 'Choice is everything.' The definitive identity of the kingdom of today's world is to be a consumer, and the exquisite moment of being a consumer is to have the thrilling experience of choice. We want a new shirt. We can have it in cotton, we can have it in poly-cotton, we can have it in linen, we can have it in silk, we can have it in organic viscose with recycled poly-unsyphonated styrotex …. Shopping isn't about wearing; it's about choosing. And choice is just a nice word for power. Consumer society is like a drug that fills our minds with so many trivial choices that it exhausts our appetite for exercising real power. But if Christ is king, choice is about giving power away. God gave up his power of choice when he chose us. God already made his choice. He chose us. If Christ is our king, we have given up the titillating power of choice because we have already chosen him. Choice means keeping your options open. God's options *aren't* open. He's chosen *us*. If Christ is our king, *our* options aren't open. We've chosen *him*.

Finally, Pilate's kingdom says, 'Eat, drink and be merry, for tomorrow you die.' And now we discover what the real issue is. The real issue is death. Death seems to demolish everything about life. And in the face of death, Pilate's kingdom invents compelling words, like hurry, justice, responsibility and choice, words that offer to manage or distract from the horror of death. These are the words that dominate our imaginations, dominate what we think is thinkable, if we live in Pilate's kingdom. Which in many ways we all do. But if Christ is king, then death reigns no more. If Christ is king, death is not the end but the beginning. If Christ is king, we don't need to manage or distract from death, because our life is in Christ's hands, and those are the safest hands we will ever know.

And this is how Christ is king. Christ is like a great jazz trumpeter. Christ is playing a tune, a song of love, and longing, and desire for us. And we are like a mindless cellphone that rings discordantly and threatens to ruin the whole of this coruscating creation. And Christ pauses. And there's that moment of dramatic tension and grief and anger and loss, which we could call judgement. And then slowly, painstakingly, but eventually thrillingly and joyfully, Christ weaves us back into the improvised melody until all is resolved and in harmony for ever. That's out of this world. That's the gospel. That's what it means to say Christ is king.

Note

K. B. Jones, *The Jazz of Preaching*, Nashville, TN: Abingdon Press, 2004.

100

Sonnet for Christ the King

MALCOLM GUITE

Our King is calling from the hungry furrows
Whilst we are cruising through the aisles of plenty,
Our hoardings screen us from the man of sorrows,
Our soundtracks drown his murmur: 'I am thirsty.'
He stands in line to sign in as a stranger
And seek a welcome from the world he made,
We see him only as a threat, a danger,
He asks for clothes, we strip-search him instead.
And if he should fall sick then we take care
That he does not infect our private health,
We lock him in the prisons of our fear
Lest he unlock the prison of our wealth.
But still on Sunday we shall stand and sing
The praises of our hidden Lord and King.

PART FIVE

Compline and Seasonal Prayers

JIM COTTER

Order One

RECOGNITION

We have injured your love:
Binder of wounds, heal us.

We stumble in the darkness:
Light of the world, guide us.

We forget that we are your home:
Spirit of God, dwell in us ...

God is Joy,
we rejoice in you.

You run to meet us
like a welcoming friend,
you laugh with us
in the merriment of heaven,
you feast with us
at the banquet,
Clown of clowns,
Fool of fools,
the only Entertainer of Jesters.

**God of Joy,
we rejoice in you.**

PSALMS

ETERNAL Spirit,
flow through our being
and open our lips,
that our mouths
may proclaim your praise.

Let us worship
the God of Love:
Alleluia. Alleluia.

From the deep places of my soul
I praise you, O God:
I lift up my heart
and glorify your holy name.
From the deep places of my soul
I praise you, O God:
how can I forget
all your goodness towards me?
You forgive all my sin,
you heal all my weakness,
you rescue me
from the brink of disaster,
you crown me
with mercy and compassion.

You satisfy my being
with good things,
so that my youth
is renewed like an eagle's.
You fulfil
all that you promise,
justice
for all the oppressed.
You made known
your ways to Moses,
and all the people
saw your deeds.
You are full
of forgiveness and grace,
endlessly patient,
faithful in love.
You do not haunt us

with our sins,
nor nurse grievances
against us.
**You do not repay
evil with evil,
for you are greater
than our sins.**
As vast as the heavens are
in comparison with the earth,
so great is your love
to those who trust you.

**As far as the east is
from the west,
so far do you fling
our sins from us.**
Just as parents
are merciful to their children,
so are you merciful
and kind towards us.
**For you know
how fragile we are,
that we are made
of the dust of the earth.**
Our days are
like the grass,
they bloom like
the flowers of the field.
**The wind blows over them
and they are gone,
and no one can tell
where they stood.**
Only your merciful goodness
endures:
age after age
you act justly
**towards all who hold
your words to heart
and fulfil them.**
For you have triumphed
over the power of death,
and draw us to your presence
with songs of joy.
We hear the ego of your angels

praising you,
and the whole communion
of your saints,
those who have walked
in your narrow ways,
and heard the voice
of your yearning,
whose food
is to do your will
and in whom
you take great delight.
From the widest bounds
of the universe
to the depths
of my very being,
the whispers and cries of joy
vibrate to a shinning glory,
O God,
our beginning and our end.

READING

Poverty

BLIGHTED are those
who crave more and more possessions:
they will be crushed by the weight
and burden of them.

Blessed are those
who are ready to do without,
to be empty, to be nothing,
to be humble and open to receive,
knowing their need of God:
they have found the secret of living,
and are rich indeed ...

Grief

BLIGHTED are those
who wallow in self-pity:
they will sink into bitterness and despair.

Blessed are those
who accept their experience of sorrow:
they will grow in courage and compassion.

Struggle

BLIGHTED are those
who have ceased to care
and be disturbed,
and are now too much at ease:
they will be bored,
and will disintegrate into dust.

Blessed are those
who hunger and thirst and strive
for what is just and good:
they will be made whole,
and will be well content ...

Insecurity

BLIGHTED are those
who, in their insecurity,
look anxiously for appreciation
from others:
they claim everything for themselves,
and yet possess nothing,
wandering unhappily
and belonging nowhere.

Blessed are those
who have accepted their insecurity,
and are content to go unrecognized
and unrewarded,
claiming nothing for themselves:
the freedom of the earth is theirs;
never exiled,
they are everywhere at home ...

HYMN

HAIL, gladdening Light,
of God's pure glory poured,
Who is the great Creator,
heavenly, blest,
Holiest of holies,
Jesus Christ who reigns.

Now we are come
to the sun's hour of rest,
The lights of evening
round us shine,
We hymn the God of Love,
Eternal Spirit divine.

You are worthy, O God,
at all times to be sung,
With clear and truthful voice,
Light of Light,
Giver of life, alone!
Therefore in all the world
your glories, Christ we own.

INTO YOUR HANDS

INTO your hands
I commend the whole of my being,
for you have redeemed me,
body and soul,
O God of truth and love.

Keep me, dear God,
as the apple of an eye,
hide me under the shadow
of your wings.

ANTIPHON TO THE NUNC DIMITTIS

PRESERVE us,
dear God,
while waking,
and guard us
while sleeping,
that awake
we may watch
with Christ,
and asleep
we may rest
in your peace.

NUNC DIMITTIS

PRAISE be to God,
I have lived to see this day.
God's promise is fulfilled,
and my duty done.

At last you have given me peace,
for I have seen with my own eyes
the salvation you have prepared
for all nations,
a light to the world
in its darkness,
and the glory
of your people Israel.

Glory be to God,
sustaining, redeeming, sanctifying,
as in the beginning,
so now, and for ever. Amen.

KYRIES

KYRIE eleison
Christe eleison
Kyrie eleison

PRAYING IN CHRIST

ETERNAL Spirit,
Life-Giver,
Pain-Bearer,
Love-Maker,
Source of all that is
and that shall be,
Father and Mother
of us all,
Loving God,
in whom is heaven:

The Hallowing of your Name
echo through the universe.
The Way of your Justice
be followed
by the peoples of the world.
Your Heavenly Will be done
by all created beings.
Your Commonwealth
of Peace and Freedom
sustain our hope
and come on earth.

With the bread
we need for today
feed us.
In the hurts
we absorb from one another
forgive us.
In time of temptation
and test,
strengthen us.
From the grip
of all that is evil,
free us.

For you reign in the glory
of the power that is love,
now and for ever. Amen.

I WILL LIE DOWN IN PEACE

I WILL lie down in peace
and take my rest,
**for it is in God alone
that I dwell unafraid.**

Let us bless the Life-giver,
the Pain-Bearer, the Love-Maker;
**let us praise and exalt God
above all for ever.**

My God's name be praised
beyond the furthest star,
**glorified and exalted
above all for ever.**

[PARTICULAR PRAYERS]

PRAYING WITH MARY

Rejoicing with you,
grieving with you,

Mary, graced by God –
Love's Mystery did come to you –
of our race we deem you
most the blessed,

save but the Blessed One,
the Child
who came to birth in you.

Woman holy,

trembling at the Presence
of the Angel,

willing the rare
and marvellous exchange,

in the darkness
holding the Unseen,

bearing forth
the Word made flesh
for earth's redeeming,

hold to your heart our world,
and pray for humankind,

that we with you
be bearers of the Christ,

through this
and all our days
and at the last.

FOR THIS HOUSE

BE present, Living Christ,
within us,
your dwelling place and home,
that this house
may be one
where our darkness
is penetrated by your light,
where our evil
is redeemed by your love,
where our pain
is transformed in your suffering,
and where our dying
is glorified in your risen life.

BLESSING

GOD of love and mystery,
grant us, with all your people,
rest and peace.

The divine Spirit dwells in us:
Thanks be to God.

Order Two

INVOCATION

THE angels of God guard us
through the night,
**and quieten
the powers of darkness.**

The Spirit of God
be our guide
**to lead us to peace
and to glory.**

It is but lost labour that you haste to rise up early, and so late take rest,
and eat the bread of anxiety. For those beloved of God are given gifts even
while they sleep.

OUR help is in the name
of the eternal God,
**who is making
the heavens and the earth.**

THANKSGIVING

DEAR God, thank you
for all that is good,
for our creation
and our humanity,
for the stewardship
you have given us
of this planet earth,
for the gifts of life
and of one another,

[for the people and events
of this day]

[for the communion of saints]

For your Love,
unbounded and eternal ...

O Thou
Most Holy and Beloved,
**my Companion,
my Counsellor,
my Guide upon the Way.**

RECOGNITION

We repent the wrongs we have done:

**our blindness
to human need and suffering;**

**our indifference
to injustice and cruelty;**

**our false judgements,
petty thoughts
and contempt;**

**our waste and pollution
of the earth and oceans;**

**our lack of concern
for those who come after us;**

**our complicity
in the making of instruments
of mass destruction,
and our threatening their use ...**

ETERNAL Spirit,
living God,

in whom we live
and move
and have our being,

all that we are,
have been,
and shall be
is known to you,

to the secrets of our hearts
and all that rises
to trouble us.

Loving Flame,
burn into us;

Cleaning Wind,
blow through us;

Fountain of Water,
well up within us,

that we may love and praise
in deed and in truth.

PSALM

Eternal Spirit,
flow through our being
and open our lips,
that our mouths
may proclaim your praise.

Let us worship
the God of Love;
Alleluia, Alleluia.

As a deer longs
for streams of living water,
so longs my soul
for you, O God.
My soul is thirsty
for the living God:

when shall I draw near
to see your face?
My tears have been my food
in the night:
all day long they ask me,
Where now is your God?
As I pour out my soul
in distress,
I remember how I went
to the temple of God,
with shouts and songs
of thanksgiving,
a multitude
keeping high festival.
Why are you so full
of heaviness, my soul,
and why so rebellious
within me?
Put your trust in God,
patiently wait for the dawn,
and you will then praise
your deliverer and your God.

My soul is heavy within me;
therefore I remember you
from the land of Jordan
and from the hills of Hermon.
Deep calls to deep
in the roar of your waterfalls;
all your waves and your torrents
have gone over me.
Surely, O God,
you will show me mercy
in the daytime,
and at night
I will sing your praise,
O God of my life.
I will say to God, my rock,
Why have you forgotten me?
Why must I go like a mourner
because the enemy oppresses me?
Like a sword piercing my bones,
my enemies have mocked me,
asking me all day long,

Where now is your God?
Why are you so full
of heaviness, my soul,
and why so rebellious
within me?
Put your trust in God,
patiently wait for the dawn,
and you will then praise
your deliverer and your God.

O God, take up my cause
and strive for me
with a godless people
that knows no mercy.
Save me from the grip
of cunning and lies,
for you are my God
and my strength.
Why must I be clothed in rags,
humiliated by my enemy?
O send out your light and your truth,
and let them lead me,
let them guide me to your holy hill
and to your dwelling.
Then I shall go to the altar of God,
the God of my joy and delight,
and to the harp I shall sing your
praises,
O God my God.
Why are you so full
of heaviness, my soul,
and why so rebellious
within me?
Put your trust in God,
patiently wait for the dawn,
and you will then praise
your deliverer and your God.

READING

THERE is great gain
in godliness with contentment.
For we brought nothing
into this world,
and we cannot take anything
out of it.
But if we have food and clothing,
with these we shall be content ...

For the love of money
is the root of all evils ...

So shun all this:
aim at justice, Christlikeness,
fidelity, steadfastness, gentleness ...

OPEN your mouth for the dumb,
for the rights of those
who are left desolate.
Open your mouth,
judge righteously,
maintain the rights of the poor
and the needy ...

THOUGH our outer nature
is wasting away,
our inner nature
is being renewed every day.
For this slight momentary affliction
is preparing us for an eternal weight
of glory beyond comparison,
because we look not to the things
that are seen,
but to the things
that are unseen;
for the things that are seen
are transient,
but the things that are unseen
are eternal ...

The Spirit of God is upon me, anointing me to preach good news to the poor, sending me to proclaim release to the captives and recovering of sight to the blind, to set at liberty those who are oppressed, to proclaim the time of God's grace and favour ...

HYMN

BE still in God's Presence,
Be still in God's Presence,
Be still in God's Presence,
And love and be loved.

Be still in God's Presence,
Be still in God's Presence,
Be still in God's Presence,
And love and be loved.

Fall deep in the silence,
Fall deep in the silence,
Fall deep in the silence,
The silence of God.

Fall deep in the silence,
Fall deep in the silence,
Fall deep in the silence,
The silence of God.

INTO YOUR HANDS

INTO your hands
I commend the whole of my being,
for you have redeemed me,
body and soul,
God of truth and love.

Keep me, dear God
as the apple of an eye,
hide me under the shadow
of your wings.

ANTIPHON TO THE NUNC DIMITTIS

PRESERVE us,
dear God,
while waking,
and guard us
while sleeping,
that awake
we may watch
with Christ,
and asleep
we may rest
in your peace.

NUNC DIMITTIS

PRAISE be to God,
I have lived to see this day.
God's promise is fulfilled,
and my duty done.

At last you have given me peace,
for I have seen with my own eyes
the salvation you have prepared
for all nations,
a light to the world
in its darkness,
and the glory
of your people Israel.

Glory be to God,
sustaining, redeeming, sanctifying,
as in the beginning,
so now, and for ever. Amen.

KYRIES

KYRIE eleison
Christe eleison
Kyrie eleison

PRAYING IN CHRIST

ABBA, Amma, Beloved ...
your name be hallowed ...
your reign spread among us ...
your will be done well ...
at all times, in all places ...
on earth, as in heaven ...

Give us the bread ...
we need for today ...
Forgive us our trespass ...
as we forgive those ...
who trespass against us ...
Let us not fail ...
in time of our testing ...
Spare us from trials ...
too sharp to endure ...
Free us from the grip ...
of all evil powers ...

For yours is the reign ...
the power and the glory ...
the victory of love ...
for time and eternity ...
world without end ...
So be it. Amen ...

I WILL LIE DOWN IN PEACE

I WILL lie down in peace
and take my rest,
for it is in God alone
that I dwell unafraid.

Let us bless the Life-Giver,
the Pain-Bearer, the Love-Maker;
let us praise and exalt God
above all for ever.

May God's name be praised
beyond the furthest star,
glorified and exalted
above all for ever.

[PARTICULAR PRAYERS]

LOVING GOD

LOVING God,
you have prepared
for those who love you
such good things
as pass our understanding.

Pour into our hearts
such love towards you,
that we may love you
in all things,
and love you
beyond everything

and so inherit
    your promises
    which exceed
    all we can desire,

    in Jesus Christ,
    ever-loving
    and ever-beloved.

ABIDING AND INCREASING

INDWELLING God,
strengthen your servants
with your heavenly grace,
that we may continue
yours for ever,
and daily increase
in your Holy Spirit
more and more
until we come to share
in the glory of your kingdom.

BLESSING

BLESSING, light and glory
surround us
and scatter the darkness
of the long and lonely night.

The divine Spirit dwells in us:
Thanks be to God.

Seasonal Readings and Prayers

ASCENSION

Reading

Christ reigns,
disarming
the principalities and powers,
triumphing
over evil and pain and death.
Christ is with us always,
to the end of time.

Antiphon

Alleluia.
The pioneer of our salvation
has triumphed over suffering and death.
Alleluia.
The firstborn among many sisters and
Brothers
has led the way into the presence of God.
Alleluia, alleluia.

PENTECOST

Reading

The love of God
has been shed abroad
in our hearts
through the Holy Spirit
who has been given to us.

For God has not given us
a spirit of fear,
but of power
and love
and of sound mind.

Antiphon

Alleluia.
The Holy Spirit
will teach you all things.
Alleluia.
And will guide you
into all truth.
Alleluia, Alleluia.

TRINITY

Reading

Countless angels praise you
and sing to you
with ceaseless voice:
Holy, holy, holy is God,
who was and who is
and who is to come, Amen.
Blessing and glory
and wisdom and thanksgiving
and power and love
be in our God for ever and ever.

Antiphon

Alleluia.
Great praise
and everlasting glory
be to God.
Loved, Beloved, Mutual Friend.
Alleluia.
Life-giver, Pain-bearer, Love-maker.
Alleluia, Alleluia.

SAINTS' DAYS

Reading

These are the words of the First and the Last, who was dead and came to life again; to those who are victorious I will give the right to eat from the tree of life that stands in the Garden of God, alleluia. Be faithful to death, and I will give you the crown of life, Alleluia. To those who are victorious I will give some of the hidden manna. I will give them also a white stone, alleluia. And on the stone will be written a new name, known only to the one who receives it, alleluia.

Antiphon

Alleluia.
The Lamb who was slain
has conquered.
Alleluia.
All who follow the Way
will share in the victory.
Alleluia, alleluia.

THE DEPARTED

Reading

Thanks be to God, because in Christ's victory over the grave, a new age has dawned, the reign of sin is over, a broken world is being renewed, and we are once again made whole. As we believe that Jesus died and rose again, so we believe it will be for those who have died: God will bring them to life with Christ Jesus.

Antiphon

Give rest, O Christ,
to your servant(s)
with your saints,
where sorrow and pain
are no more,
neither sighing,
but life everlasting.

Index of Scripture References